Rethinking Indian Jurisprudence

What is law? What is the source of law? What is the law for? How does law differ from other norms or codes of conduct? What is the difference between law and morality? Who is obligated to follow the law and why? What is the difference between moral and legal obligation?

This book addresses these foundational questions about the law in general, and seeks to reorient our thoughts to the specific nature of law in India, the India of today, and the possible India of the future.

This volume:

- covers relevant foundational elements, concepts and questions of the discipline;
- brings the uniqueness of Indian Philosophy of Law to the fore;
- critically analyzes the major theories of jurisprudence;
- examines legal debates on secularism, rationality, religion, rights and caste politics; and
- presents useful cases and examples, including free speech, equality and reservation, queer law, rape and security, and the ethics of organ donation.

Lucid and accessible, the book will be indispensable to students, teachers and scholars of law, philosophy, politics as well as philosophy of law, sociology of law, legal theory and jurisprudence.

Aakash Singh Rathore specializes in Legal Theory (Post-Doctorate) and Comparative Constitutional Law (LL.M.), and is currently Visiting Professor at the Centre for Philosophy, Jawaharlal Nehru University, New Delhi, India. He is also an International Fellow of the Center for Ethics and Global Politics in Rome, Italy. His publications include *Plato's Labyrinth: Sophistries, Lies and Conspiracies in Socratic Dialogues* (2018), *Indian Political Theory: Laying the Groundwork for Svaraj* (2017) and *Indian Political Thought: A Reader* (co-edited with Silika Mohapatra, 2010), also published by Routledge.

Garima Goswamy has taught Philosophy at Lady Shri Ram College, St Stephen's College, Laxmibai College and Hansraj College, University of Delhi, and at BML Munjal University, India. Currently she works in the risk-consulting industry.

'Legal philosophy has long been dominated by Western ideas and leading figures. This important new book surveys these concepts and contributions, and then brings them into conversation with indigenous Indian thought. The result is fascinating and opens up radically new perspectives for jurisprudence.'

Thom Brooks, Professor and Chair of Law and Government and Dean at Durham Law School, UK

'Finally a book which rights the wrongs inflicted upon "Jurisprudence" in Indian Law schools. Bridging classic western legal philosophy with Indian intellectual traditions and praxis, *Rethinking Indian Jurisprudence* will inaugurate a new pedagogical practice in law.'

Kalpana Kannabiran, Professor and Director, Council for Social Development, Hyderabad, India

'A lively, provocative, and accessible book, which encourages the reader to think on and explore further the mystery and miracle of legal philosophy, otherwise alien to the learning of modern law in India.'

Upendra Baxi, Emeritus Professor of Law, University of Warwick, UK and Distinguished Professor of Law, National Law University, Delhi, India

Rethinking Indian Jurisprudence

An Introduction to the Philosophy of Law

Aakash Singh Rathore and
Garima Goswamy

Routledge
Taylor & Francis Group
LONDON AND NEW YORK

First published 2018 by Routledge

2 Park Square, Milton Park, Abingdon, Oxon, OX14 4RN
605 Third Avenue, New York, NY 10017

Routledge is an imprint of the Taylor & Francis Group, an informa business

First issued in paperback 2020

British Library Cataloguing-in-Publication Data
A catalogue record for this book is available from the British Library

Library of Congress Cataloging-in-Publication Data
A catalog record has been requested for this book

ISBN: 978-1-138-63031-4 (hbk)
ISBN: 978-0-367-73532-6 (pbk)

Typeset in Sabon
by Apex CoVantage, LLC

Aakash Singh Rathore would like to dedicate his efforts behind and materialized in this book to current students of law in India, those future advocates, jurists and judges upon whom hundreds of millions of common citizens rely in their daily struggle to wrestle basic justice, equity and dignity from the merciless leviathan that is the modern state.

Garima Goswamy would like to dedicate this work to members of her family, including her dad (Kul Deepak Goswamy), mom (Geeta Goswamy) and elder brother (Vishal Goswamy), as well as to the memory of her late uncle Deepak Kumar Gaind (who introduced her to law), and to her late teacher, Chandrakanta Makhija (who introduced her to philosophy).

Contents

Preface

As far as we are aware, there are no published books on the Philosophy of Law in India. There is no shortage of literature on Indian jurisprudence in the sense that jurists mean when they analyze India's legal system and case law and attempt to reflect on its more abstract implications – the principles or even theories produced by the higher courts in the process of their legal reasoning. Some of this work is interesting and valuable. But we are not able to find a single text that deals with the philosophical background behind this jurisprudence, or the philosophical implications arising from out of this jurisprudence (at least, not since Chhatrapati Singh's *Law from Anarchy to Utopia* [1986], which is already three decades old and exceedingly difficult to find). Hence the clear pragmatic need for the present work.

This book, then, aspires to be no more than an introduction to the Philosophy of Law in India; indeed, it is at bottom just an attempt to *inaugurate* the Philosophy of Law in India. While we have innumerable jurists teaching jurisprudence in every Indian law school, the number of philosophers of law who teach the Philosophy of Law in philosophy, humanities and social science departments in India can easily be counted on one hand, with fingers to spare. We are aiming to provide at least one original Indian volume that may be used in these courses, and in order to be in a position to launch new ones. Hopefully many other such books, better, more comprehensive and more advanced ones, will follow. Only then can this neglected but exceptionally important discipline begin to flourish.

Even in the Indian law schools themselves, jurisprudence is abundant but it is far from flourishing. As will be explained at length in the Introduction, the current, standard form that jurisprudence in India takes is in desperate need of revision and reinvigoration. Lawyers are getting next to nothing out of it, and non-lawyers are getting nothing at all. It is hoped that this book, with its admittedly many flaws, will at least have the virtue of helping to rekindle the interest of law students in the intellectual core of their own discipline and trade.

Acknowledgements

Acknowledgments are due to the UGC's E-PG *Pathshala* program. The Principal Investigator for Philosophy, Professor A. Raghuramaraju from the University of Hyderabad, appointed Professor Aakash Singh Rathore as the Paper Coordinator for the Philosophy of Law. Most of the material in this book arises out of the year-long project of coordinating the Philosophy of Law paper for the E-PG *Pathshala* program. Of course, numerous changes (additions, deletions, revisions) have been made, which make this book significantly different from the E-PG *Pathshala* base out of which it originated. But this work would not have been possible without its prior avatar. Thus, we also owe profound thanks to Professor Raghuramaraju (and his dedicated support team), without whom there would be no published book available on the Philosophy of Law in India even today.

We also would like to acknowledge Alexandru Cistelecan, who reworked material from the earlier book *Wronging Rights? Philosophical Challenges for Human Rights* edited by Aakash Singh Rathore and Alexandru Cistelecan (New Delhi and London: Routledge, 2010) into a fascinating and challenging essay that appears here as Chapter 5. We must also thank Daniele Santoro, who provided some material toward part of Chapter 1.

Hilal Ahmed was kind enough to permit us to use his insightful work on *Shariat in Postcolonial India* for Chapter 9, 'The Politics of *Shariat*' in this volume. And we cannot fail to acknowledge Arvind Narrain, whose contributions practically amount to being a co-author of this book, for giving us permission to use extracted material from his wonderful and brilliant writings on *Gandhi & Law*, *Ambedkar & Law* and *Queering Law*, used herein as Chapter 10, Chapter 11 and Chapter 14, respectively. As we have rather freely edited, abridged and revised the texts of Alexandru Cistelecan, Hilal Ahmed and Arvind Narain, any faults found with those chapters would be our sole responsibility and not theirs, to whom we owe our deepest gratitude.

Introduction

This introductory text on the Philosophy of Law attempts to introduce students of Law, Philosophy, Social and Political Science to the area of study known variously as the Philosophy of Law, of course, but also Legal Philosophy, Legal Theory and Jurisprudence. There is no compelling reason to distinguish the content or aim of these variously named subjects, although each has its own nuances. Outside of India, it is often the very same material that is studied under these different titles, and the titles result not from the content but from the academic department where the material is studied. So, were the student to study the material in a Philosophy Department, the course would be entitled *Philosophy of Law*; in a History Department, then the title might be *Legal Philosophy*, or *History of Legal Philosophy*; in a Political Science Department, *Legal Theory*; and in a Law Department, *Jurisprudence*. In this book all these terms may be taken as synonymous, unless we draw distinctions for some pedagogical reason. We personally see no coherent or absolute distinctions to be drawn – at any rate, there is a great deal more overlap than there is difference.

As a philosophical enterprise, this field – howsoever titled – asks foundational questions. It does not merely ask, *What does the law say about the crime of murder?* For, to answer that non-foundational question, one would look up the relevant laws in the codes of the jurisdiction in question, and follow it up by researching the related case law, that is, the interpretations by the courts of those laws that appear within the codes. Instead, it would ask questions such as, *What is the law? What is the law for?* To answer such foundational questions does not require consulting codes; rather, it requires considerable reflection, discussion, debate, and surely any replies one gives would be subject to modification and adaptation over time.

Also note that although we treat the Philosophy of Law as a discrete area of study, its foundational questions, such as *What is the nature of law?* are organically bound to foundational questions across other humanistic studies as well, such as *Who should rule?* from Political Philosophy or *What is the nature of the good life?* from Ethics.

Indian Philosophy of Law

The Philosophy of Law asks foundational questions about the law – *What is the law? What is the source of the law? What is the law for? How does law differ from other norms or codes of conduct? What is the difference between law and morality? Who is obligated to follow the law? What is the difference between moral and legal obligation?* and so on and so forth. Thus we are concerned with the nature of the law, the origins of the law and also the direction in which it is going, the aims or ends which it seeks to realize. We are concerned, moreover, not just with what and why, but also with where and when and how. To be concrete, we are concerned not simply with the nature of law, but also with the nature of law in India, the India of today and the India of the future.

There seems to be a tension between this foundational orientation, which suggests an absolute element, and these temporal and locational elements, which suggest contingency. But bear in mind that we are not treating of natural science and immutable laws of nature; rather, the law about which we speak is made by human beings, for the regulation of human relationships, which always arise within the specificity of times and places. Such law may have arisen in supposed conformity either with so-called natural laws or divine laws, but they were drafted and are enforced, adjudicated and altered everywhere and always by human beings, culturally and historically conditioned persons.

Thus, although we might employ the fiction of unencumbered, deracinated, un-gendered, purely rational agents as the hypothetical persons who create and are subject to legal orders, we do so ultimately with the aim of understanding the nature of actual law and real legal orders – and we undertake this, ultimately, in order to be better positioned to bring about the best possible laws and legal order for us. To put this in another way, we are not simply engaged with some totally abstract Philosophy of Law as such, but also always with Indian Philosophy of Law too.

The Philosophy of Law in India – the standard model

The Philosophy of Law is rarely taught in Philosophy Departments in India. However, it is a mandatory course at all Indian law schools, where it is called Jurisprudence. There is an alarming uniformity to the course syllabus of Jurisprudence papers across the country. The standard model of an Indian Jurisprudence course syllabus looks like this:

Unit I
1. Definition, nature and scope of jurisprudence
2. Natural Law: its development and relevance in modern times
3. Analytical School
   - (a) Austin's Theory of Law
   - (b) Kelsen's Pure Theory of Law
   - (c) Hart's Concept of Law

Unit II
1. Historical School
2. Realist School
3. Sociological School

Unit III
1. Administration of justice
2. Socio-economic approach and philosophy
   - (a) Law and social change
   - (b) Legal aid
   - (c) Public Interest Litigation (PIL)

Unit IV Sources and elements of law

1. Sources of law: custom, precedent and legislation
2. Rights and duties
3. Possession and ownership
4. Persons[1]

Certain prominent Indian legal theorists (e.g. S. N. Dhyani, Upendra Baxi) as well as judges (V. R. Krishna Iyer) have argued that jurisprudence as presented in the standard model is saturated with Anglo-American legal theories that were cultivated on foreign soil. These concepts and principles emerged from contexts profoundly dissimilar from the Indian one, but they have been superimposed upon Indian academic treatment of the nature of law in India. For this reason, the approach that we take in this book differs considerably from the standard model.

The nature of the legal system in India is profoundly hybrid, and is characterized by what may be termed multi-form hybridity. By hybrid, we refer to a mix and blend of foreign and indigenous elements, a fusion of ancient and modern elements, and other crossovers of local, customary practices interwoven with formal, national law or even international law. By multi-form, we refer to the way that the hybridities are not static, but have evolved over time in such a manner that what we refer to as 'foreign' may actually be deeply domesticated, and what legal or cultural elements get mixed and fused can be layered one over the other, and continue to evolve and become integrated over time. Writings within the Philosophy of Law take still shots of what is actually in constant flux.

To take a concrete example, think of the Indian Constitution. This amazingly complex document blends indigenous ideals (for example, its mention of 'duties') and institutions (e.g. panchayats) with colonial British ideals and institutions (Parliament, Supreme Court, etc.), which by 1950 were already well on their way to being regarded as authentically Indian, and then fuses these hybrids with borrowed norms and principles from, to cite a few, American, Japanese, French and German Constitutional law and practices. On top of this initial multi-form hybridity that is the Indian Constitution, we get 65+ years of interpretations and re-interpretations of its meaning, both through amendments by Parliament, and judicial review by the Supreme Court – common law, case law and customary practices continue to evolve, adapt, all contributing to the multi-form hybridity of the Indian Constitution.

The Philosophy of Law in India – the model in this book

With this multi-form hybridity in view, this book on the Philosophy of Law approaches the subject from numerous perspectives, sometimes distinct and divergent, other times overlapping and cross-referencing. But in the main, there are primarily three broad domains:

1 A focus on dominant theory, if you will. That is, chapters devoted to the Philosophy of Law as it is taught and understood more or less around the world as a consequence of the overwhelming influence of the Anglo-American jurisprudence, both in theory and practice. This is a tradition that stretches from John Austin to Joseph Raz. This covers the material from Units I and II from the standard model represented above.
2 Chapters devoted to the particularities that contextualize the Philosophy of Law in India, which allow us to theorize and comprehend the distinctiveness of Indian Philosophy of Law. Such a focus is very rare and usually non-existent within the standard model.
3 Chapters treating of salient legal concepts that function as case studies illustrating the diversity and wide-ranging scope of the

Philosophy of Law. Some of these specific thematic/conceptual chapters may treat of cases peculiar to India; some, however, treat of cases relevant both to India and numerous other jurisdictions across the globe. These case studies present an alternative way of covering the material from Units III and IV from the standard model, while simultaneously introducing the student to contemporary cases, controversies and conundrums.

Chapter overviews – first domain (Part I of the Book)

Chapters 1 to 5 fall into the first domain, treating of the dominant traditions and discourses of legal theory from primarily, though not exclusively, the Anglo-American world.

1. *Law and morality* presents a broad overview of the most influential legal theories within Anglophone jurisprudence. It serves as an important prerequisite for many of the following chapters. The aim of the chapter is to help the student understand classical debates related to morality and law by examining the exchanges between H.L.A. Hart and Lon L. Fuller as well as between Ronald Dworkin and Joseph Raz.
2. *Christian sources of secular law* introduces Canon Law (ecclesiastical law, Catholic law and the like) and most importantly, suggests its significance on secular law and the long history of Western Legal Philosophy.
3. *The cannibal's guide to jurisprudence* helps us to understand different theories of Philosophy of Law by way of the hypothetical case called 'Speluncean Explorers', originally invented by the influential American philosopher Lon L. Fuller.
4. *Law and rationality* examines how legal reasoning can cope with the critiques of reason and rationality in contemporary philosophy.
5. *Wronging rights?* presents various philosophical critiques of human rights throughout their history. As India is a country with a vibrant tradition of critiquing the hegemony of human rights discourse (and indeed, also equally vibrantly championing it), this chapter serves as a transition to the second domain of study.

Chapter overviews – second domain (Part II of the book)

Chapters 6 to 11 fall into the second domain, devoted to the particularities that contextualize the Philosophy of Law in India, which allow us to theorize and comprehend the distinctiveness of Indian Philosophy of Law.

6 *Towards an Indian Philosophy of Law* introduces the idea of an Indian Philosophy of Law as a field of study.
7 *From Dharmashastra to Modern Hindu Law* aims to sketch salient elements of the rich history of Hindu Law and its development.
8 *The persistence of caste* addresses questions of caste discrimination associated with Hinduism and offers an understanding of legal provisions against such discrimination under provisions of Hindu Law and more recent Indian legislation.
9 *The politics of Shariat* sheds light on the multiple political meanings of the term 'Shariat' in postcolonial India, especially with reference to the debate on Muslim personal law.
10 *Gandhi's affirmation of law* introduces students to the Gandhian conception of the law beyond his critique in *Hind Swaraj*.
11 *Ambedkarite jurisprudence* delves into an Ambedkarite vision of the law, beyond simply the epithet of being 'the father of the Constitution'.

Chapter overviews – third domain (Part III of the book)

Chapters 12 to 17 fall into the third domain, treating of legal concepts and thematic studies that function as case studies illustrating the diversity and wide-ranging scope of the Philosophy of Law, still aiming to inaugurate an Indian Philosophy of Law, while applying Legal Philosophy to Indian cases.

12 *Free speech and All India Bakchod* presents some classical arguments for free speech and discusses the All India Bakchod Knockout event, an unregulated artistic form of free speech, whose organizers face criminal charges.
13 *Equality and reservation* allows us to understand the importance of the concept of equality to legal theory in general, and then moves on to discuss the right to equality as entitled to citizens of India under Article 14 of the Constitution.
14 *Queering law* introduces students to Queer Legal Theory in the Indian context and case Law.
15 *Rape and security – a Buddhist vantage point* reveals important features of the Philosophy of Security in relation to the increasing instances of violent crimes against women; the features are,

namely, detection, delay, deterrence and response. These key concepts from security are reinterpreted from the vantage point of Buddhism.

16 *The ethics of organ donation* asks ethical questions about organ transplantation; in particular, the moral feasibility of compensated organ donation in India is discussed.

17 *Indian Supreme Court jurisprudence: five exemplary cases* offers students a brief overview of several of the most important cases of the Indian Supreme Court, especially those that have abiding jurisprudential relevance. Each of the five cases chosen for discussion here relates back to one of the topics of concern in the earlier chapters from either Part I or Part II. This illustrates to the readers how the philosophical issues within the Philosophy of Law correlate and intertwine with the concrete judgements of the Indian Supreme Court.

Conclusion

As you can see, there is an enormous range of material covered in this book. This is as it should be, given the points discussed above regarding the multi-form hybridity of the legal situation in India. If there is an overarching moral to be gleaned from the entire arc of this book, it would be to encourage the student to contribute to the continued efforts to cultivate an approach to the Philosophy of Law in India that supersedes the standard model; an approach that is *authentic*. What is the meaning and significance of this authenticity?

The task of authenticity within the Philosophy of Law in India would mean to continue to broaden the sweep of humane and egalitarian legal thought and practice that has been consistently developing in Indian jurisprudence, while at the same time reforming and rewriting our laws in a manner that reflects the best practices of our own traditions, both customary and written. These must of course be consonant with our emerging tradition of legal philosophy, such as that found within the ideology of PIL (Public Interest Litigation). We must balance our ancient law and values with our modern sentiments and institutions. At the same time, the indigenous legal system and thought must continue to evolve and adapt to newly emerging shared values and new needs, based on the experience of our own people, but even including those developed in other progressive countries or jurisdictions, if they have inherent worth.

To summarize all of this in terms of the structural arrangements that we have been using here in the Introduction: the task of cultivating an authentic Philosophy of Law in India lies in having the second domain (Part II of this book) eventually substitute and phase out the first domain (Part I of this book), such that all the cases in the third domain (Part III of this book) could be adequately and fruitfully theorized not on the basis of foreign schools of thought, but within the horizon of our own fully ripened tradition.

Note

1 This precise syllabus is taught at a seemingly endless number of law programs across India, from Kurukshetra University to Nagpur University to IHP Law College to University of Udaipur to University of Pune and so on all across the country.

Part I

Elements of the Philosophy of Law

1 Law and morality

Natural law theory and its contribution to legal philosophy

As discussed earlier in the Introduction, legal philosophy is a branch of philosophy whose primary focus is on understanding the nature of law, its fundamental concepts and the criteria that distinguish it from other social phenomena.

Legal philosophy in the modern tradition draws upon a long-standing legacy whose origins can be traced back to the distinction between the natural law governing the natural order, and the laws of the *polis*, which govern the economy and the arrangement of commerce. The roots of a philosophical reflection on the essence and function of law can be identified in the works of Plato and Aristotle. However, the first systematic reflection on this subject is credited to Thomas Aquinas, who conceived of the law as part of the natural and rational order established by God which could be discovered by means of reason. Aquinas's 'Treatise on Law' constitutes a significant portion of his important theological and philosophical work called the *Summa Theologica*.[1]

From the Greek-Roman world perhaps the most important inheritance legal philosophy gained was the conception of natural law, which is still very much alive in contemporary legal philosophy. John Finnis, one of the most influential defenders of this tradition, argues that the criteria by which a law should be judged right or wrong 'are prior to any human choices, whether individual or collective, and cannot be repealed, no matter how much they can be violated or ignored' (Finnis, 2011: 91). In *Natural Law and Natural Rights*, Finnis claims that the essence of the law consists in the securing of the fulfilment of some basic goods grounded in human nature, and which persons value for their own sake. Among them, Finnis includes knowledge, play, aesthetic experience, sociability, reasonableness and even religion. These goods – along with the principles for their realization – provide the criteria of evaluation of the morality of the law. The history of contemporary legal philosophy can be identified with the first systematic attempt to define the essence of law in contrast to the natural law tradition. This attempt developed into the doctrine called legal positivism, to which we now turn.

The law as a command backed by a sanction: John Austin

In its most general understanding, legal positivism is the doctrine according to which there are no criteria which are prior to or dependent (at least to some extent) on moral or metaphysical conceptions. As Brian Bix puts it, legal validity is 'disentangled from proposals and prescriptions for which laws should be passed or how legal practice should be maintained or reformed' (Bix, 2005: 30). The law, according to legal positivists, is rather a social phenomenon whose criteria of validity rest either on the form and hierarchy of the law, or else on the general and stable obedience to social rules. What is valid according to the law is posited by law itself, and any regulatory function of norms does not need to refer to an established natural order. This, remember, is in opposition to the conception of law within the natural law tradition. In a related sense, many legal positivists claim also that the subject of law is the law as it *is*, not the law as it *should be*, meaning by this that the scientific study of law should concern the explanation of empirical legal facts, the observable tendency of persons to obey the laws, not the justification of their supposed morality. If there is a sense of 'should' or 'ought' with respect to the law, it is only in relation to making more cogent, rational and systematic legal regimes, and the supposed injections of morality are irrelevant to the task.

Legal Positivism in this form dates back to the 19th century works by John Austin, a student of the great utilitarian philosopher Jeremy Bentham. In *The Province of Jurisprudence Determined* (1832), Austin wrote that '[t]he existence of law is one thing; its merit or demerit is another. . . . A law, which actually exists, is a law, though we happen to dislike it' (Austin, [1832] 1995: 157). On Austin's general view, every law is a command, issued by a sovereign and backed by a sanction (Austin, [1832] 1995, Lecture I: 21), 'to whom people have a habit of obedience' [I: 28].

The law as a union of primary and secondary rules: H.L.A. Hart

Contemporary legal positivists in the Anglo-American tradition have criticized this view as oversimplified. In particular, H.L.A. Hart, in

The Concept of Law ([1961] 1994[2]: 18–78), while recognizing the importance of Austin, has claimed that the command theory could not explain many aspects of even the actual legal system. Hart's conception of law can be interpreted as an improvement on Austin's theory. While Austin's approach was reductive (all laws are commands backed by a sanction), Hart insisted that legal systems include 'primary rules', that is norms that impose duties on all citizens, and rules that confer powers, for instance on officials in executing procedures, but also on citizens for creating contracts and wills. These second kind of rules serve to identify, modify and apply the primary rules, and thus are not commands themselves. Hart called them 'secondary rules'. A key element of Hart's theory is what he calls the 'Rule of Recognition'. The Rule of Recognition is a secondary rule whose specific function is to determine whether a primary rule is properly part of the legal system. For Hart, a legal system exists if, in addition to primary and secondary rules, there is a Rule of Recognition accepted by the public officials, and if the valid rules according to the system are also generally obeyed (Hart, [1961] 1994: 116).

Legal Formalism: Hans Kelsen

In addition to the development upon Austin made by H.L.A. Hart, a second strand of later legal positivism is that of Hans Kelsen (1967), perhaps the most important legal philosopher in 20th-century Continental Europe. Kelsen's work has several points of contact with Hart's theory, but his philosophical background lies in Immanuel Kant's transcendental philosophy. Kelsen's effort is to determine the nature of validity. He does so by exploring the logic of normative reasoning. According to Kelsen, normative inferences are those where a particular injunction or rule is derived from a more general normative premise. Normative premises of these inferential deductions can be of two forms: general propositions or imperatives dictated by an authority. It follows that the validity of a particular norm will depend on the validity of the more general or authoritative norm from which the particular norm can be derived. In this sense, Kelsen has a monothetic view of the law, meaning by this that for him the source of validity of the entire legal system is one fundamental and basic norm, an authorization to officials to impose sanctions. Such a norm does not necessarily need to be posited (perhaps it could not even be asserted), but must be necessarily presupposed in order to conceive of a legal practice as a normative system. Following Kant's idea of 'pure' reason, Kelsen refers to his own position as a 'pure' theory of law.

The separation of law and morality

As mentioned earlier, the opposition between natural law theory and legal positivism rests on the role that moral considerations should play in the establishment of the law. Unsurprisingly, all legal positivists deny to a larger or lesser extent, that law and morality are necessarily connected. This claim is known as the thesis about the Separation of Law and Morals. For instance, Hart writes that 'in the absence of an expressed constitutional or legal provision, it could not follow from the mere fact that a rule violated standards of morality that it was not a rule of law' (Hart, 1958: 55; see also Coleman 1982: 141). The importance of this thesis should not be underestimated. Most of the debate in contemporary legal philosophy focuses on whether such a statement should be read in a strict or loose sense. In particular, two views of legal positivism have emerged in relation to the Separation Thesis. One labelled 'exclusive' legal positivism claims that the legal validity of a norm can never depend on moral considerations, and therefore any overlap between moral and legal judgements is merely contingent or coincidental. This is the more classical and strict legal positivist position. The second, called 'inclusive' positivism, concedes that moral considerations can provide content to legislation, but that such overlap is always partial and does not define the content of the law as a whole.

There are numerous occasions throughout history where laws have been called into question from the point of view of morality. The holocaust during the Second World War offers a particularly striking example. The horrific events that took place during it led to a serious analysis of the concepts of 'law' and 'morality' and the relationship between the two. The holocaust raised many philosophical issues that became an integral part of a legendary debate in the history of the Philosophy of Law, regarding the separation of *what is* from *what ought to be*. Here, 'what is' was called law and 'what ought to be' was called morality. The school of legal positivism advocated separation. A law would be considered a legal rule if it was made in the manner recognized by the legislative power of the state; it would be valid irrespective of its content. Natural law, however, rejected this viewpoint. The validity of man-made laws depended upon their compatibility with a higher power, which may be God or a moral code.

Gustav Radbruch, who was of Jewish origin, and who was one of the most prominent German philosophers of law of the 20th century, 'converted' from being a legal positivist to adhering instead to natural law theory as a consequence of his experiences with the Nazi Regime and the holocaust. This switch, and the reasons behind it, were of decisive significance in the famous debates on the relationship/separation of law and morality called the Hart–Fuller debate.

The Hart–Fuller debate

H.L.A. Hart paved the way for a debate after one of his lectures was published in the *Harvard Law Review* in 1958. The paper was entitled 'Positivism and the Separation of Law and Morals', a position which Hart wished to defend by countering the criticisms of his predecessors. Lon L. Fuller then published 'Positivism and Fidelity to Law – A reply to Professor Hart' in the same publication. This led to a series of publications, with Hart's reply in his book, *The Concept of Law*, to which Fuller then replied in his book *The Morality of Law*. Further replies appeared in another article in the *Harvard Law Review* and another reply was subsequently published in the second revised edition of Fuller's *Morality of Law*.

In 'Positivism and the Separation of Law and Morality', Hart addresses critiques of Bentham and Austin who, like Hart himself, professed a distinction between law and morals. Hart demarcates the critiques into three categories: the first by those who disregard the distinction by pointing at the inadequacies of what is called the command theory. The command theory considers a command to be law. The second is voiced by those who present what is called the problem of penumbra. This problem refers to that fact that occasionally judges are confronted with the proposition to interpret some words where an established meaning seems obsolete in the given context, and thus they decide what the rule is from what it ought to be. This compromises the distinction that positivists seek to maintain. The third is an emotional appeal to morally bad laws like the ones formulated during the Nazi regime, the correction of which requires the intervention of morals into law.

Hart defends what he understands to be a 'minimum content theory of natural law'. According to this position, there is space for some degree of morals in law. However, he says that not much should be read into this, for there are repressive laws as well as situations in which 'what ought to be' is not necessarily moral. For example, in the case of a poisoner's decision to choose which poison to use in order to kill, the decision to choose 'what ought to be used' is anti-social. He reiterates this example elsewhere too. Hart also mentions that

> critics say that this distinction blinds us to the true nature of law and its roots in social life. Some also say that this distinction is

> misleading and corrupt in practice as it breeds disrespect of the law and may imply weakened resistance to state tyranny or absolutism. (1958: 594)

Indeed these criticisms and some more have been levied by Fuller.

In 'Positivism and Fidelity to Law – A Reply to Professor Hart', Fuller interprets Hart's paper, critiques some arguments of positivists and some specific arguments of Hart. He appreciates that Hart's account provides both intellectual clarity and moral integrity. However, to him, it is unclear whether for Hart, the distinction really is or ought to be, to preserve 'a precious moral ideal' (Fuller, 1958: 630–31). Fuller calls this 'fidelity to law' and he believes Hart too accepts it but denies its logical implications. Throughout the essay he reiterates the importance of attempting to realize the ideal of fidelity to law. According to Fuller, there is internal morality and external morality and law making requires conformity to principles of internal morality, which make laws competent and the legal system respectable. In Fuller's words:

> Law, considered merely as orders, contains, then, its own implicit morality. This morality of order must be respected if we are to create anything that can be called law, even bad law. Law by itself is powerless to bring this morality into existence.[3]

In 'Positivism and Fidelity to Law – A Reply to Professor Hart', he gives a thought provoking illustration to support his proposal.

He introduces a fictional absolutist, selfish and forgetful monarch who does not check if his orders are followed or not. On an odd day, when he does begin to pay attention to his own orders, he gets distracted while phrasing his orders to the effect that his orders are inaudible and ambiguous. So his subjects do not really know what he wants. According to Fuller, in order for his words to be meaningful, the monarch has a responsibility to 1. accept some self restraint so that there is a meaningful connection between his words and actions and 2. accept responsibility of his position instead of issuing another futile command.

Fuller (1958) believes Hart is aware of internal morality too, only he calls it 'justice in the administration of laws' (646).

Some arguments within the debate require special mention:

The problem of the core and the penumbra

Hart explained this problem by means of an example. Imagine that there is a law that vehicles are not permitted in a public park (the core of the law). What if a judge is faced with a situation where he or she must decide if a bicycle is permitted in the park – is a bicycle a vehicle within the purview of the law? (The penumbra.) By plain definition, it would seem to be the case. But it is pretty clear that it ought not to be the case. What is the nature of that ought; is it a moral ought? Not according to Hart. Hart believed that the intelligent decision which positivists oppose to mechanical or formal decision is not necessarily identical with decisions defensible on moral grounds. According to Fuller, on the other hand, resolution of the problem of penumbra requires putting oneself in the shoes of the drafters of laws to understand what the rule ought to be in a particular case. As Fuller cannot imagine formulation of law without a moral basis, he interprets some of Hart's examples where he used ought in a non-moral sense as 'immoral morality'.

The informer case

One particular case discussed was that of an informer wife who had been punished for having illegally deprived her husband of his freedom. The wife had informed the authorities of her husband's disrespecting of Hitler, which had carried the death penalty during the Nazi regime. After the war, when the informer wife was tried, she claimed that she was simply adhering to the existent laws of the time. The court's decision was that the statute under which the wife was claiming protection was contrary to sound conscience and all sense of justice for any decent human being. It was reasoned that she could not be given protection under the previously existent statute. Similar reasoning was followed in some other cases and seemed to hail triumph of the doctrine of natural law over positivism.

This case did pose a dilemma as articulated by Hart. At one end, in the Nazi regime, there was a moral obligation to obey law and on the other end, the laws to be obeyed violated morals. Fuller makes a case in order to attempt to refute the distinction between laws and morals, and he presents a distinction, following the German legal theorist Gustav Radbruch, between order and good order. He does not hesitate in demoting Nazi laws which were detrimental to morality to the status of non-laws. This is because, he believed, they lacked what he called the internal morality required in the law-making process, which gives laws respect and makes them obligatory to follow.

As per Fuller, both Hart and Fuller agree that retroactive legislature was apt in the case of the informer wife. It is noteworthy that Hart simply states that it is the best alternative if one thinks that the woman had to be punished legally. He considered this action as one giving up a precious principle of morality (that of respecting the law) in order to choose between two wrongs. Fuller also added that Hart would have sympathized had the woman not been punished. Fuller's reason to accept the court's verdict as per his own admission is not because this was a lawful way of making unlawful laws illicit, but because it isolates a 'clean-up operation' (Fuller, 1958: 661) from the normal functioning of the judicial process. This allows there to be respect for both law and morality, necessary for the ideal of fidelity of law, which Fuller advocates.

In the notes to Hart's *Concept of Law*, Dr Pappe's 'On the Validity of Judicial Decisions in the Nazi Era' finds mention. Dr Pappe showed that Hart's narration of the case should be considered strictly as hypothetical. For in the actual case there was indeed acceptance of the possibility that the Nazi statutes were unlawful if these contradicted the natural law. However, it was proposed that the Nazi statute in question did not violate it. It was the accused who caused unlawful deprivation of liberty since she had no duty to inform, but did it for personal reasons and therefore her actions given her intention were 'contrary to sound conscience and sense of justice of all human beings' (Hart, 1961, 1994: 304). It seems that might have been the case. However, Hart's narration even if hypothetical paved the way for an important discussion on the relation of morality and law.

Hart's *The Concept of Law*

As a legal positivist, Hart insisted on the separation of law and morality. However, he developed a much more sophisticated model than Austin's to explain the nature of law. In *The Concept of Law*, Hart focused more on explaining the nature of law by distinguishing between primary and secondary rules. These formed the basis of a functioning legal system. As mentioned above, primary rules either impose legal obligation or grant powers. Secondary rules are concerned with the operation of primary rules and include rules of recognition, change and adjudication. For law to function everyone must accept primary rules and public officials must accept secondary rules. While he did not wish to give morality the basis of law making, he did admit that although a morally reprehensible law must be valid, it need not mean that it should be obeyed. However, obedience for Hart would then seem to be a matter of an individual's choice.

It might be correct to wish that a legal system ought to show some conformity to justice or morality but it does not follow that legal validity rests on justice or morality. Hart does mention though that there are certain rules of conduct which any society must contain to be viable. These rules based on the 'human condition' are required to protect person and property and to insist that promises are kept. The human condition includes human vulnerability, approximate equality, limited altruism, resources and understanding as well as strength of will. Hart regards these as 'simple truisms' which disclose the core of good sense in the doctrine of natural law.

Fuller's *Morality of Law* as a critique of Hart's *The Concept of Law*

In *The Morality of Law* Fuller introduces eight particular principles which make up an inner morality of law and help to describe a procedural version of natural law. Law according to Fuller must be 1. existent, not ad hoc, 2. promulgated, 3. prospective rather than retrospective, 4. clearly stated and comprehensive, 5. consistent with each other, 6. possible to be obeyed, 7. constant or relatively long lasting and 8. applied and administered as stated. For Fuller, law must serve a purpose and the purpose is to achieve social order by subjecting individuals' conduct to the guidance of moral rules. Failure to comply by the principles would not render the laws invalid, but would result in something which couldn't be qualified as a legal system.

In *The Morality of Law*, Fuller defines law as an enterprise of subjecting human condition to the governance of rules. Hart in his review of this book points out that the outer boundaries of this wide conception cannot be determined from this book with any precision, since the author does not give us an account of what rules are.

Hart's review did not criticize in particular any of the eight principles that Fuller put forth, but he did assert that Fuller was unjustified to consider them morality. Fuller, Hart believed, confused efficacy of the legislative system with morality. He once again gave the example of poisoning. He identified it as an activity with a purpose and said that a poisoner could develop principles to effectively poison. But it would still not be considered a moral act. Fuller counterargues by an illustration of authoritarian states whose actions violate the external morality of law, such as the apartheid regime in South Africa, which also violates the inner morality of law.

Tommaso Pavone in 'A Critical Adjudication of the Fuller Hart Debate' points out that these examples should demonstrate that it is not possible to commit social evils while fulfilling the requirements of the inner morality of law. For if it is shown that inner morality ensures external morality, then it makes the latter a derivation of the former and one may question the purpose of this distinction.

Further points of contention between Fuller and Hart

According to Fuller, Hart's conception of law is incomplete and requires definition so that the importance of fidelity to law is highlighted. Fuller appreciates Hart's warning that if the distinction between law and morals is overrun, morality infused with law may not be as per one's liking or beliefs. He rejects an assumption which he held Hart to have made, that evil aims may be as coherent as inner logic. Fuller contends that Hart and other defenders of the distinction do not give an alternative to prevent infusion of immoral morality, should the distinction weaken. He asks a question and provides as answers two options: will a judge suspend the statute of an evil law by evoking a higher power or explaining law as law? In the context of the informer case of the Nazi Regime, Fuller chooses the first option, whereas Hart was likely to prefer the second. Fuller talks about hesitation to include immorality or cruelty in laws and explains that this arises from identification as opposed to the distinction of laws and morals. He also talks of 'law is law' formalism practised in Britain. He admits that while Hart may be critical of the same, his position actually seems to endorse it.

From Hart and Fuller to Dworkin and Raz

Fuller seems to claim that Hart's idea of a minimum content of morality in law is a common meeting ground between the two in their long-standing debate. It is noteworthy that Hart, like the utilitarians Bentham and Austin, did not deny that the content of law mirrored moral rules or principles. They didn't deny that law may include moral principles. To quote Hart,

> First, they never denied that, as a matter of historical fact, the development of legal systems had been powerfully influenced by moral opinion, and, conversely, that moral standards had been profoundly influenced by law, so that the content of many legal rules mirrored moral rules or principles. It is not in fact easy to trace this historical casual connection, but Bentham was certainly ready to admit its existence, so too Austin spoke of the frequent coincidence of positive law and morality.
>
> (1958: 589)

They did state that just because something is morally desirable, it does not necessarily become a law. If standards of morality are violated and there is no expressed constitutional or legal provision regarding it, the violation is not in conformity to law. This is mentioned in the very first paper Hart wrote on the topic.

In what followed during the debate, he may have introduced the concept of minimum content of morality in law to reiterate similar views. Only Fuller noticed it much later. And while Fuller is no more, the debate is still viable, as currently there are many scholars who continue to carry it forward.

The Dworkin–Raz debate

Two of the greatest figures of contemporary legal philosophy, Ronald Dworkin and Joseph Raz, have spent much of their philosophical work in arguing over the Separation Thesis. In numerous writings, Dworkin has presented strong and sustained attacks against positivism, both in broad, general strokes, and also contradicting many particular theses held by positivists. The inclusive positivist position has largely been an attempt to adopt some of Dworkin's trenchant minor critiques in order to overcome the bulk of his overall rejection of positivism. Raz, however, has steadfastly defended the positivist tradition against all of Dworkin's attacks and has remained committed to exclusive legal positivism. In the next sections, we shall first discuss the position of Dworkin, and then move on to Raz.

The interpretive stance and the role of principles: Ronald Dworkin

Ronald Dworkin has been a long-standing opponent of legal positivists. He defends an articulated conception of the moral content of the law based on the fundamental rights that the Constitution and the judges are meant to protect. Dworkin does not claim that morality is the foundation of the law, but that the interpretation of the law inevitably appeals to moral and political considerations when rights and principles are at stake in difficult decisions. One of his most famous illustrations of this is within his discussion of 'hard cases' decided by the Supreme Court. Dworkin's considerations are particularly salient for the systems of common law, where the judicial power of judges often involves rule-making according to the interpretation of substantive principles, thus blurring the distinction between what the law is and what it should be.

However, the philosophical significance of Dworkin's contribution is far more general. This is particularly true of his conception of principles in matters of legal justice. In *A Matter of Principle* (1985),

Dworkin insists that the dimension of principles has been overlooked by legal positivists, in favour of legal rules. Yet, Dworkin argues, principles are different from legal rules. Principles provide the judges with a general guide in deciding hard cases. Crucially, and contra the positivist's dogma, principles have a moral dimension. Such a dimension, for Dworkin, is the outcome of the best moral and political interpretation of past judicial and legislative decisions in the relevant domain. In short, then, the moral and political tradition of a community provides content to the very principles that guide judicial decision-making and this helps to explain the intimate connection between law and morality erroneously denied by legal positivism.

The authoritative force of the law: Joseph Raz

The final important figure in this law–morality debate is Joseph Raz. In his *The Authority of Law* (1979) Raz defends an exclusive view of positivism. The authoritative force of law – he claims – does not depend on moral authority And yet he grants that some fundamental moral codes, such as the prohibition of murder and rape, could not possibly be authorized by any valid legal system. However, the content of these fundamental rules (even those that seem to be adoptions of moral codes into the law) actually depends exclusively on the authoritative character of the law. You might ask, in what does such authority consist? According to Raz, an authority is legitimate if and only if it offers a resolute guide to comply with a given rule. To be clear, those who follow the law follow it based upon the authority of the law, and not by figuring out the reasons behind the law. If we act on the reason behind the law directly, then the authority behind the law is void of legitimacy. But Raz also adds that the legitimacy of a rule follows from the way it helps people in acting in better compliance on the balance of reasons. Let us try to understand what this means.

Raz elaborates this view within a fine-grained account of practical reasoning. According to Raz, there are two kinds of reasons: first-order reasons and second-order reasons. A first-order reason is a reason for acting (or refraining from acting). A second-order reason is a reason one has for acting on the basis of a given reason or for refraining from so acting. Moreover, an exclusionary reason is a negative second-order reason, i.e. a reason to refrain from acting for some reason. The core tenet of Raz's theory is that rules are both first-order reasons for action and exclusionary reasons not to act on certain conflicting reasons. Therefore, reasons against a rule can be excluded by the rule. As Raz puts it, exclusionary reasons exclude conflicting reasons by kind.

Since rules serve as exclusionary reasons, rules may prevent certain reasons to be considered in the cost-benefits calculation we would be prone to make in the absence of a legal system. The function of exclusionary reasons is to prevent certain first-order reasons from being overridden by other stronger reasons. In other words, their function is not to affect the balance of reasons, but to exclude certain actions on the balance of reasons.

Conclusion

Legal philosophy is a distinctive field of knowledge at the crossroads between law and philosophy. Its main purpose is to explore the nature and function of the law in its most general sense. This chapter identifies the two main traditions that have held the field in contemporary debate, natural law theories and legal positivism. It focuses on the main philosophical conundrum of legal philosophy, the distinction between law and morality, and outlines some of the most important contributions to this debate in historical perspective.

Notes

1 Thomas Aquinas. *The 'Summa Theologica' of St. Thomas Aquinas*.
2 H. L. A. Hart. The Concept of Law. Oxford: Oxford University Press, 1961, 1994.
3 Lon Fuller. (1985). 'Positivism and Fidelity to Law – A Reply to Professor Hart,' p. 645.

2 Christian sources of secular law

Canon Law refers to a body of rules accepted by the Christian church and was prominent in governments where the dominant religion was Christianity. It has an ecclesiastical significance, for it was either sanctioned or adopted by ecclesiastical authority. The term *Ecclesia* is derived from the Greek word *ekklesia* and refers to a society founded by Jesus Christ. This is described by writers of the *New Testament*. The term also refers to a Christian place of worship, or the church.

As the political status of the Church developed in European history with the Roman Empire and the Papal States, Canon Law evolved. The adopted part of Canon Law refers to certain elements which the Church borrowed from civil law or from writings of lay individuals who had no authority internal to ecclesiastical society.

Canon Law has survived to contemporary times and is relevant even today. There is evidence to believe that Canon Law has exerted a significant influence on the Western tradition of legal philosophy, and the natural law tradition of legal theory that we discussed at length in Chapter 1 (Law and morality) is especially indebted to certain ideas fully developed under Canon Law. For this reason, it is important to gain some familiarity with Canon Law. This chapter will refer to various Canon Laws and their development through different periods of history.

Meaning

Etymologically, the term 'canon' is derivative of the Greek word *kanon*, which in Hebrew is *kaneh* and in Arabic is *Qanun*, and means 'straight'. It refers to a grounding principle or rule or norm or measure. This word can be traced back to AD 325 with the Council of Nicea, where 'canon' implied measure or rule that binds conscience to authority.

During the very early period of the history of Christianity (the 2nd and 3rd century), 'canon' meant the foundation of the faith and the order of the life of Christians, while from the 4th century onwards it stood for church law or the decisions of the synods (i.e. special councils of church leaders). The Catholic Canon Law includes elements from the 1st century and during its history it became a complex and sophisticated system. The need for such a system endowed with general authority was present from the very beginnings, as uncertainties or disagreements arose together with the geographical expansion of Christianity. These regulations went back to the Apostolic tradition and were fed by the conviction that the answers to these disputes concerning the most basic questions of Church discipline were clarified by Christ or the apostles in the Scripture or in unwritten canons. So, in cases of uncertainty, the decisions of the Church relied on these traditions as normative sources or adapted them to the new conditions. From the 3rd century onwards, the role of adjudicating the correct decisions in the cases of ambiguities was taken over by synods, and the laws created through these synods formed the body of Canon Law. The decisions of the synods already represented a wide consensus of the bishop's present, who equally made the decisions, applied and enforced them. In the beginning, the synods did not create a systematic scheme of Church discipline. However, systematic documents were created in the 6th century onwards.

According to Reverend P. Charles Augustine, who wrote a *Commentary on the Code of the Canon Law*, the term Canon Law is properly reserved for church laws since the 12th century and those who interpret this ecclesiastical law were referred to as *canonistae*. He defines Canon Law as 'the complex of rules which direct the exterior order of the Church to its proper end' (Augustine, 1918: 2). This definition points to the authoritativeness of these holy rules. Many scholars on the topic have also emphasized this point. For instance, R.H. Helmholz in his review of Professor Norman Doe's book, *The Legal Framework of the Church of England* mentions how by 'enabling the Church to fulfil its mission in the world' (Helmholz, 1997: 1456) Canon Law gets its special characteristics when compared to secular law. However, scholars also believe that besides the divine and natural law aspect, Canon Law also contains elements of positive law which are subject to invalidity or change.

Some prominent historical texts of Canon Law

Different documents in history illustrate the development of Canon Law. We shall look briefly at several important collections from the past one thousand years, and then turn to the way that this vast history of Canon Law was finally systematized in the 20th century.

Justinian's Text

Most of early Canon Law, which developed simultaneously with ancient Roman Law, was integrated into the legal system of Byzantine. It was compiled by order of the Byzantine Emperor named Justinian in the 6th century AD. As per Professor Peter Stein, this material reflected centuries of legal development. During the early Middle Ages, it became necessary that all clerics acquire formal education in law. Justinian's Text, and with it Roman Law, was thus deeply influential on the legal traditions in Italy throughout the late Middle ages, and in France during the 16th century, in the Netherlands during the 17th century and in Germany in the 19th century.

Dictatus Papae

The Gregorian reform movement (11th century) brought about the creation of several systematic collections in which the main achievements of the reform were presented. One significant text during this period was called *Dictatus Papae*. While there is debate between scholars as to whether it was actually written by Pope Gregory VII (reigned 1073–85) or inserted at a later date, the *Dictatus* is said to present a strong case to establish the Pope's supremacy and the infallibility of Canon Law. The Gregorian reform movement paved the way for the emerging science of Canon Law in the 12th century. This was the era when the difference between Civil Law and Canon Law became deeply significant. The reform movement laid the foundation for the subsequent jurisprudential work of the monk named Gratianus.

Decretum Gratiani

The *Decretum Gratiani* is a 12th-century collection of Canon Law. It was partially compiled from earlier sources, and partly freshly written by the monk Gratianus. The *Decretum* was later taken up as the first of six volumes representing the whole body of Catholic Canon Law which developed from this period in the 12th century all the way up to 1918, when it was replaced by a revised and codified version.

The *Decretum* was written to harmonize aspects of both Civil and Canon Law. Civil lawyers had been arguing that civil law was a superior tool for understanding the technicalities of any kind of law, including Canon Law. As per Professor Stein (2004), while the civil law had answers to almost all legal questions, its applicability was restricted not necessarily to the courtrooms but more specifically to where the 'local law was lacking' (Stein, 1999: 50). On the contrary, Canon Law, though divine, was applied in the courts in all matters regarding ecclesiastical jurisdiction. Thus, it did not deal with all legal matters. The harmony effected by Gratianus included stating in the *Decretum* that civil law was to be followed for all matters not specifically defined within the Canon Law.

Liber Extra *and* Liber Sextus

In 1234, Pope Gregory IX had a text edited by Raymond of Penaforte by compiling various parts of five Papal Decrees that had been issued between 1188 and 1226. This collection, that included 1,971 chapters divided into five books, was called *Liber Extra*, which could be translated as *The Book with Extra*. For the book had many extra rules other than those present in the *Decretum*. The contents of the *Extra* included rules relating to judges and their powers, legal proceedings, marriage, clerical issues and crime. By 1298, *Liber Sextus* (the *Sixth Book*) was added to *Liber Extra*. It is noteworthy that a famous principle of natural law that is often quoted in political debate 'what touches all should be approved by all' originates in the *Liber Sextus* (Stein, 1999: 51). This raises the point of the relationship between Canon Law and natural law.

Natural law and Thomas Aquinas

Thomas Aquinas (1225–74) was a philosopher and theologian much influenced by the philosophy of Aristotle, whose work was regarded as authoritative by the Church. There was a well-known decree of the Pope entitled, *Encyclical letter of our holy father by divine providence Pope Leo XIII on The Restoration of Christian Philosophy, according to the Mind of St. Thomas Aquinas, the Angelic Doctor*, published on August 4, 1879. This letter asserts that in all Catholic institutions where Philosophy is taught, St. Thomas Aquinas's system is deemed as the right one. Moreover, in the 1917 Code of Canon Law, Aquinas is the only name mentioned with regards to training the priests in accordance with his 'method, doctrine and principles'. As per the 1983 Code of Canon Law too, Aquinas is to be regarded as the teacher of priests.

Most of Aquinas's work tried to establish the truth of the Christian faith by taking recourse to reason. So, for instance, in his capacious work, *Summa contra Gentiles*, arguments were addressed to a non-Christian reader with the aim to introduce the truth of Christianity. To quote an excerpt from the *Summa contra Gentiles*:

> My purpose is to declare the truth which the Catholic Faith professes. But here I must have recourse to natural reason, since the gentiles do not accept the authority of the Scripture. Natural reason, however, is deficient in the things of God, it can prove some parts of the faith but not others. . . . Whatever is demonstrable is, so far as it goes, in accordance with the Christian faith, and nothing in revelation is contrary to reason.
>
> (Russell, 2009: 454)

So, it becomes appropriate to highlight some of his views regarding law and jurisprudence.

In his masterpiece, *Summa Theologica*, Aquinas defines law as 'nothing other than an ordinance of reason for the common good, made by him who has the care of the community and promulgated' (Deutsch, 2008: 116). More specifically, Aquinas posits that there are four kinds of law: the eternal law of God, natural law, human law and divine law.

Aquinas maintains reason to be a coextension of God, and natural law to be a reflection and participation in God's eternal law. He believed that God is the legislator of eternal law. Natural law forms a part or a subset of eternal law.[1] Natural law is applicable to human beings who are guided by freewill and governed by reason. It is noteworthy that the natural law theory of Aquinas does not exclude positive law which is called, in Aquinas's terminology, human law. Human laws must not be unjust. As per Aquinas, these too follow from natural law and hence subsequently follow from the eternal law of God. Finally, divine law is the law promulgated in the words of the Pope. As Aquinas summarized this:

> Human Law has the nature of law in so far as it partakes of right reason, and it is clear that, in this respect it is derived from eternal law. But in so far as it deviates from reason it is called an unjust law and has the nature, not of law, but of violence. Nevertheless even an unjust law, in so far as it retains some appearance of law, through being framed by one who is in power, is derived from the eternal law, since all power is from the Lord God, according to the *Book of Romans*.[2]

Codification of Canon Law

Despite the evolution of Canon Law throughout the centuries, the real process of thorough, systematic codification did not begin until the 20th century. Up to the late 1910s, the *Corpus Iuris Canonici* (Body of Canon Law) was in use together with the disciplinary decrees of the Council of Trent (i.e. a 16th-century Council that was called to deal with the problems raised by the Protestant reformation), as well as by other legal documents produced as follow up to the Council. In 1917, the first Code of Canon Law was promulgated. It was called *Codex Iuris Canonici* and was implemented in 1918. It had important influence in strengthening the church externally and internally. For example, by dealing with the concordats (i.e. agreements, like treaties), it defined the proper relationship between state and church. However, the *Codex* (just like the *Corpus* before it) became outdated, probably as its main audience were scholars of Canon Law rather than the millions of laymen under the authority of the Church.

In 1959, during the process of the Vatican II reforms, Pope John XXIII expressed his wish to revise the *Codex* of Canon Law. This process began in 1963 and took two decades. In 1983 the second *Codex Iuris Canonici* was implemented, and it stands as authoritative for the Catholic Church today.

The second and current *Codex* is much simpler than the 1917–18 Codex, containing merely 1,752 canons. It also contained several rules and regulations that were of interest to laymen and not just jurists and theologians. For example, sexual abuse policy was given importance in the revised code. Canon 1395 set out the punishment for a clergyman should he be found sexually abusing a minor. Canons 1717–19 set out the nuances of investigations in cases of sexual abuse by Church officials.

In 1990, Pope John Paul II publicized a distinct document for the Eastern churches (*Codex Canonum Ecclesiarum Orientalium*), meant to harmonize the Canon Law for the Roman Catholic and the Eastern churches, including India. This united Canon Law has been updated and developed, with major revisions in 2010. The idea is that today, the global Catholic church stands united under one all-encompassing Canon Law.

Significance of theology in law and politics

We now turn from the history and development of Canon Law to a particularly significant debate relating to Canon Law, theology and the civil law of the modern nation state. This debate questions whether Canon Law is purely theological or if it can be taken as a full-blown form of Christian jurisprudence. Scholars like R. Sohm argue that Canon Law is not 'law' as we understand it, but is purely theological in nature (Coughlin, 2007: 1). On the other hand, John J. Coughlin (2007) considers Canon Law to be a mature form of jurisprudence. In 'Canon Law', Coughlin argues that the tradition of revelation was linked with the human community of the church. Canon Law had two forms – inward and outward. While the inward could be said to be spiritual, or the faith in revelation, the outward form is one which is manifest in a judicial structure as Canon Law.

One compromise position in this debate is to regard Canon Law, which brings religion and law together, as belonging to the discipline of practical theology, which understands the practice of theology in the (secular) world. Practical theology includes the theology of law, the history of law, and theory of canon law. The need to emphasize the importance of synthesizing law with theology is expressed by Coughlin in *Canon Law and the Human Person* (Coughlin, 2003) in the following manner:

> Theology without law leaves the ecclesiastical community bereft of an ordered life. Law without theological meaning surrenders its moral persuasiveness and deteriorates into rigid legalism.
>
> (2)

One unique position running alongside this debate is presented by the important legal and political theorist Carl Schmitt. In his famous and very important book *Political Theology*, Schmitt presents an extreme view which makes Canon Law significant in the political theory of contemporary nation states. He asserts that the Canon Law of Roman Catholicism forms the basis of the concept of the nation state, as parallels may be drawn between the structure in which the Canon Law was implemented and the structure of the modern nation state. The Pope is akin to the authority figure of a nation state such as a president or prime minister, and the Canon Laws are secularized into civil legislation. Just as god has the power of performing miracles, the sovereign enjoys exceptional powers such as the authority to declare a state of emergency. Schmitt contends:

> All significant concepts of the modern theory of the state are secularized theological concepts not only because of their historical development – in which they were transferred from theology to

> the theory of the state, whereby, for example, the omnipotent God becomes the omnipotent lawgiver – but also because of their systematic structure, the recognition of which is necessary for a sociological consideration of these concepts. The exception in jurisprudence is analogous to the miracle in theology. Only by being aware of this analogy can we appreciate the manner in which the nation state developed in the last centuries.
>
> (1985: 36)

Conclusion

While several texts contain provisions of the Canon Law, the process of its codification took place formally only in the 20th century. Canon Law not only presents aspects of natural law, eternal law or divine law, but also has provisions for positive law. Although primarily meant for theological purpose or control of the Church over its jurisdiction, Canon Law is significant in the history of Western legal and political developments, not only in historical perspective, but also, as Carl Schmitt argues, in shaping the legal structure of modern nation states. Again, one of the primary significances of Canon Law is that modern legal theory is deeply influenced by the history and evolution of Canon Law.

Beyond a doubt, we need to remain attuned to the Christian origins and sources seeping in to secular law, even as we know it in India. We cannot possibly begin to work towards an authentic Indian Philosophy of Law without understanding the diverse historical and theological sources of our contemporary legal regime.

Notes

1 As per the terminology used by Susan Dimock in 'The Natural Law Theory of St. Aquinas' from Joel Feinberg. *Philosophy of Law*. CA: Wadsworth (2000).

2 Ibid.: p. 123.

3 The cannibal's guide to jurisprudence

'The Case of the Speluncean Explorers' is a paper written by Lon L. Fuller and published in the *Harvard Law Review* in 1949. This hypothetical case, which centres around an act of cannibalism, has drawn a great deal of theoretical interest. Since its publication, besides the five opinions presented in Fuller's original paper, several publications have expressed their opinions on the case. This case is hypothetical, but based on one or two historical cases. Fuller represents an idealized version of the case so that he can present judicial decisions that represent various schools of judicial interpretation based on rival legal theories. First we shall present the facts of the case, and then the rest of the chapter covers a wide array of (fictional) judicial or academic responses to the case. By reading each of the different responses, we can learn that judgements about the very same facts produce radically different results. Some judges acquit, some condemn, some recuse themselves (that is, step down from the case), all based on the very same events. What accounts for all these different decisions and approaches is the *legal philosophy* in the background of the judges'/scholars' thought processes. Therefore, reading each of the differing responses to this case exposes us to the widest possible array of rival philosophies of law. This wonderfully provocative case about Speluncean (i.e. cave) explorers thus serves as a cannibal's thorough guide to jurisprudence!

Facts of the case

In this particular case, four explorers are tried for the crime of murder, because they have killed and eaten another explorer who was with them, named Roger Whetmore. They engaged in this act in order to survive in a trapped cave while rescue efforts were still underway. The idea of killing and eating one of their own party was actually initially suggested by Whetmore himself. The reason for this terrible decision was because medical experts, who were able to communicate with the trapped explorers, informed them that cannibalism was a possible means of survival until the time they could be rescued. The experts had told them that there was 'little possibility' that they would survive for more than ten days without food (Fuller, 1949: 2).

Whetmore asked all those above ground with whom they could communicate how the trapped explorers should decide which one of their party they should kill and eat. However, no rescuer, doctor, judge, member of government or priest offered any advice. Whetmore then suggested throwing dice. The group of trapped explorers agreed, but before the dice was thrown, Whetmore himself backed out from this plan. The others threw the dice on his behalf, and he was the one who lost.

During the rescue efforts, ten rescuers were killed by landslides, but the rescue efforts succeeded and the four surviving explorers were saved. They were rescued on the 32nd day, and it was learned that they had killed and eaten Whetmore on the 23rd day after their entrapment in the cave. This means that as per the advice of the medical team, they probably all might have survived even if they had not killed and eaten one of their party. However, they had no way to know this. After their rescue, the four surviving explorers were tried for murder. The first court convicted them of murder. They appealed to the Supreme Court. What follows are the decisions of the judges of the Supreme Court on appeal.

The views – Chief Justice Truepenny

According to Justice Truepenny, the law states that 'Whosoever shall wilfully take the life of another shall be punished by death' (Fuller, 1949: 4). Considering 'law to be law', a view held mostly by legal positivists, the case of the Speluncean Explorers does not allow for an exception. However, clemency could be an alternative for the chief executive to consider so that the law's verdict is not too rigorous given the unusual circumstances. This approach will disregard neither the spirit nor the letter of the statutes in the *status quo*. At the same time, this approach shows complete regard for the law. In short, then, the chief justice upholds the conviction based on a legal positivist approach, but he also suggests that the chief executive (for example, president or prime minister) could be asked to pardon the convicted.

Justice Foster

Justice Foster is critical of Chief Justice Truepenny's opinion on this case. In the spirit of a natural law theorist, he believes that the conduct of the men on trial could not be considered a crime given the specific circumstances of the case. Nor does he appreciate expediency in this case. He tries to justify acquittal of the defendants on the following two grounds:

1 This case is governed by the law of nature and the enacted or positive law of the commonwealth, which includes statutes and precedents, is inapplicable in this specific case. He believes that the maxim of 'the reason for the law ceasing, the law ceases itself' (Fuller, 1949: 5) is applicable to this exceptional case. Positive laws assume the coexistence of men in a society. In this specific case, it was impossible without killing one man. Therefore, precedents and statutes do not exist, or rather they should not. In this case, then, the statute regarding murder is not supported by common sense, for the legal order was remote for the defendants just as if they were geographically miles beyond the boundaries of their state. He felt that the men were not guilty of any crime. Justice Foster also noted that their action was in fact proposed by Whetmore, whose life was taken. He also asserted the importance of contracts to the effect that governments were historically formed by contracts. He also mentioned that the absolute value of life is overrated in this case. However, he also showed the irony that in the rescue efforts of the five explorers, the lives of ten rescue workers were lost. He believed that the ten men sacrificed their lives for they were aware of the possible risks of undertaking the mission and they still went ahead with it. And if it is not wrong for the rescue workers to attempt to save five lives, why should it be considered wrong for four explorers to carry out an arrangement which would have saved four lives at the cost of one?
2 Accepting for argument's sake that this particular case falls under the dictates of positive law instead of the law of nature, Justice Foster says that often the statutes are not followed to the letter. This is mainly because in certain cases contingencies do not permit us to apply the statutes as stated. Reference is made to the *Fehler v. Neegas* case, in which the position of the word 'not' in the final and crucial section of the act by error changed the intended meaning of the law proposed. And so in this case, the court must dismiss a literal statutory interpretation. In addition, the exception of killing by self-defence, though recognizable in the court of law, does not find an exception in the statute which states that 'it is a crime to take a life.' Justice Foster understood the case of the defendants as a case of self-preservation and used the same logic used

in the case of self-defence to justify their act of self-preservation by means of taking one life. As per him some legislative oversights and errors need to be corrected and not adhered to, and in this case not to consider it an exception to the statute about what considers murder will be one such correction.

Justice Tatting

Unable to make a decision, Justice Tatting withdrew himself from this case for he believed that the case was counterbalanced by opposing views that lead in opposite directions. He was of the view that the prosecutor should not have brought this court to trial unless there was a law against cannibalism. There are too many circumstances in this case that made it difficult for him to determine the scope of exception to the statute of murder. Some of these include considering different scenarios postulating *what if* questions. *What if* Whetmore had refused to participate in the plan? *What if* no plan had been adopted? *What if* the plan to kill Whetmore had been motivated by personal bias against the victim? He wonders if it would be correct to put four men to death for whom ten men had died in rescue attempts. His reasons for disagreement with Justice Foster are as follows:

1. He fails to see why this case should be governed by the state of nature instead of civil society and he asks when one state ceases and another begins to be applicable.
2. He questions rhetorically if judges can take a decision when the case is governed by the state of nature. He answers in the negative.
3. He pits the instinct of self-preservation against the instinct of self-defence of the victim, which would have been possible had Whetmore shot them as they approached to kill him. He argues that if the defendants were right to kill him, he would have been unable to win the case by pleading self-defence just as a condemned prisoner is not justified to kill an executioner.
4. He did not believe that the defendants were under the code of nature. Besides, he did not accept the way the code was interpreted by Justice Foster.
5. *Commonwealth v. Valjean* was a case in which the court did not accept the justification of hunger as a reason to steal food. How could killing and eating a man be justified on a similar basis? Could someone starve to avoid a sentence? Will deterrence be served in such cases? Again, it can be argued that the stigma associated with the murder is such that had the defendants thought

that their actions would be qualified as murder, they might have waited and perhaps they might have even been rescued. Clearly, Tatting appears conflicted on whether this case will serve to deter.

6 He points out that Justice Foster has made the assumption that a statute is to be interpreted taking into account its purpose. Now, self-defence was treated as an exception to the statute as per which 'Whosoever shall wilfully take the life of another shall be punished by death' in the *Commonwealth v. Parry* case. However, in the *Commonwealth v. Scape* case, the object of a statute was retribution, while in the *Commonwealth v. Makeover* case, the object was rehabilitation of the culprit. What is to be done then, he asks, if there are many purposes (such as retribution or rehabilitation) besides deterrence?

7 He points out that while the statute concerning murder requires a wilful act, it cannot be compared with self-defence for that a response to an impulse of self-preservation. The defendants acted wilfully and with great deliberation after discussing the matter for hours.

Justice Keen

Justice Keen is critical of Chief Justice Foster's views of directing the chief executive. As per law and the proper separation of powers, he believes he cannot give any directions to the chief executive nor consider his views to arrive at a decision. He also puts aside the moral aspect of the law and focuses on the content of the statute under question. He proposes fidelity to the legislature by enacting as per the law, as per which the defendants were found guilty of murder for they willed to take the life of Whetmore. He maintains that judicial forms are understood in the light of three requisites – a purpose, a legislator and *quod erat faciendum* ('that which is to be done') to fill the loopholes in the law. He admits that neither he nor Justice Foster know the purpose of the statute. This is all right, since according to him, the importance lies in determining the scope of the statute and not its purpose. This case cannot be made an exception due to self-defence. This is because according to Justice Keen, the scope of self-defence is applicable in cases of resisting an existent threat to the party's own life. As Whetmore posed no threat to the other explorers, their acts cannot be justified on the basis of self-defence. His decision is that the defendants should get the death penalty. He is aware that this decision is not popular, may not be considered moral by some and that it goes against his wishes, but it shows fidelity to the law.

Justice Hardy

Justice Hardy maintains that the government is of the people and that men are ruled well by other men when the sentiments of the masses are given importance instead of abstract principles. His judgement is based on public opinion and the indirect knowledge that the chief executive shall not commute the sentence if it was decided that the law was not followed in this case. He does admit that rules and abstract principles are essential in some cases such as the manner of conducting elections, appointment and term of public officials, etc. However, for him a good administrator is one who applies principles and procedures to the case at hand and selects the form most suited to reach the proper result. There is efficacy and adherence to common sense in such decisions. With reference to this case, he points to its publicity in national and international media. He takes into account polling data according to which 90% of the people believed that the men on trial should be pardoned.

The original decision

Since one judge withdrew from the case (Tatting), there were only four judges left to decide. Of the four, two judges were in favour of upholding the guilty verdict (Truepenny and Keen), and two judges were in favour of acquitting (Foster and Hardy). Since it was a tie, the decision of the lower court stood, and the four men were convicted of murder and sentenced to death.

That, at least, is how the original case presented by Lon Fuller concluded. However, since that time, many other legal scholars have developed on the original case and invented many further scenarios, such as the advisory decisions of a panel of legal scholars, or a retrial and new decisions. We shall discuss all such further proceedings in the remainder of the chapter.

Further proceedings

In 'The Speluncean Explorers – Further Proceedings', Justice Anthony D'Amato (1980) attempts to examine how the right thesis applies to this case. He asks the readers to imagine that after the decision of the Supreme Court is handed, a special commission comprised by three professors is set by the chief executive. Each professor presents a recommendation on whether clemency should be extended to the convicted defendants.

Professor Wun does not recommend clemency. He believes that the defendants committed murder wilfully out of self-interest. In fact, they included Whetmore who had opted out of the plan to increase chances of individual survival.

Professor Tieu is in favour of clemency and believes that the statute regarding murder is not in violation. His emphasis is on the 'life' of the group and says that the executioner will be guilty of violating the statute 'whosoever shall wilfully take the life of another shall be punished by death' if the defendants are executed because they tried to survive.

Professor Thri believes that the defendants are neither guilty nor innocent of committing murder. And he recommends to commute the sentence of the defendants to years of compulsory service in a medical facility like a hospital where they can help save lives.

Contemporary proceedings

In 'The Case of the Speluncean Explorers: Contemporary Proceedings', seven more views are presented by the seven thinkers of this hypothetical case, where they present their views as 'judges'. These are Justice Naomi R. Cahn, Justice John O. Calmore, Justice Mary I. Coombs, Justice Dwight L. Green, Justice Geoffrey C. Miller, Justice Jeremy Paul and Justice Laura W. Stein. These new decisions introduce new movements in legal philosophy which had gained salience since the 1950s, when Fuller published the original case. For example, the new decisions also include feminist theories of the law, critical race and critical legal theories.

Justice Cahn

She presents three kinds of feminist theories before giving her verdict: 1. pragmatic feminism, 2. critical cultural feminism and 3. liberal feminism. She urges the jury and the trial judge to understand and use these perspectives to re-examine the case. Justice Naomi R. Cahn says it is possible that Whetmore's choices were not adequately represented by the judges who tried the case in Fuller's paper. She also points out that the stories of the defendants might have not been made available to the jury. Perhaps this was a case of assisted suicide. Given this uncertainty, more facts are needed to interpret 'wilfully' in the statute. Her opinion is that the jury and trial judge should consider the context in which the case arose and to also consider emotions to interpret the statute and to decide the meaning of wilfully.

Justice Calmore

He is a critical race theorist who condemns the death penalty. Although this case does not present any racial issues, he argues that racial biases are taken into account in cases of capital punishment to exercise social control and execute people of colour. He talks about oppression of blacks and Jews in the fictional Commonwealth of Newgarth. He believes that jurisprudence must include compassion, fidelity to justice and righteous decency, which does not gel well with capital punishment.

Justice Coombs

Another feminist, she notices that the judges seem to sympathize with the male defendants facing the death penalty. She ponders upon the devastating consequence of this case should a conviction take place for this may be applicable to battered women who may also wilfully take lives for self-defence. In her opinion, there should be a retrial of this case because of a procedural defect. The defendants were entitled to trial by jury and the records did not show they waived this right. Moreover, a jury verdict might be the best approach towards particularized justice, which in her opinion is needed in such cases.

Justice Green

His opinion is to confirm the conviction. He notices that the defendants represent a rather privileged group of individuals who imposed their values on another's life and presume to have a right to impose their values on others as long as the process in their view is fair. He refers to the *Commonwealth v. Valjean* case, where pardon was not granted to poverty-stricken defendants. Consequently, he affirms the conviction of this group as well. He has reservations on whether the death penalty is appropriate and suggests that the sentencing court must figure out each of the defendants' role in the killing of Whetmore and then understand their role given their life situations and circumstances. After sentencing, any sentencing error can be appealed in the court.

Justice Miller

He believes in the cost-benefit analysis and reverses the conviction on utilitarian grounds. His view is that the death of Whetmore was necessary to prevent the death of four more. Had the explorers waited for the death of another by natural causes, the health of the other four could have been negatively affected. The death of one and health of four others was a likely means to avoid further fatalities. The case presents no cause for retribution. Their release would not encourage wrongdoing. As this case is unique, it is unlikely to impact other cases. Sentencing the defendants would be costly for having deprived them of life, it would remove them from the workforce and it would cause emotional suffering. So his opinion is to reverse the conviction.

Justice Paul

After considering all the points of the judges in Fuller's paper, Justice Paul opines to reverse the conviction. He believes it would be monstrous to punish the defendants for something which could not be properly called a crime. He clarifies that this decision is not a political disposition to be critical of state-imposed violence. Moreover, his opinion regarding this case is not applicable to other cases.

Justice Stein

She believes that the defendants must be absolved of murder charges based on moral intuition. Unable to explain the basis of such intuition, she argues that much is lost and nothing is gained by issuing the death penalty for the defendants. Their conviction will not deter any troubling future behaviour nor will the sanctity of life be preserved by taking more lives. To answer her own question – namely, how can absolution be legally justified? – she says that we failed in our social obligation to them by not advising them before they committed this act, although such an advice was in fact sought. And it is unlikely, given the media coverage, that the judiciary would have been unaware of the same. Therefore, she believes that she is in no position to judge them, but she prefers to let them go free instead of recusing herself from this case.

Nine new opinions

Another important philosopher of law, Peter Suber, added nine new hypothetical opinions in his 1998 book *The Case of the Speluncean Explorers: Nine New Opinions*. Suber introduces new ways of deciding about the law, including utilitarian, deontological, feminist and economic approaches, and also adds new interpretations of positivist and natural law approaches. The nine new opinions were given as follows:

Justice Tally considers this a case of preventive killing which can be justified based on utilitarian grounds.

Justice Trumpet gives a sanctity-of-life argument. He argues that one should die before killing and therefore upholds the conviction.

Justice Burnham takes a positivist standpoint and upholds the conviction by maintaining a dichotomy between law and morals. A historical and objective approach is suggested to be adopted particularly while upholding a law in a pluralistic society with diverse moral views.

Justice Springham interprets *wilfulness* to mean that only intentional criminal conduct is punishable. And since the defendants killed from necessity, this element was absent and therefore the conviction should be overturned. Even if this is not accepted, the death penalty should be nullified and the defendants should be sentenced again.

Justice Bond points out that the meaning of words such as wilfulness is never stable so the statute cannot be decisive. Judicial discretion is unavoidable and desirable. He notices that interpreting silence is equally important in this case for the explorers did seek advice. However, none was provided. This was either due to equipment failure or to the withdrawal of the social contract of the Newgarthian society, which allowed the death to take place by throwing a dice. He recuses himself.

Justice Hellen, a feminist, argues for acquittal. She believes that the defendants need not wait until the very last moment before death to execute their plan. It is irrelevant that Whetmore was not an aggressor. It was the circumstances that necessitated his death, not his conduct.

Justice Reckon believes that crime is expensive and that punishment can make rational men obey the law. He believes that the defendants did not act out of necessity and upholds the conviction.

Justice Frank empathizes with the defendants and argues that he would have, if put in similar circumstances, joined the lottery and would have helped kill the loser and eat him. Therefore, he cannot convict the defendants because he cannot condemn others for something he would have done himself. Such imagination is part of the judge's task and is essential to lead an ethical life.

Justice Goad argues that Whetmore had withdrawn his consent so his co-workers could not infer any tacit consent to any part of the plan. They did not act in self-defence and they must take responsibility for their actions. This precludes them from arguing that it was a necessity to kill Whetmore. He does sympathize with the defendants, but upholds the conviction.

The case revisited

Six more opinions were added by the judges Alex Kozinski, Cass Sunstein, Robin West, Frank H. Easterbrook, Alan Dershowitz and Paul Butler in 'The Case of the Speluncean Explorers: A Fiftieth Anniversary Symposium' (Shapiro and Fuller, 1999). This new set of decisions is particularly interesting because all of the contributors are actual judges or legal theorists who do not just write fictional judgements. Instead, each of these very well-known judges/scholars are asked to write down how they would *really* decide this case if it came before them.

Justice Kozinski

He reads the NCSA 12-A statute literally and upholds the conviction of the defendants. Unlike common law judges, he believes that the statute is not open to interpretation. His argument is that Whetmore did not die due to illness, starvation, accident or neglect. Prior to killing him, the defendants had thought long and hard. Moreover, medical experts had advised of 'little possibility' and not 'no possibility' of survival. He gives the example of a case where contrary to doctors' predictions a patient survived nine years after life support was withdrawn. This led him to believe that a resilient human body may beat the odds. It is possible, he believes, that all may have survived. And even if all did not survive, the first one to die could have been eaten. He ponders that perhaps Whetmore may have thought of an alternate way of survival, for he did back out from his self-proposed solution, which the defendants executed. Justice Kozinski refers to a similar case and says that this case is not a legislative oversight. And even if it was, it would make no difference for one is not at liberty to 'ignore or augment legislature's words' (Kozinski et al., 1999: 1878), presuming it would have said something else had it been thought differently. He makes a case against popular appeal to acquittal by pointing out that the actions of public officials support the conviction.

Justice Sunstein

As a self-proclaimed textualist, Justice Sunstein's concern is not to uphold the conviction merely because it follows from the literal meaning of the statute in question. Instead, he upholds the conviction because after analyzing this case, its interpretation leads to no absurdity or unreasonable verdict to read the statute as such. He argues that while there is no literal ambiguity, excessive generality may have created a problem in interpretation. His approach is to analyze whether this case is like others where life is wilfully taken to protect those who may be regarded as innocent. Only then the question of an exception can be raised. However, that is not the case here for the victim did not threaten the lives of other explorers. In fact, the defendants can be condemned for killing the victim for selfish motives, that is, to save their own lives. He argues that from a Kantian, retributive and deterrence point of view, holding the conviction would lead to no absurdity. Moreover, as Whetmore withdrew his consent from the plan of cannibalism, the defendants had no sufficient legal excuse to kill.

Justice West

Justice West believes that the main purpose of the law is to protect the individual's right to equal respect. And it is this protection that gives licence to contractual freedom. She makes a reference to the state of nature and the rule of law, probably in light of Justice Foster's arguments in Fuller's original paper. For her, the protection against homicide is what distinguishes between these two states and laws are made so that individual rights are not lost in a state of nature. Such protection as provided by this statute is so vital to grant individual rights to equal respect that it cannot be overlooked due to an individual's or a group's moral or economic gain due to the utilitarian principle that it is better to sacrifice one life to save more lives. She points out that laws against suicide, assisted suicide and so forth also indicate the importance of state protection against assaultive conduct, even if self-inflicted or willed. This is not the case, for Whetmore did withdraw his consent. She argues that just like killing for organs cannot be equated to self-defence, cannibalism cannot be equated to self-defence, even if this meant saving more lives. However, while she finds the defendants guilty, she believes that they do not deserve to be given the death penalty.

Justice De Bunker (Justice Dershowitz)

Alan M. Dershowitz writes under the pseudonym of Justice De Bunker. He is critical of both natural and inalienable rights. It is Justice De Bunker's belief that all laws must be positive laws and that rights are just strongly held human preferences. Some rights are preferred over some others. Justice De Bunker's preference in the case of the Speluncean explorers is to reverse the conviction by permitting 'whatever is not forbidden'. This is because Justice De Bunker is of the view that when a tragic choice recurs and can be anticipated, and is one which has led to disagreements regarding if it be permitted, the responsibility falls on the legislature to prohibit such a choice by making it a positive law.

Justice Easterbrook

He chooses to reverse the conviction and bases his arguments on the net cost or benefit to affected parties. So the justification is utilitarian insofar as more lives would be saved by the sacrifice of one life. This justification is given for the necessity of the defendants to act in the way they did. He asserts that acting behind a veil of ignorance, it is likely that they would rationally agree to cannibalism, which may substantially reduce the risk of death due to starvation before embarking upon this risky mission.

Justice Stupidest Housemaid (Justice Paul Butler)

In Fuller's article, reference was made to a stupid housemaid by Justice Foster, so Paul Butler writes under the pseudonym Justice Stupidest Housemaid. He believes that no crime has been committed which can be morally condemned. He is also against the death penalty and argues that to kill the defendants to prove that killing is wrong is absurd. He argues that the conviction will not serve the purpose of deterrence. This is because it is odd to expect the defendants will not kill Whetmore in order to prevent themselves from ultimately dying – and so he reverses the conviction.

Conclusion

The purpose of this case is to introduce students of philosophy of law to diverse legal theories as the opinions of various scholars and judges represent the different views of natural law theorists, consequentialists, rights theorists, feminists, positivists, textualists, purposivists, realists, pragmatists, contextualists, critical race theorists, minimalists and process theorists. What students can learn is that different decisions are not just the result of different facts. On the contrary, the same facts lead to widely different results, all because of the central importance of the philosophy of law.

4 Law and rationality

The term 'legal reasoning' can refer to different domains of activity and process. We can speak of the type of reasoning and argumentation of litigators, such as prosecutors and defence attorneys, working within a court of law. One level 'higher', we can speak of the type of reasoning of the judge(s) within that same court of law, or alternatively, of lawmakers/legislators within a parliamentary body. At a still 'higher' level, we can speak of the reasoning of members of a constituent assembly, those tasked with debating and determining the most basic questions of law, the drafting of a constitution. The 'legal' sense of legal reasoning in all these different domains is self-evident, but what is the sense of 'reasoning', what is the model of reasoning or rationality understood to be?[1]

There is a classical understanding about the nature and normativity of reasoning which asserts that competent reasoning operates in line with rules derived from the established canons of rational inference, such as classical logic, probability theory and decision theory. This is what Edward Stein refers to as the 'standard picture':

> According to this picture, to be rational is to reason in accordance with principles of reasoning that are based on rules of logic, probability theory and so forth. If the standard picture of reasoning is right, principles of reasoning that are based on such rules are normative principles of reasoning, namely, they are the principles we ought to reason in accordance with.[2]

The standard picture of reasoning has been subject to increasing attack ever since its promulgation in the Enlightenment period (that is, starting in the 17th century in Europe). This attack achieved devastating results in the 20th century, when philosophy, logic, mathematics and cognitive science each, independently but simultaneously, put forward such intensive critiques of rationality, especially of the human's cognitive capacity to reason in accordance with the norms of reasoning, that the very notion of 'reasoning' has become suspect.

This chapter will explore the implications for legal reasoning amidst such critiques of reason and rationality. Towards the end, it will also attempt to lay out some of the implications of legal reasoning for our understanding of rationality itself – that is, can legal reasoning contribute towards attempts to salvage some basic or minimal foundation for reasoning itself?

Post-enlightenment critiques of reason

Since establishing the priority and dominance of reason has been widely regarded as a major project of the Enlightenment, the critique of rationality and the authority of reason is often understood as a post-Enlightenment phenomenon. However, critiques of reason and attacks against its authority to displace earlier regnant forms of authority (God's will, for example) arose simultaneously with the project of establishing the normativity and authority of human reason during the Enlightenment.[3]

Very early, David Hume (1711–76) made remarks to the effect that the notion of 'reason' may often be regarded as devoid of meaning; rather, it is just a technique for asserting the truth or correctness of a position to refer to it as established by reason. The passions, rather, were supreme. Much earlier, Thomas Hobbes (1588–1679), generally regarded as having a robust conception of human's ability to reason, occasionally suggested – similar to Hume – that reason (or, more precisely, thoughts) acted as the 'scouts and spies' of passion, and that reason is a merely instrumental tool, that can be exploited towards any ends, even wicked ones, as is evident in crime.

The great German philosopher G.W.F. Hegel (1770–1831) also served to undermine the classical conception of reason even as he aimed to establish the fundamental rationality of the external world. After all, throughout Hegel's writings, and articulated most clearly in his *Logic*, we find that the classical canons of reason are grounded in the principle of identity and the principle of non-contradiction, neither of which offers anything substantive about the true nature of things in the world. Reality is fluid, and only dialectical thought can capture the nature of things, which in themselves entail the simultaneous suspension of contradictions, not just identity, but the identity of identity *and* difference. Reacting against Hegel's rationalism, even its non-standard dialectical or contradictory form, Soren Kierkegaard

(1813–55) passionately appealed that nothing important in the world gives relevance to reason. Reason has no bearing on everything that is truly significant, such as faith, love, art, friendship and so on.

An even more shocking critique of reason was put forward by the German social philosopher Theodor Adorno (1903–69), who did not remark on the ineffectiveness or uselessness or impossibility of rationality, but rather suggested that reason in its Enlightenment form culminates in evil. The Nazi death camps, for example, are a high and consistent expression of rationality. Some implications of the prolific writings of French philosopher Michel Foucault (1926–84) also serve to dethrone reason from its authoritative position. After all, humans simply have no such faculty of reason as classically conceived; that is, as transcendent, objective, gender neutral, class neutral, culture neutral, timeless, disinterested and so on. Such a critique is in part shared by the American pragmatist Richard Rorty (1931–2007), since reason is nothing like the substantive, transcendent, eternal, objective cognitive capacity pictured in the standard model, but rather empty, precautionary – summed up in the admonition to be cautious, to double check, to concentrate and draw valid inferences from given propositions. Jacques Derrida (1930–2004) too further specified the critique of reason in terms of pointing out that reason is only justified circularly, and circular reasoning violates valid reasoning, it is a fallacy. If reason is justified by reason, then how do we exclude supplanting self-justified authorities such as emotion or feeling? Someone may suggest that feeling is more authoritative or trumps reason, arguing that we need to feel it to understand.

Cognitive science as a critique of reason

Adding a great deal of force to the post-Enlightenment critiques of reason is the empirical evidence on just how rare the appearance of reason actually is. That is, even if we granted reason its traditional normative status, experiments within clinical psychology and cognitive science show preponderantly that people just do not follow the rules of logic, do not have cognitive access to the principles of probability theory, do not make rational decisions. We find these results arising from experiments related to selection tasks, the conjunction fallacy, base-rate neglect and over-confidence. Let us briefly sketch each in turn.

In the 1960s, Peter Wason conducted a study of standard reasoning problems known as the 'selection task'. The study subsequently sparked so much research that scholars suggest that the selection task is the most deeply researched problem in the psychology of reasoning.[4] The task subjects are faced with is to select answers to problems in order to determine the subjects' apprehension of basic laws of formal logic, such as *modus ponens* and its variations, *modus tollens* and so on. What research has consistently found over the years is that the vast majority of people perform very poorly on selection task problems, suggesting that the laws of logic or the basic principles of soundness and validity in reasoning are not cognitively accessible to people in actual experience.

The command that most people – highly educated as well as average persons – have over basic laws of probability is also meagre. Studies, even including Harvard Medical graduates and Stanford University professors, repeatedly show that in working out probabilities, people routinely commit formal as well as informal fallacies, including the notorious conjunction fallacy. This fallacy arises when subjects assume that a compound state of affairs is more probable than one of the components of the compound. For example, if asked to rank the probability of threc circumstancc, such as:

1 I am a philosopher of law
2 I am a male
3 I am a male philosopher of law

subjects preponderantly and routinely rank 3 as a higher probability than 1 or 2 although clearly in order to be a *male* philosopher of law I must first be a philosopher of law.

Another set of experiments has decisively illustrated that people have strong tendencies to substitute bias, stereotypes and prejudices for factual, base-rate information during reasoning and calculation. For example, assume that in a sample of 100 persons, 20% are business men and 80% are farmers. When subjects are asked about the likelihood that one of these persons, who happens to be wearing an expensive watch, is a business man or a farmer, the answer preponderantly and routinely provided is that he is more than 50% likely to be a business man. This ignores the base-rate information that the answer is clearly more likely that he is a farmer (80%), substituting our casual assumptions and stereotypes for hard data.

Another worrisome phenomenon observed by psychologists of reasoning involves the degree of confidence that people have in their responses to even very difficult factual questions. For example, in a study, subjects were asked:

> In each of the following pairs, which city has more inhabitants?
>
> (a) Las Vegas (b) Miami
> (a) Sydney (b) Melbourne
> (a) Hyderabad (b) Islamabad
> (a) Bonn (b) Heidelberg

After each answer subjects are also asked 'How confident are you that your answer is correct?' They are given the options of 50%, 60%, 70%, 80%, 90% and 100%. Typically, the cases where subjects say they are 100% confident, only about 80% of their answers are correct.[5]

To put the results of such studies together, what we see is that not only do people lack the cognitive capacity to reason in accordance with the standard normative picture of rationality, but they are also overconfident about their abilities of judgement. There are numerous further studies within cognitive science related to the failure of people to use reason, the prevalence of subjective bias over principles of formal logic, that call into doubt our basic cognitive capacities to reason in line with the standard picture. These are not performance errors that can be fixed or improved given more time or better experimental conditions. Rather, these studies question whether we have the basic cognitive capacity to reason in line with the classical assumption that human beings are rational animals.

The status of reason in logic and mathematics

It is not uncommon for those who are aware of the many and varied radical critiques of reason enumerated above to still hold out some hope for the status of reason, by assuming that the vibrant disciplines of 20th-century logic and mathematics nevertheless attest to the robust existence of reason and rationality beyond the death grip of deep scepticism. However, this assumption is false in certain decisive respects. Far from rescuing reason from attack, contemporary logic and mathematics can be seen as supporting the large-scale attacks on the Enlightenment authority of reason.

Twentieth-century logic has in fact made the progress it is reputed to have made precisely by abandoning a robust and normative understanding of reason. Earlier, reason was regarded as transcendent, universal, objective – in short, able to judge between rival and alternative systems, for example, in terms of the 'highest' level of legal reasoning, able to judge between or amongst rival conceptions of basic constitutional regimes, rationally choosing one as superior to others. But this higher faculty of judgement has been undermined in the post-Enlightenment critiques of reason, leaving us with a frail, functional notion of reason as the faculty for drawing inferences from given premises. The inherent worth of premises is not a task reason can confidently adjudicate. Truth is sacrificed for validity. Semantics is eschewed to rescue syntax.

And thus it stands with contemporary logic. The great advances it has made have occurred precisely as a consequence of abandoning truth for validity. Reason is regarded as an instrumental rule-following, inference-drawing capacity, with no scope to judge the soundness or truth of the system, or to choose amongst rival systems, alternative logics. Thus the proliferation of non-standard logics, such as those which reject the basic principles of classical formal logic, like the principle of excluded middle. Internal to these logics, consistent, valid inferences can be drawn and the systems enjoy their own utility and thus justification. As for selection between them, or between non-standard and standard logic, this reason has not the authority to do. Thus, 20th-century logic can be seen to support the critiques of reason over and against supporting the former authority of reason itself.

In this respect, 20th-century logic followed from developments of 19th-century mathematics, specifically, geometry. For two millennia, mathematicians attempted to prove Euclid's parallel postulate, the fifth of ten axioms made explicit in classical plane geometry. While unprovable, the axiom was regarded as 'worthy' to be accepted ('worthy' being roughly the meaning of the root of the term 'axiom' in Greek) as it accorded with the conception of reason that prevailed; reason that could judge between value systems, that stood above in some significant respects its quotidian inferential function. The effort to prove the parallel postulate by showing the contradictions that arise by rejecting it were as doomed to failure as the effort to prove it positively. However, the frequent attempts to prove by contradiction opened up the door to establish geometries that proceeded without the fifth postulate at all – non-Euclidean geometries. Now, the utility of non-Euclidean geometries to the natural sciences is beyond dispute (the utility of non-standard logics is far less apparent); one need only look at Einstein's work to see this. But one point to note is that the process of dethroning Euclidean geometry's assumptions about the nature of reason hit the intellectual culture hard. From Dostoevsky (who had Ivan Karamazov emote anxiously about the demise of the fifth postulate of Euclid) to Arthur Conan Doyle (who gave Sherlock Holmes's diabolical nemesis

Dr Moriarty a Ph.D. in non-Euclidean geometry), to Lewis Carroll (who showed us a wonderland liberated from the classical conception of reason), the advance of geometry was regarded as a swansong for the transcendence or resplendence of reason. Reason was not entitled to choose or arbitrate between axioms; it could only make inferences based upon them.

Antinomies of supporting and refuting reason

We have discussed critiques of reason arising from different disciplines and perspectives. The attempt to defend reason from such critiques faces a problem of internal contradiction, insofar as the justification of reason relies upon reason, and this is a circular argument. At the same time, the critique of reason itself suffers from being stated in terms of reasons; that is, the critique of reason deploys basic rational forms, arguments, syllogisms. Further, any absolute judgements about the limitations of reason are also self-contradictory, as to declare the limit of reason only to inferences is a use of reason transcending inferences. Both supporting and refuting reason seems to result in internal contradictions, impasses or what Kant referred to as antinomies.

Notice that the strong critiques of reason in philosophy, cognitive science, logic and maths are most detrimental to the 'highest' tier of legal reasoning, that of constituent assemblies, who must adjudicate between different systems altogether, preferring certain axiomatic sets over others. The local reasoning employed by litigators is hardly open to attack, in that the reduced conception of reason as instrumental and inferential is consistent with the legal reasoning internal to a (legal) system, which is all that is expected from prosecutors or defenders, and other litigants. The real question is about the middle level, the judges and lawmakers: is it possible that they make rational choices, free of bias, objective, laws reflecting rational considerations? Or is there no way for judges and lawmakers to overcome the biases from which reason seems empirically to suffer, or the class and caste and other identity interests that seems to bound the reasoning of persons?

Avoiding antinomies: natural justice as a procedural ground for reasoning

The adversarial nature of the legal system demands certain procedural safeguards, a sort of level playing field, upon which persons subject to the law can at least minimally recognize the legitimate authority of the legal system. The concept of natural justice entails just this sort of procedural safeguard, a minimal threshold, an axiomatic and universal (objective, transcendent, etc.) set of conditions that must be followed to ensure that we are engaged with a legal system at all (as opposed to an arbitrary exercise of tyrannical power).

By natural justice we are referring to the procedural rules against bias, requiring a fair hearing of both parties, and demanding that all orders be 'speaking' orders, which is to say, reasoned orders articulating the rationale and justification for the decision reached.

Natural justice is the name for the principles and procedures that govern the adjudication of disputes between persons or organizations, that the adjudication should be unbiased and given in good faith, and that each party should have equal access to the court/tribunal/authority and should be aware of arguments and documents adduced by the other. In modern jurisprudence natural justice is construed to include following three procedural safeguards:

1 *Nemo debet esse judex in propria causa.* No one should be made a judge in his own cause, popularly known as rule against bias.
2 *Audi alteram partem.* No one shall be condemned unheard or let the other side be heard as well or both parties shall be heard before taking decision, popularly known as the rule of fair hearing.
3 *Reasoned decision/speaking order requirement.* Every decision must be based on reason.

Whence derive the principles of natural justice? That is just the point: nowhere; or, alternatively, everywhere. What is of fundamental importance to these principles is that they are not constructed out of some rarefied thought experiment, such as the well-known political philosopher John Rawls uses the idea of the 'original position' to generate the two principles of justice. The generation of the principles of justice in Rawls occurs in a process begun behind a 'veil of ignorance', where those who proffer the principles are deracinated, genderless, class neutral, casteless, religionless and lack all identifying features of real flesh-and-blood human persons. So many critiques of Rawls's work are based on the problem of this construction, totally utopian and flying in the face of precisely what is most important to so many: their gender, their religion, their identity.

Natural justice, on the other hand, is a demand of everyone by everyone through the fullness of their identities: its principles are not constructed without regard for race, gender, caste, class, religion, but rather, are demanded by the persons of those various genders, races, classes, castes, religions, themselves. No one enters a court of law and readily submits to having his or her side of the story ignored, or to being judged by his or her adversary in the dispute, or to being commanded without articulated reasons. The beauty of natural justice is that it is not imposed upon us; rather, it is almost everywhere and almost always demanded by us.

Conclusion

Legal reasoning amidst critiques of reason turns out to be not only salvageable, but also possibly a source of some comfort for disciplines or domains beyond the law. In the first place, turning away from the substantive inability for us to confidently adjudicate between rival axiomatic sets, an earlier privilege enjoyed by reason that has now been undermined in post-Enlightenment critiques of reason, we recuperate at the procedural level what we lost at the substantive. With natural justice, we have an axiom 'worthy' to be accepted by anyone who is subject to the domain of law. Within legal reasoning, the lowest tier of litigation has anyway hardly been subject to challenge: this is the most limited, inferential variety of reasoning locally that has not been called into question – indeed, the critiques of reason themselves rely on appeal to this minimum inferential ability in order to articulate their critiques.

At the highest tier, members of a constituent assembly have access to an axiom set that is not merely arbitrary: while reason has been disrobed of its claims to highest authority, universality, objectivity, transcendence, the choice by a constituent assembly that their Constitution shall be grounded in the axiom set implied by natural justice is hardly open to rival logics. And even if it is, given the elementary expectation that we have that the rationale for the appropriateness of the rival logic must be laid out, it does not take too much imagination to see where the balance of reasons would lie (i.e. not in theocracy, not in tyranny, but in a system of self-governance).

Whether judges and lawmakers can make rational and reasonable decisions is still somewhat puzzling – and perhaps this is the tier where the cognitive science critiques of our cognitive abilities is most damning. However, at least what a procedural as opposed to a deontological notion of reasoning (that is, the idea that we reason in accordance with pure norms, like Rawls generates his principles of justice) provides us with is the opportunity to aim towards reasoning that transcends the particularities and biases of identities. As we have seen, this is not in order to annul identities (through some lofty, objective, universal conception of reason), but rather to pay them due respect and consideration.

Notes

1 These levels of legal reasoning are presented by Peter Suber in his 1997 paper 'Legal Reasoning after Post-Modern Critiques of Reason'. This chapter is inspired by and also relies heavily upon the project proposed by Suber in his paper, how to think about legal reasoning amidst radical critiques of reason.
2 R. Samuels, S. Stich and L. Faucher. (2004). 'Reason and Rationality,' section 3.2.
3 Peter Suber. (1997). 'Legal Reasoning after Post-Modern Critiques of Reason.'
4 R. Samuels, S. Stich and L. Faucher. (2004). 'Reason and Rationality,' section 2.1.
5 R. Samuels, S. Stich and L. Faucher. (2004). 'Reason and Rationality,' section 2.4.

5 Wronging rights?[1]

The tradition of criticism of human rights is just as long and rich as the tradition of human rights itself. The first critiques to be formulated blamed the abstraction and arrogance of the *Declaration of the Rights of Man and the Citizen* (1789). For conservatives like Edmund Burke or utilitarians like Jeremy Bentham, the problem with human rights, as couched in the *Declaration*, is, first, that they focus on the needs of the separated individual, and thus compromise social or communitarian values; second, that their abstraction and unconditionality can become a source of opposition to the existing social order, thus eroding the very political institutions that can guarantee their enforcement. For Karl Marx, instead, the abstract individualism of the discourse on human rights is the expression of an alienated society subjected to the impersonal domination of capital. Contemporary critiques of human rights, like those formulated by Hannah Arendt or, later, Giorgio Agamben, have focused on the paradoxical tension between 'man' and 'citizen' as the bearers of rights. This original tension had the effect that precisely those most in need of protection – the stateless, the refugees, 'man' as such – were denied these rights that apparently apply only to citizens. Post-colonialist thought also accused the false universalism of human rights, which is an expression of its Western bias and which obscures the suffering of the non-Western other. Finally, Slavoj Žižek and Jacques Rancière have also emphasized the tension between the abstract universalism of the *Declaration* and its particular application, but saw in this tension the very source of its political efficiency.

Modern critiques – Edmund Burke

The first critiques of human rights started to appear immediately after the *Declaration of the Rights of Man and the Citizen*. In his *Reflections on the Revolution in France* ([1790] 2009), Edmund Burke accused the abstraction and the arrogance of the natural and inalienable rights of man. He thought that it was arrogant and limiting for the drafters of the *Declaration* to cast aside traditional notions that had stood the test of time. Burke did not deny the existence of natural rights; rather he thought that the a priori reasoning adopted by the drafters produced notions that were too abstract to have application within the framework of society. In stating that 'the pretended rights of these theorists are all extremes; and in a proportion as they are metaphysically true, they are morally and politically false', Burke argued that abstract rights are meaningless without a societal framework: 'What is the use of discussing a man's abstract right to food or medicine? The question is upon the method of procuring and administering them' (Burke, 2009: 50).

It was not the rights themselves, as much as the level of abstraction and the placing of them above government which Burke found dangerous. He stated that, 'those who pull down important ancient establishments, who wantonly destroy modes of administration, and public institutions, are the most mischievous, and therefore the wickedest of men' (Burke, 1827: 197). For Burke, politics had no simple answers, and definitely no overarching, universal maxims such as those expressed in the *Declaration*. Rather the rights afforded to individuals were to be assessed in the context of the social framework. However, he acknowledged that the simplicity of the *Declaration* was attractive and feared its ability to undermine social order. Burke believed that the absolute nature of these principles of abstraction was inherently revolutionary; they were uncompromising and any derogation from the principles constituted a reason to rise up in arms. This was a problem because 'all government . . . is founded on compromise and barter. We balance inconveniences; we give and take; we remit some rights that we may enjoy others' (Burke, 2005: 222). The natural rights 'against which there can be no prescription; against these no agreements is binding' (Burke, 2009: 32) gave the revolutionaries the tools to destroy the very society that Burke believed afforded them with rights.

Modern critiques – Jeremy Bentham

The 18th-century utilitarian philosopher Jeremy Bentham criticized the *Declaration of the Rights of Man and the Citizen* in his text 'Anarchical Fallacies' ([1791] 1843). One of the critiques Bentham levelled against the *Declaration* was its assertion of rights in the form of absolute and universal norms. He argued that absolute rights possessed by everyone equally are meaningless and undesirable. They lack meaning because if everyone has, for example, unbounded liberty, there is nothing precluding them from using that liberty to impinge on the liberty of another. In this way 'human government and human laws' are required to give some bounds to rights in order for them to be realized. However, since these rights are declared to be imprescriptible, this means any interference of the laws and existing government is excluded from the outset. In addition to this contradiction, Bentham warned of the dangers of couching rights in absolute terms. A government that is able to protect every person's right absolutely and equally is a utopian aspiration, but the *Declaration* couches it as the conditions for its legitimacy. 'Against every government which fails in any degree of fulfilling these expectations, then, it is the professed object of this manifesto to excite insurrection' (Bentham, 1791: 506).

Not only did Bentham think that there was no logical basis for the theory of natural rights, he believed that their individualistic approach was harmful to society. Bentham thought that society was dependent upon people's ability to pursue the greater good, not just the short term satisfaction of their own desires. The advancement of natural rights, which he saw as celebrating selfishness, was to provide the means to break down the social community that makes human life bearable.

Modern critiques – Marxist critique of human rights

Karl Marx also took issue with the individualistic bias of the *Declaration*. However, contrary to Bentham, he did so not in order to oppose this individualism to the social community, but in order to read in it the expression of the existing bourgeois society and ideology. In *On the Jewish Question*, he claims:

> Above all, we note the fact that the so-called rights of man, the *droits de l'homme* as distinct from the *droits du citoyen*, are nothing but the rights of a member of civil society – i.e. the rights of egoistic man, of man separated from other men and from the community. . . . Security is the supreme social concept of bourgeois society, the concept of the police, the whole society exists only to ensure each of its members the preservation of his person, his rights and his property.
>
> (Marx, 1844)

Thus for Marx, liberal rights and ideas of justice are premised on the idea that each of us needs protection from other human beings. Therefore, liberal rights are rights of separation, designed to protect us from such perceived threats. Freedom in such a view is freedom from interference. What this view denies is the possibility – according to Marx, the fact – that real freedom is to be found positively in our relations with other people. It is to be found in human community, not in isolation. So insisting on a regime of rights encourages us to view each other in ways that undermine the possibility of the real freedom we may find in human emancipation.

Marx argued that the society that gives rise to the idea of rights is the same as that which gives rise to the commodity form. They are two sides of the same coin. It is a society based on production by independent producers whose contact with each other is mediated through the exchange of products in the market. These producers are formally free to produce what and how much they wish. They are formally equal in that no producer can force others to produce against their will or expropriate their products against their will. They are self-interested in that they are all entitled to pursue their own private interests regardless of what others think or do. Their contact with other producers takes the form of free and equal exchanges in which individuals exchange their property in return for the property of another and this exchange of unneeded things in return for useful things appears to be done for the mutual benefit of each party.

The juridical figure of the Person, so central and foundational for the discourse of human rights, is thus the superstructural expression of an atomized society in which the private labour of each individual is blindly socialized 'at his back' via the fluctuations of the capitalist exchange. The individualism and abstraction of human rights are thus not an error of method, but instead express correctly the alienation and impersonal domination of capitalist society.

Contemporary critiques – Hannah Arendt, Giorgio Agamben

Closer to our time, human rights have been criticized not so much for their philosophical stature (abstraction, arrogance and so on), but for the way in which they (mis)functioned in real events.

Prior to World War II, millions of people have been deprived of their citizenship not only in Nazi Germany, but also in many democratic countries of the West. Compounded by the refugee crisis brought about by the war, this created a situation in which countless people were left practically without any legal statute or defence. Hannah Arendt (1973) saw in this extreme situation a logical possibility inscribed in the *Declaration of the Rights of Man and the Citizen*, namely, the curious division of the bearers of rights into 'men' and 'citizens'. This split was already problematic in the *Declaration* itself, since it assumed that these natural and inalienable rights – which should, thus, apply to any person – are somehow restricted or particularized, and apply only to citizens. Hence, these natural rights seem to apply only under a certain political condition – namely, citizenship. This paradoxical imbalance inherent in the initial *Declaration* exploded in dramatic fashion during the war, when it was clear that the inalienable rights of man are indeed conditioned on the statute of citizenship. Thus, precisely those most in need of protection through these rights – the stateless people, the displaced, the refugees – were denied this 'natural' right.

Hannah Arendt's critique of human rights was revisited more recently by Giorgio Agamben, who saw in this imbalance inherent in the original *Declaration* – between natural men as such, and men as citizens, as the only bearer of rights – the classical biopolitical operation, by means of which political sovereignty is grounded in the opposition between bare life and political life and is instituted through the exclusion of the former. Thus, the contemporary crisis of human rights, first analyzed by Arendt in the refugee crisis, is, for Agamben, nothing but proof that the classical mechanism of sovereignty does not function anymore. The concrete outcome of this dramatic breaking down of political sovereignty, the derailment of the operation of articulating a political life on the basis of an excluded bare life, is the camp, which thus constitutes, for Agamben, 'the paradigm of modernity' (Agamben, 1998: 73).

Contemporary critiques – post-colonialist critiques

Another trend of criticism of human rights comes in our time from the post-colonialist tradition, where Indian legal theorists like Ratna Kapur and Upendra Baxi have been active. The general argument consists in accusing the false universality of human rights as Western particularism.

Ratna Kapur, in 'Human Rights in the 21st Century' (2006), for example, argues that 'assertions about the universality of human rights simply deny the reality of those whom it claims to represent and speak for, disclaiming their histories and imposing another's through a hegemonising move' (Kapur, 2006: 674). The abstract universality of human rights is, in fact, a 'discriminatory universality', and one can see this in all the attempts of the West to relate to its other. There are three such attempts, and they are all equally discriminatory:

> The first is through the assumption that the difference can be erased and the 'Other' tamed and assimilated through some form

> of cultural or racial strip. The second is to treat the difference as natural and inevitable. And finally, there is the response that justifies incarceration, internment or even annihilation of the 'Other'.
> (Kapur, 2006: 675)

Therefore, be it assimilation, tolerance or violent rejection – in all its logical possibilities, the proclaimed universality is discriminatory. According to Kapur, the problematic gap between the assertions of rights and 'those whom it claims to represent and speak for' can only be reduced by the '*centring* of excluded subjects, excluded zones and excluded histories' (Kapur, 2006: 687). The story of human rights must 'be told from the perspective of transnational migrants' (Kapur, 2006: 686), for example, because of the 'urgency of re-reading human rights from alternative locations, the excluded zones or from the perspective of excluded subjects' (Kapur, 2006: 685). As Kapur puts it emphatically, they – the excluded ones – are 'the creditors'. Unless the West opens the door, repays its debt of 'cultural erasure' and allows them to tell the story as it really is, that is from their own perspective, there is no chance to 'put some life back into a project in desperate need of resuscitation and to give this body [the legacy of human rights] a soul' (Kapur, 2006: 687).

For Upendra Baxi (2002), the starting point in his critique of human rights is rather similar to Ratna Kapur's: the modern conception of human rights was based on the 'discursive devices of Enlightenment', which were in fact 'devices of *exclusion*' (Baxi, 2002: 29). The passage from modern human rights to contemporary human rights is a passage from an exclusionary to an inclusionary approach, which is accomplished by '*taking suffering seriously*': 'No phrase except a romantic one – *the revolution in human sensibility* – marks the passage' from the first to the second. Baxi claims that the previous, formal and abstract conception of human rights was in fact 'essentialist'; while the contemporary one, based on the concrete experience of pain and on the direct access to difference, is not. The unending task that lies ahead of us is, for Baxi,

> one of *humanizing human rights*, going beyond rarefied discourse . . . to histories of individual and collective hurt. . . . To give language to pain, to experience the pain of the Other inside you, remains the task, always, of human rights narratology.
> (Rathore, 2011: 76)

A similar yet more complex operation of de-abstractization of human rights is accomplished by Gayatri Spivak (2008). She is perfectly aware that there is a certain tension between the need to give a soul to the body and replace the abstract rights with morality (or, in her own terms, the need to effect the passage from rights to responsibility to the Other) and her own theoretical deconstructionist background. Witness her repeated confessions that the suffering of the rural poor of the global South is impossible to translate in the language of academic theory and scholarly research: 'writing this piece has almost convinced me that I was correct in thinking that I should not make it part of my academic discourse'; or, 'I am not able to give scholarly information. . . . I do not usually write about this activity'; or,

> I leave this essay with the sense that the material about the rural teaching is not in the acceptable mode of information retrieval. The difficulty is in the discontinuous divide between those who right wrongs and those who are wronged.
>
> (Rathore, 2011: 104)

For Spivak, the discontinuous divide between those who right wrongs and those who are wronged is such that the suffering of the latter cannot be translated into the language of the former. But this radical divide is, according to Spivak, inherent in the very project of human rights, which is why the project of human rights is nothing but a kind of 'social Darwinism'.

> 'Human rights' is not only about having or claiming a right or a set of rights; it is also about righting wrongs, about being the dispenser of these rights. The idea of human rights [carries within itself the idea that] the fittest must shoulder the burden of righting the wrongs of the unfit.
>
> (Rathore, 2011: 79)

For Spivak, the only chance to correct this structural injustice of human rights is through the appeal to responsibility, which is an 'antonym of right' and whose possibility is 'underived from rights'. The responsibility approach entails a process in which the dispenser of rights learns directly from the subaltern, and in which the educator as educated takes the form of humanities teaching. 'This is the different way of epistemic access, this the teacher's apprenticeship as suturer or invisible mender.' 'Obviously, in the end, this alternative or supplementary project remains virtually untranslatable and almost impossible to communicate: it is just a "licensed lunacy in the name of the unnameable other."'

Contemporary critiques – liberal critiques

In their anti-foundational approaches to human rights, Richard Rorty (1998) and Michael Ignatieff (2003) argue that universal human rights are not to be based on a belief in a 'metaphysical' idea of human rationality, but on a pragmatic idea of sensibility to cruelty. Although they both try to hold on to crucial ingredients from the original project of human rights (the Enlightenment utopia for Rorty, its universalism for Ignatieff), the way to achieve these goals is, for Rorty and Ignatieff, by discarding the maximalist claims to human nature and universally shared rationality and by replacing them with 'the most we can hope for' – a minimalist account of resistance to cruelty. In both cases, this shift towards minimalism and sentimentalism is grounded on a pragmatic basis: as Rorty argues, 'the best, and probably the only, argument for putting foundationalism behind us is [that] it would be more efficient to do so, because it would let us concentrate our energies on manipulating sentiments, on sentimental education' (Rorty, 1998: 176). At first glance, sentimental education seems to do the whole job: 'Producing generations of nice, tolerant, well-off, secure, other-respecting students of this sort in all parts of the world is just what is needed – indeed *all* that is needed – to achieve an Enlightenment utopia.' On more careful inspection, the shared sensibility to cruelty is not the only necessary ingredient, since it has a condition of possibility of its own – security. 'Security and sympathy go together, for the same reasons that peace and economic productivity go together.' As it turns out, sentimental education, as vital as it is, is only the moral superstructure that drags along the even more vital base, namely, the shared peace and security of our shared mode of production.

This liberal criticism of human rights has been, in its turn, criticized by Wendy Brown (2004), who accuses the depoliticizing effect – with crucial political implications – of this 'minimalist' liberal rearrangement of the doctrine of human rights. First, argues Wendy Brown, human rights discourse, as imagined by Ignatieff,

> not only aspires to be beyond politics (notwithstanding his own insistence that it is politics), but carries implicitly antipolitical aspirations for its subjects – that is, casts subjects as yearning to be free of politics and, indeed, of all collective determinations of ends.
> (Rathore, 2011: 138)

Second, human rights 'are not simply rules and defences against power [as Ignatieff claims], but can themselves be tactics and vehicles of governance and domination'. In the best-case scenario, what they amount to is 'a form of "empowerment" that fully equates empowerment with liberal individualism'. And third, human rights are not just an innocent defensive tool attached to a pre-existing subject, but they actually produce the subject to whom they are assigned.

> In its very promise to protect the individual against suffering and permit choice for individuals, human rights discourse produces a certain kind of subject in need of a certain kind of protection. . . . [T]he point is that there is no such thing as mere reduction of suffering or protection from abuse – the nature of the reduction or protection is itself productive of political subjects and political possibilities.

Contemporary critiques – post-Althusserian critiques

Another trend of critical reappraisal of human rights comes from the post-Althusserian perspective. Here, human rights are analyzed on the model of the Althusserian 'ideological interpellation' – namely, focusing on the way in which the declaration of human rights creates its subjects by means of its symbolic efficiency. In this framework, the inadequacy of the declaration of human rights – the tension between their abstract, natural bearer and their concrete, particular referent – which was blamed by Arendt or the post colonialists, becomes the very source of their political efficiency.

Thus, for example, instead of criticizing the distorted abstraction that these rights represent, Slavoj Žižek (2005) directs his attacks exactly in the opposite direction, namely, against the 'morality' that recent approaches try to infuse in the abstract frame of these rights. This re-naturalization of the subject's particular condition leads to the consequence that the much praised 'enlightened' West begins to assume the traits of its presumed 'fundamentalist' Other. 'What is effectively disappearing here is public life itself, in which one operates as a symbolic agent who cannot be reduced to a private individual, to a bundle of personal attributes, desires, traumas and idiosyncrasies' (Rathore, 2011: 151). The other target of Žižek's critique is the very conceptual core of the morals of human rights, the notion of free choice, with its underlying belief in the undisturbed spontaneity and authenticity of the subject's will. According to Žižek, in the consensual universe of naturalized particular beliefs, genuine free choice cannot be a simple and direct expression of the subject's will and substantial identity: 'a choice is always a meta-choice, a choice of the modality of the choice itself. . . . The subject of free choice can only emerge as the result of an extremely violent process of being uprooted from one's particular life-world.' It is only with this violent gesture by means of which the individual extracts himself from his immediate life context and disrupts the organic unity of the social body, that genuine universality that is 'universality for itself', is generated. Inasmuch as the abstract frame of human rights provides precisely such a space for the universality for itself, it designates

> the precise space of politicization proper. . . . What [human rights] amount to is the right to universality as such – the right of a political agent to assert its radical non-coincidence with itself, to posit itself as the 'supernumerary' . . . and thus as an agent of universality of the social itself.

Similar considerations were formulated by Jacques Rancière (2004). The French philosopher bases his reappraisal of human rights on his conceptual opposition between *politics* and *police*. While to Rancière, the police indicates the imposition of a partition on the social body which assigns to each part its own 'natural' place, politics occurs precisely when this natural partition is disturbed, when the harmonious consensus of the social body is shattered by the non-coincidence of each part with itself and by the imposition of disagreement [*différend*] as community. Human rights are an open site for both these possibilities. As an abstract inscription of formal equality, they provide the opening of an interval for political subjectivization. However, in their moralistic reappraisal which assigns to each part its right to assess its particularity and its own point of view, contemporary approaches to human rights seem to head in the opposite direction: 'supposed efforts to make inequality explicit have rigidified it. For one thing, the making explicit of sociocultural difference has tended to turn that difference into destiny (Ranciere, 1995: 54). In his essay 'Who is the Subject of the Rights of Man?', Rancière tries to engage with a more sophisticated attempt to re-naturalize difference as irreducible. The tension between the formal universal bearer of human rights and his particular actual bearer, the non-coincidence between man and citizen, between bare life and political frame – a distinction which roughly corresponds to the one diagnosed by the postcolonialists, between an abstract frame of rights and the untranslatable suffering of the excluded. This opposition, while being rightly criticized by Hannah Arendt and, lately, Giorgio Agamben, nevertheless runs the risk of being hypostatized in their writings and turned into a new destiny. However, for Rancière, this distinction between man and citizen, between the subject of the enunciated and the real referent of human rights, is not the whole story: 'the very difference between man and citizen is not a sign of disjunction proving that the rights are either void or tautological. It is the opening of an interval for political subjectivization.' This means that, besides the two equally problematic alternatives delineated by Arendt and Agamben (human rights either as a tautology or as a void), there is a third possibility: 'the Rights of Man are the rights of those who have not the rights that they have and have the rights that they have not.' But this radical non-coincidence with itself of the subject of human rights, which reveals the sphere of human rights as being a possible space of genuine political subjectivization, is not at all blocked by the abstract nature of rights, but, on the contrary, opened precisely by this formal inscription of equality and universality. 'The strength of those rights lies in the back-and-forth movement between the first inscription of the right and the dissensual stage on which it is put to test.' It is this very abstract inscription of universal equality that discloses the political space in which each part can extract itself from its organic medium, affirm its non-coincidence with itself and claim a direct access to universality.

Conclusion

While the critiques of human rights have always accompanied the institution of these rights, the stakes of these critiques varied considerably depending on the historical context and on the politico-philosophical stance of their authors. Thus, while early critiques have accused the individualism and abstraction of the human rights and tried to put back the emphasis on society and the existing political order, which can only guarantee their partial enforcement, more contemporary critiques have blamed precisely their dependence on the existing political order and accused their false universalism as merely disguised particularism.

The next part of the book will now turn to one further and more general way of thinking about this interrelation between universalism and particularism. Namely, we now move from a so-called pure Philosophy of Law (although we hope Chapters 2, 3 and 4, for example, forced you to begin to question whether there really was any kind of pure, universal approach that was not hiding behind it some particular ground or set of axioms), towards an attempt at forging an Indian Philosophy of Law.

Note

1 The material for this chapter was written by Alexandru Cistelecan. (2010). 'Which Critique of Human rights?' In Aakash Singh Rathore and Alexandru Cistelecan (eds.). The original is considerably longer than what appears here, which has been abridged, edited and slightly reworked by us, with the generous permission of the author.

Part II

Towards an Indian Philosophy of Law

6 Towards an Indian Philosophy of Law

The term 'Indian' within the title 'Indian Philosophy of Law' may be taken in numerous, all equally valid ways. We may think of it in contemporary terms: the nature and status of the philosophy of law in India today (the 21st century). This puts the focus on the idea of law in a post-independence context. But as we all know, what law in India is today owes an immeasurable debt to the era of colonization, and above all, British rule. After all, the very idea of law as we presently conceive of it in India is largely a transplant of 17th–20th-century British developments. Thus when we consider jurisprudence in India – from Constitutional law and its philosophical interpretations, to criminal law, the law of contracts and so on – we generally envision this wide historical epoch, and within it circulate our attention back and forth from the present 21st-century developments back to their 19th- or 18th-century origins, and then again return to the contemporary developments. This is a perfectly valid way of understanding the Indian Philosophy of Law.

Of course, beyond Constitutional law and other such areas, there is also the domain of what is called 'family law'. Within family law we find concepts such as 'Hindu Law', 'Mohammedan Law', 'Islamic Law', 'Modern Hindu Law', and so on. The codification of these concepts like 'Hindu Law' and 'Muslim Law' of course also date back to the British introduction of the modern legal system in India. But the source material, the customary cultural and religious practices that were codified into firm and fixed 'Hindu Law', for example, date back well before the 17th century. Various legal practices that came to be known as 'Muslim Law' flourished in several parts of India from the 13th century up until the British took over control. Thus the Indian Philosophy of Law could also be expected to refer to theorizations of aspects of Muslim Law in South Asia, its codification in the modern era and its contemporary manifestations as family law in the 21st-century Indian legal system.

And again, what is called 'Hindu Law' dates back as far as any historical knowledge of Hinduism in India. More concretely, the pre-modern legal systems of so-called Hindu kings date back to the late Vedic period, and establish legal norms and procedures that held sway in various parts of South Asia until being supplanted by modern law. For this reason, Indian Philosophy of Law could also be expected to refer to theorizations of aspects of Hindu Law, its codification in the modern era, and its contemporary manifestations as family law in the 21st century Indian legal system. Indeed, elements of what would have previously been understood as Hindu Law have also been absorbed within contemporary Constitutional law, and form an integral part of our legal and political system. Think, for example, of panchayats.

Four distinct eras that can be subsumed under the concept of 'Indian' within the notion of Indian Philosophy of Law have found mentioned: 21st century, or more broadly, post-independence; the British colonial rule, or implementation of modern law with codification of religious and cultural practices as Hindu Law, Muslim Law, etc.; the various iterations of Islamic law under regimes such as the Delhi Sultanate or the Mughal Empire; and, the ancient cultural, social, political and legal practices and norms that are often collectively referred to as Hindu, whether accurately so or not. These distinct eras mimic the divisions of Indian historians who treat of Indian history in four phases: ancient (saliently Hindu); medieval (saliently Muslim, though also with Maratha and other dynasties); modern (European colonial, and predominantly British); and, post-independence, the post-1947 Indian nation state. However, there is no need for philosophers of law to commit themselves to this representation of many historians.

Indigenous Indian Philosophy of Law

Students of Contemporary Indian Political Philosophy are likely familiar with the most recent orientation of that discipline. That is, a collective attitude that Indian political thought should articulate its concerns through native, vernacular or indigenous ('experience-near') conceptions, and begin the process of sloughing off the conceptual apparatus hitherto worked with, which has too often ensured that Indian political philosophy was realized as a derivative discourse incapable of addressing the realities of the ground situation as they seemed to present themselves. The most recent thinking in the Philosophy of Law matches this very same concern.

Certain prominent Indian legal theorists (e.g. S.N. Dhyani, Upendra Baxi) as well as judges (V.R. Krishna Iyer) have argued that Indian jurisprudence is saturated with Anglo-American legal theories, from John Austin to Joseph Raz (see Chapter 1), that were cultivated on foreign soil. These concepts and principles emerged from contexts profoundly dissimilar from the Indian one, but they have been superimposed upon Indian reflection on the nature of law in India. Not only has India seen legal transplantation, but also the transplantation of legal theories and the overall philosophy of law. But it has not at all been established that this transplantation of concepts from alien contexts bears relevance to the Indian ground situation, to Indian conditions, legal, political, social, cultural or whether they possess any real validity in India at all.

The same forces behind the development of Indigenous Indian Social and Political Philosophy have been serving as sources of momentum and inspiration for some scholars of Indian Philosophy of Law, who have been trying, against the odds, to inaugurate and cultivate a new tradition of Indian legal theory in recent years. They believe that the teaching of jurisprudence in India within law schools does not meet any of the basic tests of need or utility, as these ideas are of no use, or of ground realities, as these ideas are oblivious to the actual Indian situation. According to them, the philosophy of law tradition from John Austin to H.L.A. Hart to Joseph Raz needs to be toppled. Indian Philosophy of Law, rather, should look to reflect the real ideas and best practices of the Indian people. Indian jurisprudence should be Indian in origin, in content, in application – it should be *sui generis* and not merely borrowed or derivative. Further, they recognize that in India, the law has been mostly imposed from above. And certainly within the last several hundred years, it has had no roots in the authentic Indian soil, with a foreign vocabulary totally distanced from the common people. Both the actual legal system as well as the theoretical reflection related to it have lacked the imprimatur of India's cultural, climatic or geographical conditions.

But just as in the search for an authentic, indigenous political philosophy, how we identify the authenticity and indigeneity of Indian Philosophy of Law is open to contestation and dispute. For, indigenous could be equated to ancient, which was a common way of conceiving it for many swarajists, like Gandhi or Swami Vivekananda. This has been a central position in Indian political philosophy. However, within the Philosophy of Law, although there has been a temptation to link indigenous and authentic with ancient (at times, even simply Hindu), for the most part, jurists and legal theorists recognize the fundamental modernity of our primary legal (and political) institutions, and opt rather for a hybrid approach, which fuses some of the values and traditions of the ancient view, with the profoundly egalitarian, pluralist and progressive elements enshrined in the Indian Constitution.

But the question, *What is authentic or indigenous Indian Philosophy of Law?*, is a challenging one, and the temptation of leaping back to a presumed glorious age, that 'wonder that was India', remains strong in current theoretical discourse.

Ancient ('Hindu') legal theory and practice

Ancient Indian philosophy, Hindu or otherwise, contained numerous reflections of the nature of law (dharma). There is a widely and frequently cited passage from the Brihadaranyaka Upanishad that is often used as example:

> Law is the king of kings, far more rigid and powerful than they; there is nothing higher than law; by its prowess as by that of highest monarch, the weak shall prevail over the strong.
>
> (Gajendragadkar, 1965: 119)

The ancient world was replete with tracts articulating various moral, religious and customary laws which, when enforced by the sovereign authorities, held the status of law. Examples are the Dharmashastras and more particularly the Manusmriti. It is worth noting that, according to these texts, the king was almost universally regarded as subject to the law(s), and not – as in the Austinian or Schmittean legal theories – sovereign over the law. This notion, that the king bore duties and obligations towards the welfare of his subjects, is termed Rajya Dharma.

The concept of dharma has been the privileged social, political, moral, religious and legal term within ancient Indian thought. But the diverse or possibly even divergent manner whereby dharma had been practised as custom or implemented as law is largely a mystery for us today. What is now referred to as Hindu Law emerged as customary, and was reflected or refracted through sruti and smriti. What is codified in Manu's laws, in the codes or writings of Narada, Brihaspati, Katyayana, Yajnavalkya, etc., may or may not have reflected actual practices. That there were conflicting norms and practices is clear, since there was a well-established principle of how to decide between conflicting rules of smritis; that is, reasoning along the principles of equity (yukti).

But explicating the scope and content of Hindu Law is well beyond the point of this section (see Chapter 7 for more on Hindu Law). Rather, our interest is to consider instead the proposal that the codified remnants of Hindu Law available to us represent in any way the authenticity of Indian law; whether, in our attempt to cultivate an Indian Philosophy of Law that is not merely derivative, a resurrection of the Dharmashastras and smritis represent a viable option. Interestingly, it was in the very process of wiping out indigenous Indian legal practices – both formal and informal – that the British simultaneously ossified certain customary social, cultural and religiously mandated practices of pre-British India into the form of family law. But English statutory and common law saturated all other Indian codes and statutes. The Indian Penal Code, 1860, the Indian Contract Act, 1872, the India Evidence Act, 1872, the Code of Civil Procedure, the Code of Criminal Procedure, and so on, all served to supplant whatever common penal, contractual, procedural, criminal customary practices that were traditional all over India by alien (i.e. British) juristic concepts, customs and institutions.

But a century earlier, the British – through the Company and not the Raj – had already instituted a policy of so-called non-intervention in personal matters of the Hindus and Muslims. This meant that ancient custom became a source of modern law. Rules promulgated in 1772 and again in 1793 established that courts must apply Hindu personal law for Hindus, and Muslim personal law for Muslims. The Act of Settlement, 1781, laid down that the 'laws and usage' of Hindus and Muslims would be binding for those communities for questions of inheritance and contract. Even into the 20th century, the Privy Council maintained that ordinary law should give way to customary practices when no supervening interests were at stake.

In this context, it is important to note that the contemporary practice and theorization of law is firmly rooted much more in modern thought, traditions and institutions than in ancient ones. However, one integral part of the modern system – family law – is in some respects the ancient made modern. Nevertheless, the lure of the ancient – and even the Hindu – remains a strong pull. For example, consider Justice Iyer's claim from the Supreme Court case *Mohammad Giasuddin v. State of Andhra Pradesh* – 1977, when he wrote:

> Perhaps the time has come for Indian criminologists to rely more on Patanjali sutra as a scientific curative for crimogenic factors than on the blind jail term set out in the Penal Code, and that may be why western researchers are now seeking Indian yogic ways of normalising the individual and the group.

Legal theory and practice post-independence

With the adoption of the Constitution, Indian Philosophy of Law acquired a new paradigm. The concepts of liberty, equality and fraternity, though of 18th-century provenance, took on new meaning, or, rather, for the first time assumed real meaning, rather than hypocritical words without substance or traction. The Constitution was understood by many, including the Chairman of the Drafting Committee, Dr B. R. Ambedkar, to be the means of legal social revolution. Recent legal theorists as well as sitting judges supported this vision, most especially since the 1980s onward. They saw law as the means to the end of justice, and a great deal of the sense of justice was Ambedkarite social justice. This was visible in numerous Supreme Court decisions by Justice Krishna Iyer, and reflected in the legal philosophy of Upendra Baxi. The underlying motivation is in forging a home-spun jurisprudence, not simply a mere mimicry of British legal norms and practice. In this way there has been an effort to further the needs of the common people of India in the spirit of social service, and some have referred to this as being *nyaya darshaka* to the great Indian masses. This is a return and reinvigoration of the social change envisioned in the Constitution.

According to the self-understanding of judges and jurists, Indian Philosophy of Law is inflected by Gandhian conceptions, his profound concern for non-violence and his humanism (see Chapter 10 on Gandhi), as well as Nehruvian socialist impulses, and firmly grounded in Ambedkarite egalitarianism (see Chapter 11 on Ambedkar). Justice Krishna Iyer referred to this as *antoyodaya* jurisprudence or poverty jurisprudence. This suggests that both in theory (legal theory) as well as in practice (court decisions), Indian jurisprudence has a decidedly and distinctively pro-poor, pro-ordinary person, pro-underdog orientation, holding at bay the vested interests, powerful parties, the elite. In this respect, the words of the Indian Supreme Court case *Bidi Supply Co. v. Union of India* – 1956 are often cited:

> I am clear that the Constitution is not for the exclusive benefit of the governments and States; it is not only for lawyers and politicians and officials and those highly placed. It also exists for the common man, for the poor and the humble.

Such thought has culminated in India developing a robust practice of Public Interest Litigation. PIL is not unique to India, nor an Indian invention. All across the globe, we can find ‘social action litigation’ or 'social cause lawyering' or other terms used for what is essentially what we know as PIL. Throughout the world, PIL is initiated by NGOs or other groups who use the courts in order to bring about systemic policy change in society. The groups undertake this on behalf of individuals who are underrepresented or disadvantaged. In most of the world, this usually means women, the poor and ethnic and religious minorities. In the United States, for example, as part of a social change strategy for historically marginalized groups, PIL has focused on issues like school finance reform, reproductive choice and land-use planning, and has resulted in the reform of public education and extending the fair treatment of immigrants. PIL is not only for making law, but is equally a tool to enforce laws and to seek compliance with pre-existing unenforced decrees. For example, in the United States, this has applied to issues like racial desegregation, Native American treaty obligations and women's rights.

In India, PIL is much more robust and explicitly dedicated to the poor and downtrodden. Both legal theorists and jurists have come to recognize that in India, justice has been denied or inaccessible to the poorest of the poor, the illiterate, unorganized labour, women (especially from the lower strata), the disabled, the Dalits and adivasis. The philosophy behind the PIL, then, is consistent with the home-spun sort of Indian Philosophy of Law that regards the authenticity of Indian legal theory as referring to representing and pursuing the interest of the Indian masses, rather than merely the return to the ancient.

Conclusion

Some Indian philosophers of law and prominent judges suggest that India, since Independence, has rejected the legacy of English statutory and common law, and instead begun to evolve its own legal thought and principles in line with the indigenous needs and ethos. In the Supreme Court case *Rattan Lal v. Vardesh Chander* – 1976, Justice Krishna Iyer wrote, 'Free India has to find its conscience in our rugged realities and no more in alien legal thought. In a larger sense, the insignia of creativity in law, as in life, is freedom from subtle alien bondage.' Indeed, Justice Krishna Iyer has been the path breaker in this respect, refusing to remain tied down to the English traditions of practice or Austinian traditions of theory, which have been associated with colonial, autocratic and authoritarian law, rather than pursuing the post-Independence goals of law for the masses. Indeed, Justice Iyer has gone so far as to lay down a test, one of Gandhi's, for guidance in this respect. In the Supreme Court case *Moti Ram v. State of Madhya Pradesh* – 1978, he wrote:

> Where doubts arise the Gandhian talisman becomes a tool of interpretation: 'Whenever you are in doubt . . . apply the following test. Recall the face of the poorest and the weakest man whom you may have seen, and ask yourself, if the step you contemplate is going to be of any use for him.' Law, at the service of life, must respond interpretatively to raw realities and make for liberties.

One of the foremost elements of India's newly emerging indigenous Philosophy of Law is that it must be consistent with our plural society – with the common, shared fate of our diverse internal cultures and traditions. The essence of Indian unity and the best part of our heritage has been a continuous evolution and acceptance of diverse religious beliefs, linguistic habits, regional variation and so on, harmonizing all this within the mosaic of an Indian nation. When legal philosophy seeks authenticity, it does so with diversity and not exclusion in mind.

Indian philosophers of law who seek authenticity in the field know that Indian thought must not be slavish imitation of English or Anglo-American law and thought. Nor, throughout the strongly socialist era, were the communist systems to be mimicked. No foreign modes should be simply taken up without consideration of their fit with the unique Indian focus on the masses, the common man and our internal diversity. For example, Justice Krishna Iyer was quite specific about this in the Supreme Court case *Ediga Anamma v. State of Andhra Pradesh* – 1974, when he wrote:

> We confess to the impact made on us by legislative and judicial approaches made in other countries although we have warned ourselves against transplanting into our country concepts and experiences valid in the West.

However, just the same, foreign best practices, developments in law around the world, must not be eschewed just on account of its foreignness. Even Justice Krishna Iyer was very fond of citing the *United Nations Universal Declaration of Human Rights*, and numerous relevant cases of other jurisdictions, including the Anglo-American world, if the occasion were opportune.

In the end, the most reasonable task of an authentic Indian Philosophy of Law is to continue to broaden the sweep of humane and egalitarian legal thought and practice, while at the same time reforming and rewriting our laws in a manner that reflects the best practices of our own traditions, both customary and written, provided these themselves pass muster. That is, they must be consonant with our emerging tradition of legal philosophy, such as that found within the ideology of PIL. We must balance our ancient law and values with our modern sentiments and institutions. At the same time, the indigenous legal system and thought must continue to evolve and adapt to newly emerging shared values and new needs, based on the experience of our own people, but even including those developed in other progressive countries or jurisdictions, if they have inherent worth.

7 From Dharmashastra to Modern Hindu Law

According to J.R. Gharpure, author of *Hindu Law* (1931),

> Hindu Law is a personal law and follows and is attached to persons wherever they go. It applies to Hindus proper and others roughly described as Hindus; that is to the Brahmos, Cutchi Memons, Sunni Borahs of the Dhaundaka Taluka, Molesalam Girasia, Jains and Sikhs.
>
> (Gharpure, 1931: 6)

Law in India or rather Hindu Law has a history as diverse as that of India, which has seen an influx of rulers including the Mughals, the British and others, besides the Aryans. It is fascinating that while in the contemporary nation state model of Indian democracy, Hindu Law enjoys the status of personal law applicable to a section of Indian citizens. It has survived a history of different political and social changes.

Right from the Vedic period, India had a legacy of legal framework in place. There is reason to believe that during the Bronze Age as well as the Indus Valley Civilization, there was a legal system present. According to John Dawson Mayne (1906), Hindu Law based on customs existed prior to the compilation of the Vedas and independent of it. The Aryans may have accepted similar or the same law without modifications, rejecting only those that were incapable of being assimilated. Initially, facts may have been stated as such and religious influence may have been a later development. The divine character accorded to classical Hindu texts might have been given to these texts too. Law eventually was often structured based on religious practices and philosophical doctrines.

Different philosophical schools including the Nyaya, Vaisesika, Samkhya, Yoga, Vedanta, Jaina and Buddhism preached different doctrines. Accordingly they had rules that had the power of a law in the kingdom where these schools enjoyed royal patronage. The Mimamsa school in particular is known to have strong implications on the legal system. The significance of the Purva Mimamsa School of philosophy is that they provide hermeneutics, that is, they help to interpret various texts of the Dharmashastra tradition by providing in-depth information about the manner in which Vedic texts are to be interpreted. As the population was predominantly Hindu, laws during these times may be categorized as Hindu Law.

Different regions and different rulers were associated with what can be called secular law. In ancient India, court systems were primary features of ruling dynasties where both civil and criminal cases were dealt. For instance, during the reign of the Mauryas (321 BC to 185 BC) as well as the Mughals (16th to 19th century AD) secular courts were well established. These of course greatly preceded the current system of Indian common law.

In this chapter, the origins of Hindu Law will be traced through ancient literature and the changes undertaken during the British Raj in order to understand and implement Hindu Law in relation to modernity.

It is to be noted that Hindu Law during the ancient time was very different from Hindu Law under the current Indian Constitution. This is because while it was probably applicable and enforced to its fullest in different kingdoms, today, it merely enjoys the status of personal laws which may be called family law and are enforceable only in matters such as marriage, divorce, adoption, succession and so forth. In this chapter, Hindu Law will be classified as Classical Hindu Law, Anglo-Hindu Law and Modern Hindu Law.

Relationship of the ruler or king in Hindu Law

Hindu jurisprudence, more specifically, Classical Hindu Law, is quite different from its European counterparts. This is because obedience to law was not primarily due to authority of its arbiter. The commands found in the authorless divine texts such as the Vedas were revered. The law was interpreted from these and explained to the general public. The interpretations of these texts were quite frequently in conformity with the belief of the authority of the Vedas among the theist schools of Indian philosophy, which gave Classical Hindu Law a universal appeal. In Classical Hindu Law there is a distinct relation between law and politics. One of the reasons for this can be that there was a distinct scheme of values. Moreover, unlike in the West, where the king is the sovereign, in Classical Hindu Law, the king too had a *dharma* or duty which was known as *Rajya Dharma*.

The king merely gave political sanction to laws written by private individuals based on their interpretation of the texts. A just ruler was also a good judge who often arrived at verdicts seeking the assistance of his council, which included philosophers or religious ascetics. However, most cases rarely reached the king's court and were sorted out within small communities or groups.

While the king was given the responsibility to ensure social stability by observing dharma, it was his sacred duty to ensure dispensation of justice. If, however, there was any miscarriage of justice, the ruler responsible for it was liable to get one quarter of the sin.

Classical Hindu Law

While it is true that Classical Hindu Law was based on religious or rather sacred philosophical texts and that scholars of these texts therefore played a critical role, in actual practice it was both decentralized and diverse and differed from community to community based on different locations, vocational groups and castes.

According to Werner Menski (2001: 14) Sanskrit does not have a single word that means 'law'. The word *dharma* in Sanskrit, which is equivalent to *dhamma* in Pali, is what is used for law. Etymologically, *dharmais* derived from *dhri* which means to 'hold together'. Dharma is meant to hold the human race together. Its meaning is multifarious and is used to mean duty, morality, obligation and law and need not have only a religious basis. Dharma comprises court procedures and activities such as regimes for personal hygiene, ritualistic purifications and so on, apart from law. The mistake most scholars make, according to Menski, is to search for a definition or concept of Hindu Law modelled after the understanding of European law, particularly the search for preferably codified form of state-made rules. He opines that the purpose of ancient Hindu texts is to offer guidance for negotiating dharma and not to lay down fixed rules. It is one of the *purushastras*, the objective or guiding principles for men by which human beings are supposed to lead a systematic and disciplined life. According to Ludo Rocher (1978), the Sanskrit term *vivada* corresponds to substantive law and the term *vyavahara* corresponds to legal procedure. These terms too are met with a lot of ambiguity.

Vyavahara, which also has different meanings like 'doing, performing, conduct, action, behaviour or practice' has been interpreted by many thinkers as a formal legal procedure. Menski however understands it to mean settling a doubt in the context of Hindu Law, which may vary from sorting out a mental doubt to a formal court hearing before a king.

Menski believed that 'Law is never a given and must be constantly negotiated' (Mensi, 2007: 132) and in this respect, the concept of dharma got it right for its consciousness of plurality is a feature of Hindu Law.

Danda or punishment did not only have a deterrent effect. It was given with the aim of reformation of the person who was punished. The punishment took into account the nature of the offence, its motive, antecedents as well as the culprit's character. No individual was condemned for life.

Sources of law

There are three sources of law – *shruti*, *smriti* and *achara*. Of these three, the ultimate authority is of the shruti texts which include the Vedas and are said to be of divine origin. In fact smriti and achara, which are man-made, get their authority from the Vedas or the shruti texts. In case of any dispute, the words of the shruti texts are considered. However, according to Menski (2003), there is hardly ever any dispute between shruti and smriti.

According to the Yajnavalkya, shruti and smriti, usage among the good, one's own inclination and a desire based on good motive, is the origin of dharma. This suggests that the sources of Hindu Law are shruti and smriti. Shruti means what is heard while smriti refers to what is remembered. These are either written or unwritten.

According to Donald R. Davis Jr. (2005), sacred Indian texts were rarely used within the Indian legal system in the administration of law. Although there is no single positive precept which could be used as a rule of conduct within the Vedas, according to the Dharmashastras, the Vedas are the root of dharma.

Shruti comprises ancient Sanskrit texts, including the Vedas and the Upanishads. The Vedas are four in number namely Rig Veda, Yajur Veda, Sama Veda and Atharva Veda. These are divided into Samhitas (hymns), Brahmanas (rituals), Shakhas (branches) and Upashakhas (subdivision of branches).

Only a few learned individuals were given access to the shruti texts and smriti texts were compiled to teach others. The smriti texts are based on shruti texts. As per Manoj Kumar Sinha (2005), there are 18 main smritis. He regards smritis to be the foundation of law in Hindu jurisprudence, and rightly so. While smritis derive their authority from shrutis, as smritis are written by humans and come with a divine sanction, they incorporate rules of conduct for every day life in view of the customs followed in society.

Smriti includes commentaries (or Sutras), digests (or Nibandhas) and Puranas. Smritis may be further classified as primary and secondary smritis. Sutras are primary smriti texts. Primary sutras include Grihasutras and Dharmasutras. In this chapter, we are concerned with Dharmasutras. Dharmasutra means a string or thread of righteousness. It is written as prose. The texts are guidance on dharma with steps to be followed for rites and rules of conduct. Dharmasutra reflects on the four *ashramas* (stages) of life, the *bramacharya* (stage of a student), *grihasthashrama* (stage of the householder), *vanaprastha* (stage of the forest dweller) and *sannyasa* (stage of renunciation). Other topics covered include duties of kings, rites to be performed by them and court procedures to be followed; information about crime, punishment, sacrifice, rituals to be performed at funerals and the correct diet to be followed and so forth. Primary Dharmasutras are those written by Gautama, Bandhyana, Apastambha, Vasistha and Vishnu. Principal smritis include those of Manu, Yajnavalkya and Narada.

Dharmasutras and smriti texts often require to be interpreted; therefore, commentaries are written to make them meaningful. A commentary may be exclusively written for a singular text. For instance, there are several commentaries on *Yajnavalkyasmriti* as well as *Manusmriti*. Unlike commentaries, digests may refer to a compilation of topics, subject matter or different themes and are not limited to only one text. So a digest may refer to many Dharmashastra or smriti texts to cover one topic. For instance, there are different digests on topics such as adoption, property inheritance, litigation, rites and ritual, and the functions ascribed to a king. Digests and commentaries were derived from smriti texts, which in turn, were said to have their origins in shruti texts. Supremacy of the shruti texts was to be maintained. However, there was rarely any conflict between shruti and smriti texts, for the subject matter of these two differed considerably.

Significant smritis are *Manusmriti*, *Katyayanasmriti*, *Brhaspatismriti*, *Naradasmriti*, *Yajnavalkyasmriti* and *Vishnusmriti*. It is unclear if these texts, comprising verses, are to be ascribed to a single author or multiple authors.

In classical and medieval India, the first order of legal discourse was achara (customs). In order to preserve the importance of shruti and smriti texts, the customs of those who were learned in Vedic texts were considered valid.

According to Henry Thomas Colebrooke, there were primarily two schools of law, the Dayabhaga and the Mitakshara. Other less prominent schools were the Benaras School, the Dravida School, the Mithila School, the Bombay School including the Maharashtra school, the Gujarat School and the Bengal School.

Anglo-Hindu Law

The development of Anglo-Hindu Law can be divided into two periods in Indian history. The first is from 1772 to 1864. During this period the British adopted rules to administer justice in Bengal. The second period is from 1864 and ends in 1947 when India finally gained independence. In the first period, judges in courts of law initially relied on pandits to interpret Dharmashastra texts so that Classical Hindu Law could be applied to Hindus. Eventually, their use became irrelevant due to development of case laws where precedent cases were referred to. Moreover, compilation and translation of some Dharmashastra texts was undertaken by scholars including William Jones, J.C.C. Sutherland, Harry Borrodaile and Colebrooke, giving Hindu Law its codified character.

During the second period, the Dharmashastra texts lost their significance in the Indian legal system when the British realized that the idealized legal system of the Dharmashastra was not connected with customary legal practices which were followed among various regions and communities. Codification of various laws and acts took place and Hindu Law was reconstructed into the modern form of the legal system followed in England. Much has changed except what is known as family law or personal law. This was because the Hindus, who comprised a majority in India, followed different personal laws from the Muslims. The Hindu Law applicable in this sphere was one based on customs and Dharmashastra texts. The subject matter of Modern Hindu Law included marriage, adoption, succession of property and property inheritance.

Werner Menski provides an interesting insight into this period for he believes that this was the period when Classical Hindu Law was misinterpreted and misconstrued. To quote him:

> Starting off with imperfect assumptions about the nature of law, and having sought the wrong kind of expert help by asking misconceived questions of their Native Law Officers, as the *pandits* in their service were called, the British engendered a complex process of distortion. The morass of Hindu law got deeper and eventually the 'monstrous hybridity' of Anglo Hindu Law was produced.[1]

Glorifying Hindu Law or rather Classical Hindu Law, Menski says:

> Hindu Law represents a culture specific form of natural law. It is an ancient chthonic legal system. At the same time, as a holistic legal system it emphasises and instrumentalises the intricate connection between different interlinking elements of the whole experience of human life. Hindu Law thus falls firmly within the theoretical parameters of the historical school of jurisprudence, which treats legal rules as organically grown socially tested normative orders and therefore does not accept legal positivism encapsulated in the claim of the state to be able to determine and enforce rules in an authoritarian fashion.[2]

Modern Hindu Law

The end of Anglo-Hindu Law saw the codification of law modelled after the modern legal system of the British, except in the sphere of personal law. The Indian Constitution adopted principles of equality, secularism, socialism and liberty. B. R. Ambedkar, who drafted the Constitution of India, proposed a Hindu Code Bill. He intended to restructure some laws under the sphere of Hindu personal law where the distinction of various castes was taken into consideration. This, according to Ambedkar, was opposed to the spirit of equality and was therefore unconstitutional. Reforms suggested in this Bill tried to do away with the shastra or varna basis as advocated in Classical Hindu Law which was not modified under the British Raj as long as it formed part of personal Hindu Law. There was immense opposition to the Hindu Code Bill as many believed that it was partial that only the Hindu Laws were meant to change drastically as opposed to other religions. This development however was said to have been well-received by the Indian Nationalist movement and much from this period was adopted after India's independence. But despite making many changes to the Hindu Code Bill, it failed to pass. However, four separate acts were passed which were said to be part of Hindu Code Bill, namely, the Hindu Marriage Act 1955, Hindu Succession Act 1956, the Hindu Minority and Guardianship Act 1956 and the Hindu Adoption and Maintenance Act 1956.

It is noteworthy that in India, despite there being different family and personal laws for various religions, the courts where matters are adjudicated are common. The judges who preside over legal matters are common to all communities and they need not belong to a specific religious group which brings forth some matter before the court of law. The judges do not have any formal training in religious studies.

Hindu customs are significant only to help identify as Hindu a person to whom the Hindu Law may be applicable. But as per the provisions of many acts within the Hindu Law, such as the Hindu Marriage Act, it can be seen that the force of customs have been made less significant. For instance, Section 4 of the Hindu Marriage Act maintains that

> any text, rule or interpretation of Hindu Law or any custom or usage as part of that law in force immediately before the commencement of this act shall cease to have effect with respect to any matter for which provision is made in this act.

However, as the Modern Hindu Law is not completely codified, Menski notes, there are certain provisions for certain customs. For instance Section 5(iv) allows South Indian customs of cross cousin marriages while it lays down rules for prohibited degrees in marriage for North Indians.[3]

Conclusion

Hindu Law has its own history of transformation from what was known as Classical Hindu Law, where its rules were applicable in all civil and criminal matters, to Modern Hindu Law where Hindu Law became limited to the sphere of personal law or family law. Anglo-Hindu Law was the product of possible misinterpretation of classical Hindu texts as well as the purpose and incorporation of customs in what was considered to be case specific to codified form modelled after modern English law where case laws were significant. It is important to understand the historical development of Hindu Law, in order to gain an understanding of the nature of Indian Philosophy of Law.

Notes

1 Werner Menski. (2001). 'Postmodern Hindu Law,' p. 12.
2 Ibid., pp. 14–15.
3 Werner Menski. (1992). 'The Role of Custom in Hindu Law,' p. 342.

8 The persistence of caste

As might be inferred from the previous chapter, the significance of Hindu Law in India is immense considering that it forms part of personal law, which governs matters such as marriage, adoption, succession, divorce and so on. So, it becomes important to understand what is meant by terms such as Hinduism, some of its precepts and who can be termed a 'Hindu'. This will not be a problem in religions such as Islam or Christianity, which are governed by some similarities such as the presence of one holy book.

Within Hinduism, some aspects of Indian philosophy were (wilfully or otherwise) misconstrued and led to various regimes of rigid social discrimination and exclusion. In the British era, the courts did not pass any law discouraging such discrimination in cases which involved religious practices, as they had adopted a policy of non-interference relating to matters of religion and caste. However, post-Independence, national leaders took sufficient measures to ensure that the Indian legislature does not recognize any negative social discrimination due to caste. This is observed in the law practised in India today. Whether this law is correctly administered and implemented is of course another matter.

Hinduism

A lot of ambiguity surrounds the term 'Hinduism' which has been defined, modified and redefined across several centuries. Etymologically it is derived through *Sindu*, which referred to the Indus Valley Civilization in the north-western part of the Indian subcontinent. The contemporary understanding of Hinduism in a political context can be traced to the ideology of Hindutva, which is accepted by the Bharatiya Janata Party, a political party of India. The term *Hindutva* was coined by Vinayak Damodar Savarkar and is explained in detail in his work *Essentials of Hindutva*. This treatise was later renamed *Hindutva: Who Is a Hindu?* Interestingly, in the treatise, Savarkar warns that Hindutva should not be equated with Hinduism. According to him, use of the word Hindu dates back even before the word Sindu.

The need to define a unified notion of Hinduism or a Hindu arises because in Indian philosophy, there is a lot of diversity in terms of schools of thought, which were followed by different republics or kingdoms. There are six primary schools that maintain the validity of the Vedas and three unorthodox schools. The six orthodox schools include Samkhya, Yoga, Mimamsa, Nyaya, Vaisesika and Vedanta (which comprises of Advaitism and Dvaitism). The unorthodox schools include Buddhism, Jainism and Charvaka. The teaching of the scriptures, the Vedas, was oral and the Vedas were said to be authorless.

Commentaries on these texts were in the form of verses or notes taken down by students. Each orthodox school interpreted the teachings of the Vedas differently and each school had its own metaphysics and occasionally its own ethics. However, there was no single text which could be considered the text of religious codes of Hinduism for a Hindu to follow.

Prominent members of each school sought the patronage of various kings. In fact, an interesting tradition prior to the British rule was philosophical debates that took place in various kingdoms. The one who lost received the death penalty and the one who won the debate received the patronage of the king. During the Mughal rule, which spread far and wide, especially during Akbar's reign, non-Mughals or non-Muslims were identified as Hindus.

Thinkers such as Savarkar and Swami Vivekananda considered Hinduism to be all-inclusive. Hindu Dharma as per Savarkar is both Vedic and non-Vedic. 'It is the veritable science of religion applied. This is Hindudharma – the conclusion of the conclusions arrived at by harmonizing the detailed experience of all the schools of religious thought – *Vaidik*, *Sanatani*, *Jain*, *Baudda*, *Sikha* or *Devasamaji*' (Savarkar, 2016: 41). Swami Vivekananda who maintained salient parts of Vedanta as tenets of Hinduism, tried to popularize the idea of a universal religion. To quote him from a paper he read in the Parliament in 1893:

> From the high spiritual flights of the Vedanta Philosophy, of which the latest discoveries of science seems like echoes, to the low ideas of idolatry with its multifarious mythology, the agnosticism of the

> *Buddhists*, and the atheism of the *Jains*, each and all have a place in the *Hindu* religion.
>
> (Vivekanand: 1893)

In the absence of a clear notion of a Hindu and of Hinduism, the Hindu Marriage Act 1955, Sections 2(a), (b) and (c) had to attempt to define clearly who the act applies to. The provisions of the Act apply to some sects which are predominantly considered to be a part of Hinduism (as mentioned in 2a) but also to Buddhists, Jains and Sikhs (as mentioned in 2b) as well as those who are not Muslims, Christians or Jews (as mentioned in Section 2c). Similar usage is seen in acts which are meant primarily for Hindus including the Hindu Succession Act 1956, the Hindu Minority and Guardianship Act 1956 and the Hindu Adoption and Maintenance Act 1956.

Predominance of caste distinctions based on duties (dharma)

Caste distinctions or social stratification was predominant in the orthodox tradition and it was initially a means of division of labour. There were four primary castes: Brahmins (priests), Kshatriyas (warriors), Vaishyas (traders) and Sudhras (productive and sustaining force, who performed actions constituting services). Doing one's duties according to one's occupation was to do duties as per one's varnadharma. Each person was to perform duties associated with each caste. Castes were identified according to one's birth. It was initially merely a concept of social stratification. Svadharma referred to performing duties as per one's varna. Sadharana dharma referred to common duties to be performed by all castes. One aspect of sadharana dharma was not to discriminate against anyone due to one's occupation. But this aspect was lost to many and ignoring the sadharana dharma led to a lot of inequalities and discrimination.

King Siddhartha, who later came to be known as Gautama Buddha, belonged to an orthodox system before he attained enlightenment and preached Buddhism. While Buddhism deviated from orthodox texts and teachings, there was an inherent understanding of the precepts of the orthodox schools, including caste distinctions. Buddha did not endorse caste discrimination but was aware of its usage. In the *Ambatta Sutta*, there is evidence that Buddha was subjected to caste distinction and he in turn ridiculed Ambatta, who had voiced such concerns, by proving that in fact Ambatta belonged to an inferior caste by birth. Buddha then declared these distinctions based on birth to be immaterial and full of conceit. This is evident in *Sonadanda Sutta* which mentions that the significant qualities of a Brahmin were morality and wisdom and *Agganna Sutta* which provides a fanciful account of the origin of castes and where Buddha teaches that there is no difference between Brahmins and others if they behave badly.

Although inclusion was preached in Hinduism philosophically, as is evident from the works of Savarkar and Swami Vivekananda, practically, exclusion was preached due to social stratification in Hinduism as a result of the caste system.

B.R. Ambedkar, who framed the Constitution, is known to stand vehemently in opposition to the caste system. He calls it a principle of graded inequality. In the essay 'India and the Pre-requisites of Communism' (1987) he highlights some forms of discrimination practised. To quote Ambedkar:

> Supposing an officer was distributing dole to a famine stricken people. He would be bound to give greater dole to a person of higher birth than he would to a person of lower birth. Suppose an officer was levying taxation. He would be bound to assess a person of high birth at a lower rate than he would to a person of low birth. The Hindu Social Order's motto is that in regard to the distribution of good things those who are reckoned as the higher must get the most and the best and those who are classed as the lowest must accept the least and the worst.
>
> (Ambedkar, 1987: 111)

He quotes passages from *Manusmriti* to highlight the severity of punishment to a person of a lower caste.

> A *Sudhra* who insults a *Dvija* with gross invectives, ought to have his tongue slit. . . . If he mentions their names and classes with contumely, as if he says, 'Oh Devadatta, thou refuse of Brahman'; an iron style, ten fingers long, shall be thrust red into his mouth. Should he, through pride, give instructions to Brahmins concerning their duty; let the king order some hot oil to be dropped into his mouth and his ear.
>
> (Ambedkar, 1987: 109)

Similarly the severity of punishment for crimes inflicted on members of different castes was different, as per the *Manusmriti*. For instance, a soldier would be fined 100 panas to defame a priest, a merchant would have to pay 150 or 200 panas but a Sudhra would be whipped for the same crime. This completely violates the principles of natural justice as we know it, which is based on the equal dignity of persons and equality before the law.

Polygamy was endorsed in India but caste consideration was included here as well. For instance, a Brahmin was allowed to have four wives – one from each caste, a Kshatriya three wives – one from each caste barring the Brahmin caste, a Vaishya could have a Vaishya wife and a Sudhra wife while the Sudhra could have only one wife, that is, a Sudhra wife.

Under the British rule, unified law was applied to all castes in civil and criminal cases. However, in the case of personal law, which included matters such as marriage, divorce, inheritance, legitimacy, religious endowments and so forth, religious laws were applicable. Till 1864, the courts relied on Brahmin pandits or sastris to advise judges regarding rules and their interpretation. Initially, in Hindu Law, it was accepted that usage of customs, should clear proof be provided, would outweigh the written text of the law. There were numerous instances where different laws applied for different castes especially in cases concerning law of succession, adoption and marriage. Inter-caste marriages were not valid (with the exception of marriages in Bombay). Adopting a child of a different caste was unheard of. Jurisdiction over civil cases involving caste questions was withdrawn through a regulation in 1827 in Bombay. In 1859 similar steps were taken in other provinces through the Civil Procedure Code. However, this just meant non-interference of the courts in caste matters. This gave different castes the autonomy to make rules and force social exclusion of certain members from various activities. On some occasions the courts issued injunctions to prevent members of certain castes from entering Hindu temples and awarded damages in case some ceremonies were polluted by the presence of a lower caste member. The latter was seen as an act of trespassing. If a member of an excluded caste, a Sudhra, Palshe or Lingayat Brahmin knowingly polluted a temple by his presence, he was prosecuted under a criminal law. However, if a Brahmin were to tear a sacred threat from the body of an Ahir, the verdict would be that this act did not injure the Ahir's religious beliefs but only his dignity for it was not part of his religious custom to wear such a thread.

Marc Galanter mentions in his article 'Law and Caste in Modern India' (1963) that the courts did intervene in cases pertaining to enforceable civil or property rights. However, the extent of intervention was dependent on some factors: 1. that the decision of a caste tribunal was not arrived at with bona fide motives, 2. that the decision was taken under a mistaken belief, 3. that the decision was actually contrary to the rules or usage of the caste or, 4. that the decision was contrary to natural justice.

Abolishment of caste discrimination from Hindu Law

The Hindu Code Bill was a progressive initiative to put an end to caste discrimination legally. It had several reforms to do away with the shastra or varna basis of Hindu Law. It met with immense opposition and failed to be passed despite changes made to its drafts. Dr B.R. Ambedkar resigned as the Law Minister as a result. Jawaharlal Nehru, then prime minister, managed to pass four separate legislations which sprung from the controversial Hindu Code Bill. These were the Hindu Marriage Act 1955, Hindu Succession Act 1956, the Hindu Minority and Guardianship Act 1956 and the Hindu Adoption and Maintenance Act 1956.

So while polygamy was previously allowed and the number of legal wives was based on the caste of a person, monogamy was and is the rule as per the Hindu Marriage Act 1955. Similarly, property rights were not taken away from lower caste members. Legal and monogamous inter-caste marriages became possible. Members of a particular caste are not barred from adopting a child of a different caste.

In the case of *Shri Krishna Singh v. Shri Mathura Ahir*, Justice Kirty made a commendable decision, which was appreciated by scholars on Hindu Law such as J.D.M. Derrett and Werner F. Menski. In this particular case, a deeply religious father had given away his property to a member of a lower caste instead of his son. The son filed a case and it was argued that the defendant had no right over the property for he was a Sudhra. According to the Dharmashastra, he could not become a *sannyasi*. This implied that he could not be the *mahhat* (head) of the *matt* (religious community) to which the property would belong. The Supreme Court's verdict was that

> even though as a result of custom, usage or practice or of sacramental precept *Shudra* might have been considered incapable of being a *Sannyasi* at one point, such disqualification ceased to exist long ago, and can no longer be held to exist.

Moreover, abolishment of untouchability is a fundamental right under the Constitution of India through Article 17. The Scheduled Castes and Tribes (Prevention of Atrocities) Act 1989 came into being in the light of ineffectiveness of the Untouchability Offences Act 1955 (which was later revised as the Protection of Civil Rights Act). Besides these acts punishing those that discriminate, in order to attain equality for all, a number of steps were taken by the government of India to reserve some seats in government institutions, jobs and colleges for disadvantaged castes. However, the concept of reservation has led to a debate about affirmative discrimination or reverse discrimination. The Mandal Commission was set up by Prime Minister Morarji Desai in 1978 to identify socially or educationally backward classes. Based on the commission's report, Prime Minister V. P. Singh's government declared a total of 49.5% reservation in government jobs and public universities. This led to protests highlighted by the self-immolation of Rajiv Goswami, a member of a privileged religious class. A series of protests followed and debates continue on the topic of percentage of reservation and the subsequent continuation of reservation for economically and socially backward classes in India.

Conclusion

It is noteworthy that social inequality is practised in contemporary society. Caste-based politics is often seen during election times when political leaders try to sway voters based on caste preferences. Moreover, while acts which prevent discrimination based on caste are a positive relief, the debate about the extent of reservation for economically and socially backward classes and castes in India springs a debate on reverse discrimination against what would have been considered to be privileged social groups. In spite of all efforts towards its annihilation, today's India – legally, politically, socially – is marked by the persistence of caste.

9 The politics of Shariat[1]

This chapter focuses on the place of Shariat in postcolonial Muslim political discourses. Exploring the ways in which the constitutionally granted minority rights are identified as potential sources for articulating political arguments and positions, this chapter raises two conceptual questions:

1 What are the forms in which Shariat is represented as a political issue?
2 How do these varied political forms draw legal-constitutional legitimacy?

To offer an empirical background to these abstract questions, this chapter looks closely at some crucial postcolonial debates, including the famous one on inclusiveness of Shariat, that came up during the Shah Bano controversy in 1985–86 (which reopened the issue of the Uniform Civil Code).

This chapter does not strive for tracing structured arguments. Instead, it makes a serious attempt to map out various meanings of Shariat and their complex relationship with political-legal debates. In this sense, certain politically correct positions on rights of women, progressive or regressive nature of Islam and the divinity of Muslim personal law are intentionally avoided to do away with the secular/communal binary. In contrast, an interpretative exercise is taken beyond the known meanings and definitions of Shariat to highlight certain very preliminary inferences.

The chapter, in this sense, briefly traces the 'past' of the process by which certain ideas and practices are transformed into a legally codified entity called Personal Laws in the specific context of South Asia. This is not a history of Shariat; rather it is a conscious attempt to historicize a few 'second order political questions' (Kaviraj, 2010: 39).

The story of the Quran, the nature of political belongingness in pre-British India, the relationship between historical writings and legalization of the Quran as the main source of Islamic law are all invoked to address the issues that emerged in the postcolonial period.

The chapter looks at the recent historical researches, parliamentary debates, legal documents and the publications of the All India Muslim Personal Law Board (AIMPLB), particularly the texts published in Urdu. These varied sources are put together to offer a sequence to this exploration. These texts directly address two publics – the Indian state/political class and Muslim communities – to make certain strong historical claims about Shariat and its unsettled sacredness.

What is Shariat, historically?

According to the AIMPLB:

> Qanun-e-Shariat is a collection of rules and norms that have been codified following the intentions and consent of almighty Allah (as expressed in the holy Quran) for making human life meaningful, peaceful, and successful. Any act of law making in the name of Islam must follow the orders and directions given by Allah. Following these . . . principles our ancestors performed the sacred duty of tashri-e-Islam (explanation of Islam), which is also known as fiqg and usool-a fiqh. A jamat of foqha (ulema) was born after the prophet Muhammad by the mercy and generosity of almighty Allah for this task. As Allah says in the Quran, 'Why cannot a section of people from all groups go ahead for exploring interpretation of deen'? Allah entrusted the responsibility of explanation of divine laws to foqha. Consequently, the assembly of foqha was able to produce a body of law which covers all aspects of human life. . . . The foqha never deviated from the divine will and its virtual obedience; that is because their explanation was entirely based on wahi-e-ilahi.
>
> (Rehmani, 1999: 7–12, translated from the Urdu)

This interpretation of Shariat has three interesting aspects: 1. The Quran is the fundamental source, which cannot be changed and which is relevant for all human societies. Since the guidance/legal indications given in the Quran are not entirely spelt out, the legality of Quran verses is subject to certain controlled elaborations. 2. The sunna or the life of the prophet is an important reference point in this regard because his life history embodies the legal indications of the Quran. 3. The foqha or the ulema class is entitled to reinterpret the Quran, partly because the existence of this class is recognized by Allah in the Quran and partly because this class continues to adhere to the true message of the Quran/Prophet.

The third aspect of this interpretation of Shariat needs some more elaboration because it is related to the complex and provocative idea of human intervention in the unpolluted, indivisible, indissoluble divine words and practices. The intervention of the foqha class, we must note, is legitimate because of its trustworthiness towards the authenticity of the Quran and sunna. This explanation raises a few relevant issues: what is the originality of the Quran/Sunna? Is this originality self-evident? If yes, why do we need an 'interpretation'?

If we look at the hadith literature, we find that the compilation of the Quran has a very interesting story. The Quran, during the time of the Prophet, was not available in the form of a book. The Prophet's companions would memorize the revelations word by word. Salat or prayers five times a day was the main ritual in early Islamic society for the recitation of these words. However, after the death of the Prophet, attempts were made to bring together these 'sacred' words so that a basic text of Islam based on God's revelations could be prepared. Accordingly, 114 chapters or suras were arranged and the principles of recitation of this text were clearly laid down. Interestingly, the verses were not arranged in a chronological sequence. Rather a different criterion of relevance was adopted. Thus, the Quran in its present form is neither related to the history of Islamic struggle during the time of the Prophet nor does it reflect the sequence or order in which revelations were sent to the Prophet. In fact, we have a compiled and edited version of the Quran.

This compilation of the Quran, over the course of time, transformed it into a relic or an 'intentional monument' of some kind. Its 'authenticity', that is, of the words of the revelation as well the order of the verses given to it by the early Islamic religious-political elite, consequently emerged as the most essential commemorative value. The religious elite of the subsequent generations evoked this commemorative value, especially in terms of authenticity, to produce various interpretations of the Quran. The rise of *Tafsir-ul-Quran* (explanation of Quran) literature in early Islamic history is an illustrative example. AIMPLB, however, offers us another, more context-oriented historical account:

> After the demise of Muslim rule in India, efforts had been made for the protection of Muslim personal laws in India. The Shariat Application Act 1937 was the obvious outcome of this endeavor.

This passing reference to Muslim rule in India is crucial not only for the deconstruction of the linear genealogy of the ulema class but also to underline the gradual evolution to the modern notion of Shariat.

The recent works on Indian Islam, particularly the writings of Muzaffar Alam, Raziuddin Aqil, Sunil Kumar and Richard Eaton, problematize the given historical imaginations of Muslim rule in medieval India. They argue that although a large part of the subcontinent was ruled by Muslim kings and rulers, the management of political affairs was not entirely based on the set of rules and interpretations called Shariat.

These historical explanations make two larger points: 1. The set of norms called Shariat was contingent upon the context in which a certain version of religiosity came to be recognized as Islam. 2. The relationship between this discursively constituted Shariat and actual political discourse was highly fragile and unclear. Precisely because of these two possibilities, locally evolved cultural practices emerged as the main source of Islamic religiosity in pre-British India. Interestingly, many of these practices later became 'customary laws', which were intentionally separated from personal laws!

Two very significant developments in 19th-century north India – the translation of the Quran (in Persian and later in Urdu) and circulation of *Tafseer* literature established a clear distinction between Shariat-based ideal Islam and the customary practices associated with various Muslim communities. Muslim reformers, particularly the ulema, constructed a highly idealized picture of classical Islam and started marking the actual cultural practices as un-Islamic. In fact, the term *gair-Sharai* was established as an explanatory category in religious texts. Since the Shariat-based Islam had already been recognized by the colonial state, following a secularism of strict neutrality, Marc Galanter has argued that customary practices lost their potential as a source of law (Galanter, 2001: 100). The Wakf al-ulaulad Act 1913 and the Muslim Personal Law (Shariat) Application Act 1937, in this sense, evolved from this legal schema. The struggles of the ulema, which AIMPLB's version of history talks about, also revolved around the protection of the various versions of this Shariat-based ideal Islam.

The postcolonial Shariat

The legal-constitutional justification of Shariat in postcolonial India is based on two strong hypotheses: 1. The right to religion can also be interpreted as a right to have personal law. 2. Shariat is an essential aspect of Islam as a religion.

Let us locate these conclusions in the context of the 1940s. The creation of Pakistan somehow made it difficult for the Congress Muslims to make a strong case for Shariat laws. They had to face two types of challenges. The partition of India based on religion encouraged Hindu rightists to demand that India should be declared a Hindu state. From this point of view, the demand to have separate personal laws was a reflection of intolerable Muslim 'separatism'. On the other hand, there was a strong modernist-secular lobby within the Congress which became proactive in pursuing a radical social reform agenda. For this lobby, Muslim demand was a sign of an inward-looking attitude. Despite facing these adverse political forces, the Muslim members in the Constituent Assembly managed to raise the question of Shariat in the debate on personal laws. The outcome of this debate was quite delicate: the personal laws were recognized along with other customary laws, while at the same time, the supremacy of the Constitutional law was upheld. As Ambedkar points out:

> There is nothing extraordinary in saying that we ought to strive hereafter to limit the definition of religion in such a manner that we shall not extend beyond beliefs and such rituals as may be connected with ceremonials which are essentially religious. We must all remember – Including members of the Muslim community who have spoken on the subject, though one can appreciate their feelings very well – their sovereignty is always limited, no matter even if you assert that it is unlimited, because sovereignty is the exercise of that power and to reconcile itself to the sentiments of different communities. The Government can exercise its power in such a manner as to provoke the Muslim community to rise in rebellion. I think it would be mad government if it did so. But this is a matter that relates to the exercise of the power and not to the power itself.
>
> (B.R. Ambedkar, Constituent Assembly Debates, 24 November 1948)

Ambedkar's clarification, in a broader sense, points towards the classical distinction between the state and the government. The Constitution, Ambedkar seems to suggest, is a symbolic embodiment of the idea of a sovereign state. The government, in this classical liberal formulation, is the actual governing body whose decisions are entirely contingent upon the contextual wisdom. Thus, the supremacy of the state (read Constitution) cannot be challenged by any community, because it represents a collective whole; yet, the limits to have certain community specific rights are to be decided by the government.

The meaning of religion given in Article 25 is quite comprehensive. For instance the term 'religious affairs' covers a variety of activities including the management of functional religious places of worship as well as various acts of religious nature associated with them. The Indian judiciary, however, has devised an interesting concept of 'essential practices' of religion to determine the limitations of religious institutions and the secular control of the state. The Supreme Court in various cases has observed that there is an essential part of religion that constitutes the core or the centre of the entire belief system. According to the Supreme Court, this 'essential part of religion' has to be protected and the state can intervene in other 'non-essential religious activities'.

The difference between essential religious practices and non-essential religious practices may be understood as a workable legal formula. However, it raises an important question: How could a secular judiciary based on rational principles determine the 'essential practices' and 'non-essential practices' of a religion? Or, what could be the principles by which certain practices might be designated as essential practices?

This point was raised by many scholars at the time of the Shah Bano controversy. For instance, in an article published just after the Supreme Court decision in 1985, Tahir Mahmood (*Lok Sabha Debates*, 1985) argues:

> Of course, the fault does not lie with the court. . . . The Quran – like the Holy Vedas and the Bible is a revealed book. Would any modern court anywhere in the world attempt to interpret the Rigveda or the Old Testament? Laws derived from the Quran in the distant past are found in the books of law, and the court could definitely have interpreted those books. Re-interpreting the Quran itself straight away was, however, not a task that the Supreme Court of India or any of its judges should have performed.
>
> (Tahir Mahmood, *Muslim India*, December 1989)

If we accept Mahmood's persuasive argument that the Supreme Court's decision might have been in accordance with the provisions of the Criminal Procedure Code or with the judges' conception of equality and justice but it was not in conformity with traditional Muslim Law, one might ask a straightforward question: if the Supreme Court does not have the right to interpret the Quran directly, what is the logic behind accepting the supremacy of the Constitution/Supreme Court as the protector of minority rights? After all, Shariat is always presented as a complete way of life, which also covers the criminal cases in which Muslims are involved. In other words, why is there a controlled demand for the protection of a personal law that is only concerned with civil issues?

This question was also raised by the Law Minister Asoke Sen in a parliamentary debate on a private bill presented in April 1985 by G.M. Banatwala on deleting Article 44 in the Lok Sabha. Banatwala gave a very interesting response in the *Lok Sabha Debates*. He said:

> An argument has been advanced that when the Indian Law of Crimes, which is also at variance with the Islamic Law, then why an objection is taken with respect to Personal Law? I submit that this is perverted logic. If a part is not made available, it doesn't mean that the other should be surrendered. Let me declare that we, the Muslims, are prepared to submit ourselves to the law of crimes as envisaged by Islam if the state is prepared to enforce it upon us. . . . I emphasize the word 'free' which has been used deliberately and purposely in Article 25 of the Constitution of India. . . . 'Free practice' means, when your own religion gives you certain discretion, you will be free to make your own choice. Closing the doors of discretion for an individual is not free practice of religion as contemplated by Article 25 of the Constitution. . . . I must appreciate the position taken by the government. It has been made amply clear that there is no intention on the part of the Government to bring about any changes in the personal law of the Muslims unless and until the Muslims themselves desire it.
>
> (G.M. Banatwala, *Muslim India*, May 1985)

This reply, quite obviously, overstates the case of freedom of religion by making a rather technical explanation. Yet, the distinction that Ambedkar makes between the state and the government is evoked to articulate a theoretically nuanced and legally plausible position. It is claimed that the state, in principle, recognizes the interests of the 'community'. In conformity to this recognition, the community also recognizes the state as an ultimate protector of rights. The government, Banatwala seems to suggest, has to admit this mutual trust in devising various laws.

Banatwala's explanation is not entirely rhetorical. In a recent judgement on the legality of Islamic fatwa and the existence of the Muslim personal law board, the Supreme Court made an interesting observation. The court had to decide whether the AIMPLB strives for the establishment of a parallel judicial system in India. According to the judges:

> One may not object to issuance of Fatwa on a religious issue or any other issue so long it does not infringe upon the rights of individuals guaranteed under law. Fatwa may be issued in respect of issues concerning the community at large at the instance of a stranger but if a Fatwa is sought by a complete stranger on an issue not concerning the community at large but individual, then the Darul-Qaza or for that matter nobody may consider the desirability of giving any response and while considering it should not be completely unmindful of the motivation behind the Fatwa. . . . Issuance of Fatwa on rights, status and obligation of individual Muslim, in our opinion, would not be permissible, unless asked for by the person concerned or in case of incapacity, by the person interested.
>
> (Indian Supreme Court 386/2005)

Conclusion

This chapter gives food for more thought. Primarily, four points that are raised for further discussion can be summarized as below:

1. The Shariat is a historically evolved entity, which is actually the product of human intervention. Therefore, its perceived sacredness needs to be contextualized as well as problematized.
2. The evolution of Shariat in the south Asian context is inextricably linked to the ways in which various traditions, including the Sanskrit and Persian cosmopolises, amalgamated and produced a distinctive political culture. Thus, there is a need to have an informed historical discussion on south Asian Shariat.
3. The body of norms called Shariat is a rather modern phenomenon, whose modernity could also be traced in the 19th-century Islamic reform movement.
4. The postcolonial Shariat is contingent upon the state/government distinction. The Muslim political elite, particularly the AIMPLB, offers a state-oriented legal position. It is suggested that although the state could interpret Shariat, any endeavour of this kind must take cognizance of religious authority as the legitimate stakeholder.

Note

1 The material for this chapter was written by Hilal Ahmed. The original has been very slightly reworked by us, with the kind permission of the author. The original is available on e-PGPathshala | Free PG Courses, http://epgp.inflibnet.ac.in/ and may be found at http://epgp.inflibnet.ac.in/ahl.php?csrno=27 (accessed 01 January 2018).

10 Gandhi's affirmation of law[1]

The relevance of Gandhi's ideas still continue to be debated passionately even 60 years after his death. Part of the reason why Gandhi has such an extraordinary hold, not just on the national but also on the global imagination is because of the multi-faceted nature of the Gandhian personality. There are many Gandhis, right from the Gandhi who was a lawyer in South Africa to the Gandhi who was an uncompromising disaffectionionist and non co-operator to the Gandhi who in Churchill's opinion was nothing more than a 'seditious fakir' who dared to 'parley on equal terms with the representative of the King-Emperor'. The range and expanse of his concerns both political as well as ethical and spiritual, have spawned a veritable Gandhi cottage industry with all aspects of his life and work inviting scholarly attention.

While keeping in mind the wider world of ideas and politics in which Gandhi engaged in, this chapter seeks to discuss and analyze, specifically, Gandhi's engagement with law over the course of his life. When it comes to the question of the law, undoubtedly it played a major role in Gandhi's life and arguably his training as a lawyer contributed to his larger persona. However the role of law in Gandhian thought and action still needs a deeper study.

Perhaps the reason for this relative neglect owes much to Gandhi's own disavowal of the law. For instance, in *Hind Swaraj*, Gandhi launches a blistering attack on lawyers as one of the evils of Western civilization:

> The lawyers, therefore, will as a rule, advance quarrels, instead of repressing them. Moreover men take up that profession, not in order to help others out of their miseries, but to enrich themselves. . . . It is within my knowledge that they are glad when men have disputes. Petty pleaders actually manufacture them.[2]

Gandhi goes on to argue that:

> [T]he greatest injury they [lawyers] have done to the country is that they have tightened the English grip. Do you think it would be possible for the English to carry on their governments without law courts?[3]

Can Gandhi's philosophy of law be fully contained within the hermetic limits of *Hind Swaraj*? Did Gandhi reject the law in its totality, or did he continue to engage with the law creatively, passionately and subversively?

What if we were to not read Gandhi's critique of law in *Hind Swaraj* in 1910 as his final insight into the law, but rather view it within the context of the broader corpus of his work. This work includes the seminal contribution to civil rights in South Africa (where he donned the role of a human rights lawyer), his contribution to innovating socio-legal activism by authoring the first human rights Fact Finding Report on the *Jallianwala Bagh* massacre, his contribution to the field of legal journalism where the paper becomes a vehicle to denounce legal injustice and his use of the theatrical potential of the law to challenge the colonial state. An analysis of the range of ways in which Gandhi continued to use the law even after the iconic statement of *Hind Swaraj* alerts us to another Gandhian conception of the law's potential.

Gandhi as an early human rights lawyer

After getting his law degree from the Inner Temple, Gandhi attempted the practice of law both in Rajkot as well as in Bombay. Being somewhat unsuccessful in his efforts to break into the legal profession in India, when an opportunity arose to go to South Africa to provide legal assistance to a client he took it.

The first case that Gandhi handled for a poor man was the case of Balasundaram, who had been attacked by his master. Gandhi took the injured man to the magistrate, who was 'indignant and issued a summon against the employer' (Gandhi, 1987: 98). Gandhi observes that 'it was not his desire to get the employer punished' and that 'he simply wanted Balasundaram to be released from him' (Gandhi, 1987: 98). The law regarding indentured labour was such that if the indentured labourer left the employer he was liable to suffer both criminal and civil penalties. The only way of release was by getting the Protector of Indentured Labourers to cancel the indenture, to transfer the indenture to someone else. Gandhi then proceeded to persuade the employer to transfer the indenture, to which the employer agreed. Gandhi then went one step further; he 'went off in search of an employer' (Gandhi, 1987: 98). Upon finding one, the magistrate then convicted Balasundaram's employer, and recorded that he had undertaken to transfer the indenture to someone else. This small victory in law echoed in the Indian community.

In another case handled by Gandhi, two Indians, John Lutchman Roberts and Samuel Richards, were strolling home when stopped by the police and asked for their curfew passes. The 1896 curfew law provided that 'a coloured person found wandering between the hours of 9pm and 5am without a pass from his employer, or not giving a good account of himself, may be arrested' (Gandhi, 1987: 82). Gandhi, in the course of his argument, demonstrated that the defendants had indeed given a good account of themselves (i.e. that they were well dressed and had employment) and as a result should not have been arrested. The Magistrate agreed with Gandhi's argument and dismissed the case against the defendants on the spot.

The difficulty, yet not quite impossibility of getting a measure of equal treatment in colonial South Africa is alluded to in Gandhi's legal practice. The legal route involved both using the limited statutory framework to assert some rights, as in the cases above, and the use of the authorities' non-compliance with procedure to challenge some of the laws on limited procedural grounds.

Gandhi knew that no law could be challenged on substantive grounds before a South African judiciary which had limited freedom from executive control. Though at times the only thing standing between the Indians and a state of utter rightlessness was the limited notion of procedure, and the limitations of procedure were apparent to Gandhi. The challenges to the substantive law had to be political.

Coming face to face with these limitations of the law to deliver justice, Gandhi's conception of his role as a human rights lawyer changed dramatically during the series of campaigns against discriminatory laws. Gandhi moved from being the lawyer who got his clients released on bail to becoming the accused himself as he confronted laws which were patently unjust. He decided on a new strategy of actively disobeying laws which were unjust and hence going against his conscience, divesting the power and authority he had as a lawyer and embracing the vulnerability of one who chooses to suffer the consequences of disobedience.

In the range of his legal practice, the work Gandhi did was not very different from a human rights law practitioner of today. However, where Gandhi went beyond the role of a human rights lawyer was when he became a *satyagrahi*. This involved the systematic courting of arrest. When arrested, it involved entering a plea of guilty and asking for the highest penalty under law. This of course, opened an even wider engagement with the law, exposing unjust laws before the court of public opinion.

Innovating socio-legal activism: Fact Finding

As noted above, as a lawyer, Gandhi's practice shifted law from being an instrument to serve the needs of capital to a practice that served the needs of the Indian movement in South Africa. This shifting of the objectives of the law also resulted in an innovation what in time came to be called the 'Fact Finding Report'. The need for a 'Fact Finding Report' with a strong basis in verifiable fact, which cannot be easily controverted or denied by the authorities, came from Gandhi's experience with state officials in South Africa. The challenge to which the Fact Finding Report responded to was the accusation that the grievances of the petitioner were imaginary and that the state had a monopoly on 'truth'. An excellent example of challenging the state's monopoly on truth was the Report prepared by the Indian National Congress on the Punjab Disturbances in 1919. After the *Jallianwala Bagh* massacre, the government set up a Commission of Inquiry under the Chairmanship of Lord Hunter. This commission was boycotted by the Congress as it was not seen as neutral enough. Instead of participating in the Hunter Commission, the Congress chose to conduct its own inquiry through a team headed by Gandhi. The objective clearly was to ensure that the state was not able to control the truth of what happened at *Jallianwala Bagh* through its appointed Commission. In the Report which the team came out with, Gandhi pays close attention to 'facts' and contextualizes the massacre within a larger history of British colonialism. While Churchill contended that *Jallianwala Bagh* stood in 'sinister and singular isolation' (Dwivedi, 2016: 147), the Gandhi-authored report sees the massacre as a logical end of British policy in Punjab.

The Punjab Report is the forgotten ancestor of human rights reporting in India. Gandhi drew upon his skills as a lawyer to construct an 'alternative truth' to the state-authorized truth. In producing a narrative which contextualizes the 'crime against humanity' committed at *Jallianwala Bagh* within a history of increasing provocations, Gandhi goes beyond the immediacy of the newspaper report to produce a contextual understanding. The event of *Jallianwala Bagh* is no more *sui generis* but rather becomes emblematic of a more structural phenomenon of colonialism. It is this ability to go beyond the facts and see the historical process of which the particular event is a consequence, is the essence of a good Fact Finding Report. In drawing attention to historical forces behind the incident, till today, the Gandhi-authored report stands as perhaps one of the best Fact Finding Reports authored in the Indian context.

By shedding light on a phenomenon which might otherwise have been forgotten, namely the excesses committed in the name of martial law, Gandhi highlights another essential feature of Fact Finding, i.e. keeping the spot light on violations which the state refuses to recognize. Further there is an impetus on 'truth telling' regardless of how unpalatable it may be, as seen in the condemnation of the violence by the mob and the murder of innocent Europeans. Thus 'fact finding' has to tell the truth, even if it means pointing out shortcomings and violations by the groups on behalf of whom the exercise is undertaken. This again is a challenge which 'fact finding' by civil society organizations in contemporary India continue to face.

The Gandhi-authored report continues to both inspire and challenge civil society when it comes to the question of undertaking an analytically rigorous, historically rooted investigation which can bear effective witness to the wrongs perpetrated by both the Indian state as well as society.

Law as journalism: exposing injustice

Within a few years of arriving in South Africa, Gandhi realized that arguing a matter within the confines of a court was never enough. One needed to reach beyond the court and influence the larger public. It is with this view that the very first newspaper started by Gandhi, *Indian Opinion* began in South Africa. It published articles in English, Gujarati and Tamil, thereby enabling Gandhi to reach a wider community. Key to the *Indian Opinion* was the analysis of cases of harassment and discrimination. By giving voice to the experience of injustice, Gandhi was creating the ground for 'the victim ceasing to be a victim and beginning to be a threat'.

The newspaper was an instrument which worked in tandem with the law in the struggle for justice. Thus when Gandhi returned to India, even though he did not practise law in India, he continued to engage legally with issues through his writing. In the pages of *Young India*, Gandhi again wrote about cases of injustice, so that these cases began to have a wider public profile in the 'court of public opinion'. In particular, one must refer to Gandhi's series of articles exposing the farce that legal trials had become in Punjab during the martial rule imposed in the immediate aftermath of the *Jallianwala Bagh* massacre.

Legal training conditioned both Gandhi's words and his silence in the pages of *Young India*. He had a lawyer's horror of not saying anything which he could not back up by evidence. Once the facts were apparent, Gandhi's silence on the violence in the Punjab was replaced by a torrent of print. Gandhi reproduced entire judgements and extensively commented upon them with the trained eye of a lawyer. He expected his readers to read the judgements as well as the writings on which it was based 'word for word'. The cases involved sentences of death for offences against the state, such as sedition (Section 124-A) and waging war against the state (Section 121). In all these cases Gandhi drew upon his resources of legal reasoning to eloquently argue for the release of the accused.

In Gandhi's legal writing the appeal against injustice is based on a strong analysis of the procedural law and its violation. Clearly the years of practice in South Africa wherein procedure was the route to question state authoritarianism continued to influence Gandhi's writing. Even while there is a focus on the procedural, the larger substantive point of the injustice meted out to the arrested is clearly demonstrated. The big shift from the South Africa years is the stronger reliance on the 'court of public opinion' to bring about a measure of justice to the accused. Of course what is powerful in this plea on behalf of those wrongly convicted is that the appeal is not based on emotion, but on a reason which is the heritage of 'Bentham, Austin and other English writers whose names are a watchword for liberty and independence' (Guha, 2013: xli).

The other point which can be made is the value of taking a struggle from the confines of the court to a wider public. Sometimes injustice is perpetrated within the court and the public has no knowledge of what happened. In the mind of a conventional lawyer, if one suffers an adverse ruling the conventional route is appeal to the higher authority. The public as a 'court of appeal' is not a notion readily entertained by conventional lawyers. In the Gandhian scheme of things, public opinion is central and key to the struggle against injustice and it's vital that in the appeal to the law one never forgets the 'court of public opinion'. Thus Gandhi, at all times in his career, published widely and extensively, constantly keeping the public informed of his numerous experiments including his experiments with the law.

Disrupting the link between law and justice: the sedition trial

Gandhi transcended mere 'creativity' and engaged the 'radical' potential of law when he courted prosecution for sedition. His work in South Africa in particular sees Gandhi toying with the numerous possibilities of law. As early as 1907 Gandhi experimented with a new idea – to not offer a defence, to accept guilt, and to ask for the maximum punishment. He underwent three trials between 1907 and 1913.

From these three trials in South Africa one can make two observations. First, the response to Gandhi as an accused in court changes from the first trial in 1907 in which Gandhi is not allowed to speak, to the trial in 1908 when there is a visible softening of the judge as he refused to pass the highest penalty. By the time of the third trial in 1913, Gandhi's reputation seems to have been established; the judge observed that 'it is his painful duty to pass sentence upon the conduct of a gentleman like Mr. Gandhi.' In the contest between the judge and the prisoner, the prisoner seems to have appropriated some part of the moral authority which one associates with the notion of justice. The link between law and justice seems to have been shaken, as suggested by the apologetic language of the judge. Second, Gandhi was able to supplement the silent language of protest with the eloquence of speech. He converted the courtroom into another forum for the ventilation of the grievances of the Indian community. He also began to articulate his philosophy that 'without suffering it was not possible for them to get their grievance redressed.'

The South African trials are in effect test runs for the sedition trial in Ahmedabad in 1922. Gandhi was tried under Section 124-A of the IPC on the charge of 'exciting disaffection towards the government established by law in India'. Drawing from his South African experience, Gandhi again pleaded guilty and made a statement. The statement is an eloquent summary of why 'a staunch loyalist and co-operator should become an uncompromising disaffectionist and non-co-operator' (Gandhi, 1922: 241). Gandhi challenged the legal system, arguing that it bears no inherent connection with justice. Gandhi concluded his remarks by summarizing why he is a disaffectionist, before seeking the 'severest penalty'. His statement is a powerful indictment of the entire colonial system. Gandhi succeeded in disrupting the link between law and justice; after Gandhi's speech, the colonial state's legitimacy was disrupted, and the moral centre cleaved towards Gandhi.

In the sedition trial, Gandhi converted the charge against him of 'causing disaffection' into a powerful statement on why 'exciting disaffection' against the government was 'the highest duty of the citizen'. In short, as Sudipta Kaviraj observes, 'the trial of the rebel was turned into something that appeared more like a trial of the State.'[4] In the trial of the State what is contested most seriously is the link of the State to justice. As Gandhi demonstrates in eloquent prose, not only has the 'law been prostituted to the exploiter' but even more grave is the 'crime against humanity' of an economic policy that has succeeded in reducing people to 'skeletons in villages' 'as they sink to lifelessness'. The concept of justice both economic and political is what is at stake and Gandhi demonstrates that the British state has forfeited its claim on his affection having completely violated its commitment to the Indian people. The sedition trial also invokes another history, the history of a law which cannot be reduced to precedent alone. Law in this sense is born at the moment of disobedience.

Within this understanding, law cannot purely be understood within the framework of precedent and repetition but as something which is born outside this framework. Thus, when Gandhi makes the celebrated gesture of disobeying the law, he is in his defiance reaffirming the fact that law must have a connection to justice. He is implicitly asserting that if law is to be law at all, it cannot be linked to violence and force but must instead be linked to justice. The disobedience of law is premised upon the fact that the law bears no relation to justice and for law to have a claim to a citizen's obedience it must satisfy the condition of being just.

Conclusion

After ranging over the width as well as depth of Gandhi's engagement with law, what can we say about his legal philosophy? We cannot understand Gandhi's understanding of law from the viewpoint of *Hind Swaraj* alone. What his creative and subversive engagements with law even post 1910 clearly demonstrate is that Gandhi did not seek to reject the law as an embodiment of Western civilization and colonial rule; rather, law was something to be engaged with. For Gandhi was not brahmanical in his attitude to law and never rejected the 'polluting touch of law'.

This stance of continuous engagement was consistent with Gandhi's larger philosophical outlook. As Antony Parel eloquently argues, we cannot understand Gandhi as either a saint or a politician; rather, Gandhi was both, and being both was integral to his very conception of the ideal life. In Parel's interpretation the key to understanding Gandhi lies in perceiving his life's work as an attempt to find a harmony between the four ends of life – *artha*, *kama*, *dharma* and *moksha*. These roughly translate (respectively) as: politics or wealth, sex or love, religion or duty, and salvation.[5]

How do we apply this thinking about the aims of life to the question of the engagement with law? Simply put, the law should ideally be linked to dharma but is most often not. This does not absolve us from engaging with law, but only makes an engagement more imperative. The link Gandhi draws between politics and spirituality, or the world of contemplation and action, can be read as a call for a link between legal philosophy and legal activism.

What is the philosophy which flows out of the ceaseless engagement with the law? Does the philosophy have a relation to the world of action? These are the questions which need to be answered. The most important point which emerges from an account of Gandhi's engagement with law is that legal theory and practice should not be separated but rather should emerge out of an engagement with each other.

Closely linked is the point that a worldview which produced *Hind Swaraj* could at the same time continuously, ceaselessly and creatively engage with the law. It must be noted that *Hind Swaraj* did not produce a debilitating inaction but rather continually spurred Gandhi onto further engagement with the law. The critique did not absolve Gandhi from continuing to act using the law. This, of course, can only come from one who believes that action is a true mode of engagement.

The second point one can make is that there are some striking resonances between Gandhian practice in colonial South Africa, colonial India and independent India when it comes to the possibility of creative engagements with the law. However, the extent to which some of what Gandhi said and did resonates today remains striking. The early years of Gandhian practice, in which procedure was the one shield used against the state, stands true in some areas of human rights practice. The challenge to both Prevention of Terrorist Act (POTA) and Terrorist and Disruptive Activities Prevention Act (TADA), for example, was crafted in procedural terms. At no point was the substantive legal case made that the right to life was violated, but rather that the union had no legislative competence to legislate upon matters of terrorism as that pertained to the entry on public order in the state list.

One can find striking parallels between contemporary cases of terror suspects who have been denied the right to a fair trial and the wave of arbitrary arrests following the *Jallianwala Bagh* massacre. In both cases, procedure is completely disregarded. The work of contemporary human rights activists in painstakingly documenting and exposing the repression by the police, bears some analogy to Gandhian strategy of exposing the series of false cases filed by the British post the *Jallianwala Bagh* massacre.

What all this indicates is that the patient Gandhian work of courtroom trials, fact findings as well as legal journalism must continue as one strives to eke out justice from a state which appears impervious to the cries of human suffering. However, Gandhi's engagement with the law also exposed the limitations of human rights practice. This ability that Gandhi had to be both an exemplary practitioner of human rights as well as critic who aimed to transcend the limitations of human rights is something which human rights practice in India can only aspire to.

All this we learn through an exploration of Gandhi's affirmation of law, rather than remaining satisfied with the assumption of his rejection of it.

Notes

1 The material for this chapter was written by Arvind Narain. The original is considerably longer than what appears here, which has been abridged, edited and slightly reworked by us, with the kind permission of the author. The original is available on e-PGPathshala | Free PG Courses, http://epgp.inflibnet.ac.in/ and may be found at http://epgp.inflibnet.ac.in/ahl.php?csrno=27 (accessed 01 January 2018).
2 M.K. Gandhi. (2010). *Hind Swaraj*, p. 59.
3 Ibid.
4 Sudipto Kaviraj. (2006). 'Gandhi's Trial and India's Colonial State,' p. 308.
5 Anthony J. Parel. (2006). *Gandhi's Philosophy and the Quest for Harmony*.

11 Ambedkarite jurisprudence[1]

The question this chapter will explore is whether there is something which can be called an Ambedkarite vision of the law, which was not limited to the epithet of being 'the father of the Constitution'. To answer this question this chapter will attempt to make three points:

First that the idea of law in Dr Ambedkar's corpus extends beyond state law; second that the key Ambedkarite conceptualization of law is as a counter-majoritarian force to be mobilized on the side of the Dalits against 'the law of Hindu society'; third, legal concepts Dr Ambedkar espoused such as constitutional morality have been re-discovered as tools to combat new forms of oppression as the history of the nation unfolds.

Law beyond the law of the state

One idea of law which is pervasively present in Dr Ambedkar's work is the notion that the law is a command which must be obeyed. At first glance this is similar to what every jurisprudence student is familiar with, namely the Austinian theory of law (discussed in Chapter 1). This theory has at least these three characteristics:

1 Law as a command.
2 Such a command, which is issued by a political superior to a political inferior.
3 A political superior is one who is obeyed 'by and large'.

The innovation in Dr Ambedkar's theory of law is that this notion of law as a command is not limited to the state but moves beyond what is legitimized by the state to what society sanctions. In effect there is another origin other than the determinate sovereign for the birth of law. This wider understanding of law emerges from Dr Ambedkar's understanding of how Indian society operates in accordance with the rules of caste.

> Custom is no small thing as compared to law. It is true that law is enforced by the state through its police power, and custom, unless it is valid, is not. But in practice this difference is of no consequence. Custom is enforced by people far more effectively than law is by the state. This is because the compelling force of an organized people is far greater than the compelling force of the state.[2]

What Dr Ambedkar challenges us to is to rethink what law in the Indian context is. Is it limited to the notion of state law or even custom which had the validity of law, or does it go beyond these two notions to encompass other rules which can compel behaviour, sometimes even more effectively than the law of the state?

A more detailed discussion of this idea of law beyond state law is undertaken in the germinal essay on *The Annihilation of Caste*. In Dr Ambedkar's analysis, 'what is called religion by the Hindus is nothing but a multitude of commands and prohibitions.' Hinduism according to Dr Ambedkar cannot qualify as a religion as

> the essence of religion is that it is based upon principle and not upon rules. The moment it degenerates into rules, it ceases to be a religion as it kills responsibility which is the essence of a truly religious act.[3]

Dr Ambedkar concludes that 'what the Hindus call religion is really law or at best legalized class ethics.'

> The first evil of such a code of ordinances, misrepresented to the people as religion, is that it tends to deprive moral life of freedom and spontaneity and to reduce it to a more or less anxious and servile conformity to externally imposed rules. Under it, there is no loyalty to ideals, there is only conformity to commands.[4]

Thus force and command is the basis of the law of caste.

The fact that the rules of caste enjoy the status of law in Indian society has the inverse implication that laws prohibiting caste-based behaviour suffer from a lack of social legitimacy. Hence the rules of caste enjoy greater sanction than any state-based law. In this context, Dr Ambedkar doubts whether rights which guarantee 'Untouchables' freedom from discrimination have the character of rights at all:

> Law guarantees the untouchables the right to fetch water in metal pots. Hindu society does not allow them to exercise these rights. . . . In short, that which is permitted by society to be exercised can alone be called a right. The right which is grounded by law, but is opposed by society is of no use at all.[5]

In a paradoxical sense, when it comes to the question of caste, the caste-based rules of society enjoy the status of law, with the law of the state being consigned to being nothing more than an ineffectual commandment.

Law as a counter-majoritarian instrument

The law as discussed in the previous section is a deeply weakened instrument when it comes to the question of dealing with the problem of caste. In this context that Dr Ambedkar asks the question as to how when there is a deep rooted majoritarian bias against a geographically scattered and weak minority can the law be mobilized to serve the interests of the minority? In Dr Ambedkar's analysis the coercive power of the law is a force which should be mobilized even if it be against a culturally and socially sanctioned prejudice of the majority community.

As he puts it,

> Sin and immorality cannot become tolerable because a majority is addicted to them or because the majority chooses to practise them. If untouchability is sinful and an immoral custom, then in the view of the depressed classes, it must be destroyed without any hesitation even if it was acceptable to the majority.
>
> (Ambedkar, 1945: 106)

In this context of majoritarian bias, the coercive force of the law must be mobilized on the side of right and morality. The form that the counter-majoritarian power of the law took during Dr Ambedkar's lifetime was through two legal regimes.

Making untouchability a criminal offence in the Constitution

In a speech in 1930 at the Round Table Conference, Dr Ambedkar first articulated the idea that untouchability was a criminal offence.

> First of all, we want a Fundamental Right enacted in the Constitution which will declare 'Untouchability' to be illegal for all public purposes. We must be emancipated from this social curse before we can at all consent to the Constitution; and secondly, this Fundamental Right must also invalidate and nullify all such disabilities and all such discriminations as may have been made hitherto. (Ambedkar, 1982: 532)

Within the Constituent Assembly, there was widespread agreement on the need to criminalize the practice of untouchability and Article 17 of the Indian Constitution was formally approved. Article 17 reads:

> Abolition of untouchability:
>
> Untouchability is abolished and its practice in any form is forbidden. The enforcement of any disability arising out of Untouchability shall be an offence punishable in accordance with law.

Protection of Civil Rights Act, 1955

While recognition in the Constitution of the enforcement of any disability arising out of untouchability was important, for this Constitutional prohibition to have any impact it was vital that it find statutory expression. The original Bill which was moved in Parliament was the Untouchability Offences Bill, 1954. Dr Ambedkar's responses to the Bill in a speech in the Rajya Sabha are worth noting.

Dr Ambedkar articulates his discomfort with the title and voices his preference for the title Civil Rights (Untouchables) Protection Act. The reason is because the original title of the Bill

> gives the appearance that it is a Bill of a very minor character, just a dhobi not washing the cloth, just a barber not shaving or just a *mithaiwala* not selling *laddus* and things of that sort. People will think that these are trifles and piffles and why has parliament bothered and wasted its time in dealing with *dhobis* and barbers and

> *ladduwallas*. It is not a Bill of that sort. It is a Bill which is intended to give protection with regard to Civil and Fundamental rights.
>
> (Ambedkar, 1997: 933)

What emerges through the discussion on the Untouchability Offences Bill, 1954 is the lack of seriousness of the government in putting in place, what after all was no ordinary law, but rather a law which had to combat a deeply entrenched majoritarian prejudice to ensure success. The only person who seemed to grasp the nature of this enormous task was Dr Ambedkar.

Limitations of a counter-majoritarian approach

However Dr Ambedkar is also very clear that it might be difficult if not impossible to implement the law, in the context when the offenders are not a few persons but the entire society.

> Rights are protected not by law, but by the social and moral conscience of society. . . . But if the Fundamental Rights are opposed by the community, no law, no parliament, no judiciary can guarantee them in the real sense of the word. What is the use of the fundamental rights to the Negroes in America, to the Jews in Germany and to the Untouchables in India? As Burke said, there is no method found for punishing the multitude. Law can punish a single, solitary recalcitrant criminal. It can never operate against a whole body of people who are determined to defy it. Social conscience is the only safeguard of all rights fundamental or non-fundamental.
>
> (Ambedkar, 1979: 222)

The history of implementation of these laws might support this opinion of Dr Ambedkar. However the narration of the failures of a counter-majoritarian legislation is not to disavow or reject such efforts but rather to say that a counter-majoritarian legislative effort must be supplemented by other efforts to change the very structure of Indian society.

The legacy of Ambedkar's jurisprudence: constitutional morality

There are concepts which are core and central to the thought of Dr Ambedkar which might not have enjoyed a deep relevance at the time they were propounded, but in the context of today they have achieved an added salience. These concepts have been deployed by activists and judges and have enjoyed a new lease of life as they speak to contemporary concerns. The concept which will be elaborated below from the Ambedkarite legal corpus is the notion of constitutional morality.

The particular concept contributed by Dr Ambedkar to current political discourse is the idea of 'constitutional morality'. There are at least three references in Dr Ambedkar's corpus to the notion of 'constitutional morality'. The most famous reference to the idea of constitutional morality was of course in the Constituent Assembly while presenting the draft Constitution.

Dr Ambedkar quoted Grote, the historian of Greece, who had said:

> The diffusion of constitutional morality, not merely among the majority of any community but throughout the whole, is an indispensable condition of government at once free and peaceable; since even any powerful and obstinate minority may render the working of a free institution impracticable without being strong enough to conquer the ascendancy for themselves.
>
> (Ambedkar, 1948: 38)

Dr Ambedkar goes on to say,

> By constitutional morality Grote meant 'a paramount reverence for the forms of the Constitution, enforcing obedience to authority acting under and within these forms yet combined with the habit of open speech, of action subject only to definite legal control, and unrestrained censure sure of these very authorities as to all their public acts combined too with a perfect confidence in the bosom of every citizen amidst the bitterness of party contest that the forms of the Constitution will not be less sacred in the eyes of his opponents than in his own.'
>
> (The Constitution and Constituent Assembly Some selected speeches, 1990: 116)

Dr Ambedkar concludes:

> The question is, can we presume such a diffusion of constitutional morality? Constitutional morality is not a natural sentiment. It has to be cultivated. We must realise that our people have yet to learn it. Democracy in India is only a top dressing on an Indian soil which is essentially undemocratic.[6]

Clearly, the idea of constitutional morality was a theme to which Dr Ambedkar returned to again and again. What could Dr Ambedkar have meant in his repeated invocation of constitutional morality? Plausibly the importance of the concept flowed from his experience of advocating the rights of the depressed classes. He was acutely conscious that a democracy which was based upon a majority opinion which was no mere majority but a communal majority was deeply dangerous to the very notion of democracy itself. This was particularly important as

> in India, the majority is not a political majority. In India the majority is born; it is not made. That is the difference between a communal majority and a political majority. A political majority is not a fixed or a permanent majority. It is a majority which is always made, unmade and remade. A communal majority is a permanent majority fixed in its attitude.
>
> (Ambedkar, 2010: 58)

At its heart, Dr Ambedkar's notion of constitutional morality is a response to the particular conditions of India, where democracy remains but a top soil. If majorities will be crafted purely on the basis of caste and religion, what would happen to the minorities? Would not minorities be at the sufferance of majority opinion which misunderstands democracy to be equal to popular sovereignty?

The first time the concept of constitutional morality as propounded by Dr Ambedkar found a contemporary public resonance was when it was cited by J. Shah in his celebrated decision in *Naz Foundation v. NCR Delhi* when the court ruled that Section 377 of the IPC was ultra vires Articles 14, 15 and 21.[7]

The dilemma faced by the Delhi High Court was in crafting a judgement which would secure the rights of the LGBT community against the viewpoint of representatives of religious communities that homosexuality was against their religious beliefs and hence against public morality. The Court choose to sidestep the debate on religion and sexuality by arguing that it was not a relevant consideration at all. Even if the majority of the followers of a particular religion was against homosexuality and by extension the 'public morality' was against homosexuality, even then the public morality would be trumped by 'constitutional morality'.

As Justice Shah put it,

> Thus popular morality or public disapproval of certain acts is not a valid justification for restriction of the fundamental rights under

> Article 21. Popular morality, as distinct from a constitutional morality derived from constitutional values, is based on shifting and subjecting notions of right and wrong. If there is any type of 'morality' that can pass the test of compelling state interest, it must be 'constitutional' morality and not public morality. This aspect of constitutional morality was strongly insisted upon by Dr. Ambedkar in the Constituent Assembly.[8]

The implications of this line of thinking are profound for our very understanding of democracy in what is after all a diverse, plural and hierarchical society like India. While the *Naz* decision extended the life of the concept of constitutional morality to LGBT citizens, the power of the concept lies in its possible application to other 'unpopular minorities'. In a country coming to grips with increasing Hindu majoritarianism, this call to constitutional morality and by implication the understanding that brute electoral majorities do not mean that minorities of every strip and hue can now be effectively lorded over, is even more important. We shall discuss these ideas in further detail in Chapter 14 (Queering law).

Conclusion

In returning to that idea of law beyond the law of the state, it is fitting to end with Ambedkar's apparent optimism in certain possibilities opening up in this regard. In 'What Congress and Gandhi Have Done to the Untouchables', Dr Ambedkar gestures towards a social space outside the law when it comes to the possibility of bringing about social change. Talking about the work the Gandhi-initiated Anti-Untouchability League should do, he indicates the necessity of fostering what he calls 'social intercourse'.

> I think the League should attempt to dissolve the nausea, which the Touchables feel towards the Untouchables and which is the reason why the two sections have remained so much apart as to constitute separate and distinct entities. In my opinion, the best way of achieving it is to establish closer contact between the two. Only a common cycle of participation can help people to overcome the strangeness of feeling, which one has when brought into contact with the other.

The reason for focus on social contact is because Dr Ambedkar is convinced that 'the touchables and the Untouchables cannot be held together by law, certainly not by any electoral law substituting joint electorates for separate electorates. The only thing that can hold them together is love.' Of course this idea of love is premised upon an acknowledge of the legitimacy of the just demands of the Untouchables.

In Dr Ambedkar's writing one finds a clue that to achieve this change one needs to challenge the prejudice in the inner world. This inner world is of course a world beyond the reach of the law. But it is the ground for righteous law, which, working together, would bring about the possibility for a just society:

> Do not be under the wrong impression that untouchability will be removed only by removal of a ban on personal meetings and drawing of water from wells . . . it will remove untouchability at the most in the outer world, but not from the inner world. For that the ban on inter-caste marriage will have to be removed. Once that happens untouchability will vanish from inside the house.

* * *

This look at Ambedkarite jurisprudence brings to a close Part II of the book, which has attempted to make a move towards an Indian Philosophy of Law. Chapters 6 to 11 have been devoted to the particularities that contextualize the Philosophy of Law in India, which serve as a foundation to allow us to theorize and comprehend the distinctiveness of Indian Philosophy of Law. Now we shall change tack somewhat. Chapters 12 to 18 fall into the third broad motif or domain of this book, treating of legal concepts and thematic studies that function as case studies illustrating the diversity and wide-ranging scope of the Philosophy of Law. Part III still aims to help inaugurate an Indian Philosophy of Law, but it does so while applying general Legal Theory to the specificities of Indian cases and Supreme Court case law.

Notes

1 The material for this chapter was written by Arvind Narain. The original is considerably longer than what appears here, which has been abridged, edited, and slightly reworked by us, with the kind permission of the author. The original is available on e-PGPathshala | Free PG Courses, http://epgp.inflibnet.ac.in/ and may be found at http://epgp.inflibnet.ac.in/ahl.php?csrno=27 (accessed 01 January 2018).

2 B. R. Ambedkar. (1979). 'Their Wishes and Laws Unto Us,' p. 283.

3 Ibid.

4 Ibid., p. 299.

5 B. R. Ambedkar. (2013). *Ambedkar Speaks*. Vol. 1, 'What Path to Salvation?' p. 186.
6 Constitutional Assembly Debates: Official Reports Vol.VII: November 4, 1948, p. 38.
7 *Naz Foundation v. NCR Delhi*. (2009). https://indiankanoon.org/doc/100472805/ (accessed 1 December 2017).
8 Ibid.

Part III

Applying legal philosophy to Indian cases

12 Free speech and All India Bakchod

Does the right to freedom of expression give us the right to free and unregulated expression? Should such expression be allowed? What did prominent philosophers say about it? What does the Law say? This chapter will present some arguments for free speech and discuss the All India Bakchod (AIB) Knockout event. It was performed in Mumbai by a collective of stand-up comedians with some prominent personalities of Indian cinema as guests and host. Besides gathering publicity due to the show itself, it was also highlighted for what was regarded as indecent freedom of speech due to obscene and vulgar punch lines and actions in public space. This show may be considered to be an unregulated artistic form of free speech, but as a result the organizers face criminal charges.

Philosophical thoughts

Some salient arguments by philosophers who spoke in defence of free speech, relevant to the theme of this chapter, are sketched briefly hereunder.

John Milton's Areopagitica

One of the first treatises on free Speech was called *Areopagitica*. It was written by John Milton, the great English poet and political philosopher, to express his protest against the Licensing Order of 1643. The Order established a system of pre-censorship, registration of all publications and also authorized the destruction of published material considered to be guilty of the 'great defamation of religion and government', as well as the arrest of offending authors. It is noteworthy that it was not Milton's initial contention to speak for free and unregulated speech per se. His arguments were mainly suggestive of the importance of the publication of books. To be more specific, his argument is that there should be no ban on books *prior* to publication, for there is a grave danger in prior restraint, and that false statements hold inherent value too. Penalties on authors and a ban on books should take effect only in the case of books which were 'treasonous, slanderous and blasphemous' (Morgan, 1895: 221). It is possible that one of the reasons why he held such a view was also because he was himself religious.

During his time, his work did not have any significant impact on the government. However, its influence was felt immensely in later times. The Supreme Court of the United States referred to it in interpreting the First Amendment to the US Constitution. At least, in four famous cases in United States history, reference is made to *Areopagitica* in support of a broader perspective on freedom of speech and association. These cases include *New York Times Co. v. Sullivan*, *Times Film Corp. v. City of Chicago et al.*, *Sheriff v. Baird* and *Communist Party of the United States v. Subversive Activities Control Board*. Some of these US Supreme Court judgements in turn influenced the judicial assessment of free speech in other parts of the world, and Indian courts have themselves had recourse to cite them.

John Locke's A Letter Concerning Toleration

In *A Letter Concerning Toleration*, John Locke primarily argues that governments should not coerce individuals to follow Christianity, which was considered the one true religion. However, while he believed that the choice of religion was free and voluntary, practising the same must be governed by some rules of society which call for toleration. Some of these considerations can ground imposing restrictions. The same argument from the religious sphere extends to the domain of free speech. To quote Locke,

> Forasmuch as no society, how free soever, or upon whatsoever slight occasion instituted, whether of philosophers for learning, of merchants for commerce, or of men of leisure for mutual conversation and discourse, no church or company, I say, can in the least subsist and hold together, but will presently dissolve and break in pieces, unless it be regulated by some laws, and the members all consent to observe some order.[1]

So clearly while he did not support coercive practices or imposition of restrictions on speech, completely unregulated free speech would not be supported by Locke since unless regulation is provided in some minimal form, a complete breakdown of order could result.

'I disagree with what you say but I will defend to the death your right to say it.'

Voltaire was the pen name of François-Marie d'Arouet, a French philosopher who propounded liberal thoughts that may be said to have defined the era of Enlightenment. According to J.B. Shank (2009), Voltaire did not really write a text on the topic of freedom of speech. However, it is clear from his political life and philosophical writings that he was an ardent defender of free speech. Voltaire is well known for his position that the 'the liberty of speech is sacred and cannot be violated.' He is most famously associated with a quote which ironically he did not precisely say: 'I disagree with what you say but I will defend to the death your right to say it.' Roughly such a statement was made in reference to Helvitius, a fellow French philosopher and author of *De l'espirit* (*On the Mind*), a controversial book, copies of which were publicly burnt. One of the reasons for the burning and its condemnation by the Parliament was that the views expressed therein seemed to oppose religion and morality. The idea presented was that men choose a particular course of action bearing in mind an estimate of possible pleasure and mitigation of pain. While Voltaire did not agree with the author and had many counterarguments, he supported his right to free speech.

John Stuart Mill's On Liberty

Mill in his Introduction to *On Liberty* speaks of an 'appropriate region of human liberty' (Mill, 1869: 7). No society, he believes, irrespective of its form of government, is completely free if certain kinds of liberties are not respected. The first of these is the absolute freedom of thoughts, feelings, opinions and sentiments on 'all subjects'. Even despite the absolute nature of this freedom, restrictions to express and publish one's opinion are feasible especially if the content of such expression or opinion involves others. The exception is of course, unless the other referred to provides 'free voluntary and undeceived consent' and is willing to participate. The second is liberty of tastes and pursuits according to which we may do what we like as long as we are willing to follow the consequences of our actions. As long as no harm is done to others, there should be no obstruction of free speech even if society thinks the conduct to be 'foolish, perverse or wrong'.

The third refers to a freedom to unite for any purpose as long as no harm is done to anyone.

One of Mill's main arguments is that silencing any opinion is illegitimate and harmful, for it robs society of a differing view. In case the opinion wished to be silenced is justified, censorship will rob society of the truth. In case such an opinion is unjustified, it robs the dissenter of the opportunity of furnishing arguments in his defence.

To begin with, it cannot be said with surety whether an opinion is false. And even if can be so said, it is still an 'evil thing' to stifle such an opinion. Those who wish to suppress an opinion have no authority to judge for the rest of mankind. By silencing an opinion, absolute certainty about an issue is implied. Mill is not, however, opposed to the idea that some opinions may be condemned. A criticism considered by Mill is that it may be argued that it is important for people to fight for their convictions. Mill's counterargument is that belief in one's conviction implies the belief that such convictions could be defended even in the presence of differing opinions. Addressing these differing opinions, instead of silencing them, becomes all the more important then. Another criticism in favour of censorship is that governments have a duty to uphold certain beliefs that are important for society. This view is often counterargued. It can be said that this view assumes infallibility of a belief. He shows that Socrates and Jesus Christ were exemplars for they had been victims of such an assumption that their prosecution was essential to protect the society because the views they expressed were not in sync with beliefs held as important. Some views may be considered to be too radical for a time, but are these views wrong and is it right to censor such views?

Mill then considers the criticism which rests on a hopeful worldview: if an opinion is truth, it will survive despite prosecution. This sentiment is unjust to those characters in history who have been wrongfully incarcerated for upholding true ideas. And to uphold such a view that the truth will survive persecution also undermines the value of the contributions of such people. It may take time for truth to re-emerge after it is unjustly suppressed. He gives the example of the time it took for Martin Luther's attempts to be successful with respect to the Christian Reformation. Dissenters might not be put to death. But still, the fear of legal prosecution and social disapproval may prevent novel true ideas from being expressed and shared. And this will be harmful for intellectual growth.

Even if public opinion is right, in order for it not to become 'dead dogma' dissent is important. In fact it is important to hear a view that one opposes in order to be able to forcefully oppose a view one disagrees with. It exercises political rationality.

Indian Constitution, freedom of speech and reasonable restrictions

In the Constitution of India, Article 19(1) (a) states that all citizens have a fundamental right to freedom of speech and expression and so the Indian Judiciary feels the need to uphold its sanctity above some conflicting directives. However, reasonable restrictions are imposed on this freedom in Article 19(2).

As per Article 19(2)

> Nothing in sub clause (a) of clause (1) shall affect the operation of any existing law, or prevent the State from making any law, in so far as such law imposes reasonable restrictions on the exercise of the right conferred by the said sub clause in the interests of the sovereignty and integrity of India, the security of the State, friendly relations with foreign States, public order, decency or morality or in relation to contempt of court, defamation or incitement to an offence.
>
> (K.N. Munshi, Constituent Assembly Debates. 1 December 1948, Part 1)

The irony of the same was discussed in debates when the Constitution was being drafted. Then, these articles were referred to as Article 13(1) and Article 13(2) respectively. Some of the liberal thinkers who were against the restrictions to be included at the time included K. M. Munshi, Sardar Hukum Singh and Mahboob Ali Baig. What the liberals did manage to do was get the word 'sedition' deleted, which was originally suggested from what is currently known as Article 19(2) of the Indian Constitution.

In one famous debate among members of the drafting committee in favour of deletion of the word sedition, K. M. Munshi argued thus:

> now that we have a democratic Government, a line must be drawn between criticism of Government which should be welcome and incitement which would undermine the security or order on which civilized life is based, or which is calculated to overthrow the state. Therefore the word 'sedition' has to be omitted. As a matter of fact, the essence of Democracy is criticism of Government.

All India Bakchod and AIB Knockout Roast Show – the background

AIB refers to a stand-up comedy organization. This comedy collective is represented by Gursimran Khamba, Tanmay Bhat, Rohan Josh and Asish Shakiya and has a large following on the website YouTube. In December 2014, inspired by the format of a Roast Show,[2] which is said to have originated in America, a similar show took place in Mumbai. Within a few days of the event, once its video was uploaded on YouTube, it received mixed reactions. In less than four days, the show had 4 million hits. While most viewers liked the show, some dissenters filed First Investigation Report(s) (FIRs) against the organizers, the Bollywood actors and personalities who formed part of the show, including some eminent personalities. It is noteworthy that some dissenters did not view the video while some could not sit through the entire show as they were shocked and disgusted by its content and considered it against Indian culture and morality. In Mumbai, an advocate filed a Public Interest Litigation in the Criminal Case category. Some of the accused contested the PIL and FIRs so filed.

As per the format of the show, guests (invited Bollywood actors) are subjected to humorous insults by a panel of comedians and the show host; towards the end they get a chance to take a dig at the members of the panel and the host. To quote the organizers, 'We managed to bring together consenting adults who were willing to be made fun of by other consenting adults in a crowd full of (wait for it) consenting adults.'[3]

Some jokes about the Christian religion and the Parsi community were made. While all jokes were offensive (as per the format of the show), some jokes could be characterized as sexist, some as racist. Jokes were made about homosexuality, masturbation, the promiscuity of one of the stars, poor relationship and professional choices of some actors (some of whom were on stage and some who sat in the audiences), the professional credibility of a journalist on the panel, etc.

Crude gestures were made in some portions of the act. For instance, Raghu Ram was portrayed as a person in the habit of hurling a lot of abuse and it was suggested that he would probably masturbate by scolding his penis. A suggestion about doing a movie led Singh to bend over in front of Johar, only to have Johar walk away from him, reach the podium and revert, 'this is my position Ranveer.'

Some of the content which may have been considered hate speech or seen as hurting religious sentiments or may be otherwise seen as bullying, was not regarded as such by the very so-called 'victims' of this hate speech – for most of the 'victims' of the jokes joined in the laughter and did not complain about being bullied or insulted. Upon realizing that some jokes may have hurt members of the wider Christian community, the organizers issued an unconditional apology. To quote, 'While performing our acts, no matter the subject, we never intend to hurt anyone, though as an unfortunate consequence of the nature of our profession we sometimes do. We are sorry' (All India Bakchod, 2015).

Legal ramifications and possible consequences

The show and its organizers and participants including 14 persons were charged under various provisions including Section 292 (prohibiting obscene content), Section 294 (which prohibits obscene acts or songs), Section 509 (which prohibits words or gestures made with the intent to insult the modesty of women), Section 120 B (which sets out the punishment for criminal conspiracy to commit offences under the IPC), Section 34 (prohibited acts done by several persons with common intention) of the Indian Penal Code and other sections under the Environment Act, IT Act and Bombay Police Act. A case was also made against YouTube.

What may protect the accused is the fact that most parties involved consented to the roast show. A warning was issued at the beginning of the video that it was appropriate for viewers above the age of 18 and the content of the show was qualified as 'adult'. A background of the roast show was mentioned in the beginning of the video. A cautionary warning was also given which indicated that the roast was 'filthy, rude and offensive' as was customary in a roast format. The roast master, Johar, announced to the crowd present that 'those who are easily offended or are even difficultly offended should leave immediately as a lot of foul things are going to be said publicly.' In a Facebook statement too, the organizers maintained that 'No one was forced to watch it (AIB Knockout video), we didn't buy airtime on every single TV channel on Earth to broadcast it. YouTube videos do not magically auto-play in front of you.'

As per Section 295A of the Indian Penal Code, 'hate speech' is punishable with arrest, fine or both. Hate speech is basically when hateful comments are made against any religious community. However, this section prohibits defamatory speech against a religious community and not particularly against a caste. The Sindhi Community (which is considered a caste and not a religion) is not protected even under a similar section 153A because this section talks about persecution if words lead to disharmony or feeling of enmity between different communities.

The apology to the Christian Community may help the AIB group avoid being prosecuted under Section 298 of the IPC, which protects religious communities from deliberate intent to wound religious feelings.

Scrapping of Section 66A of the IT Act 2000 (amended in 2009) might bring the AIB group some relief, for as per this act people could have been arrested for posting offensive comments on the internet. AIB had publicly mentioned that the show was meant to offend. The Supreme Court deemed this section unconstitutional as it opposed the spirit of freedom of speech and expression contained in Article 19(1) of the Indian Constitution. Section 19(1) might protect the accused in the AIB controversy unless Article19(2) is given precedence.

In the past Indian courts have taken decisions in favour of pre-censorship of films, censorship of forms of art including books and films and have particularly seen motion pictures as having a greater power to influence in comparison to other forms of arts.

One internationally studied case was *S. Rangarajanv. P. Jagjivan Ram* (1989). The Madras High court had revoked the U certificate issued to a Tamil film named *Ore Oru Gramathile* (*In One Village*). The national award-winning film had the political consequence of disturbing the law and order situation. An appeal against the High Court's decision was made in the Supreme Court. The verdict ruled against what is called the 'Heckler's Veto' where censorship is imposed to prevent discord by dissenters. Overturning the High Court's decision the Supreme Court held that it was the duty of the State to protect the freedom of expression and that the State could not plead its inability to handle the expected hostile audience. At the same time, it reasoned that at times a compromise needed to be reached to resolve the clash between the contending interests of freedom of expression and social harmony. The Court also explained that censorship was permissible only on the grounds set out under Article 19(2). In fact, the reasoning given in this judgement is often cited as an argument for censorship by members of the Central Board of Film Certification:

> The combination of act and speech, sight and sound in semi darkness of the theatre with elimination of all distracting ideas will have a strong impact on the minds of the viewers and can affect emotions. Therefore, it has as much potential to instil or cultivate violent or good behaviour. It cannot be equated with other modes

> of communication. Censorship by prior restraint is, therefore, not only desirable but also necessary.

Since the *Ore Oru Gramathile* case many films have been censored in India upon its grounds, including the documentary *India's Daughter*, feature films *Fifty Shades of Gray*, *Water*, *The Da Vinci Code* and *Parzania*, to name just a few.

Now, there is a possibility that the AIB Knockout show may not be seen to be an artistic work. There is no precedent for such a case. The defence counsel for the AIB plans to draw a distinction between obscenity and vulgarity and argue that the show was not obscene, only vulgar. This is probably because in *Samaresh Bose and Another v. Amal Mitra and Another*, which concerned the censorship of a Bengali novelist Samaresh Bose's novel named *Prajapati*, the Chief Presidency Magistrate at Calcutta and Calcutta High Court both ordered the destruction of offending portions of the work. An appeal was made to the Supreme Court, which dismissed the charges of obscenity and held that vulgarity was not necessarily obscene. To quote a section of that judgement:

> Vulgarity arouses a feeling of disgust and revulsion and also boredom but does not have the effect of depraving, debasing and corrupting the morals of any reader of the novel, whereas obscenity has the tendency to deprave and corrupt those minds are open to such immoral influences.

The Court also mentioned that while some sections of the novel exhibited bad taste, the reader was mature enough to draw necessary inferences. If reference to sex were to be considered obscene and unfit for an adolescent reader, the adolescent would not be able to read any novel and would instead have to read purely religious books.

If AIB Knockout is characterized as vulgar instead of obscene and charges are dismissed, it is possible that it might still be considered in 'bad taste'. It is argued by the defence that AIB Knockout represents crucial liberties; if such liberty is not respected in our society, then we cannot consider ourselves to be free. Society may think AIB Knockout to be foolish, perverse and wrong, but there should be no obstruction to free speech for this reason alone. If AIB Knockout is characterized as obscene, there is still a chance the charge of Section 292 of IPC may be dropped as was done in the case of *Raj Kapoor and Others v. State and Others* which concerned the censorship of the film *Satyam Shivam*

Sundaram which had already acquired an 'A' certificate from the censor board. However, there is also the chance that those associated with the AIB may be prosecuted.

AIB philosophy

After the controversy and after some action had been taken against the AIB organizers and participants of the roast show, the video was taken off of YouTube, but the organizers did issue a statement on the social networking site Facebook. This statement clarifies their philosophical position. The statement began with the fractured quote attributed to Voltaire: 'I may not agree with you, but I will defend to the death my right to get offended. How dare you? *Baahar mil.* (Lets settle this outside!) – *Desi* Voltaire'. They supported absolute freedom of expression and the show tried to achieve that through humour in the public sphere:

> [The jokes were] in the spirit of irony and good humour. It was just liberating to be able to say those things, things that people have thought in one form or another privately for years. A lot of the laughter [that night] came from that spirit. . . . It is performed with the understanding that none of the material is to be taken seriously – none of the performers actually mean the 'offensive' things they say to each other on the night. With the Knockout, in our own juvenile, idiotic way, we wanted to push the envelope of comedy in this country. But then the envelope pushed back . . . the world we live in is entirely too complicated to be run by silences. We still stand by our belief in the right to absolute freedom of expression for us and for anyone who has anything to say about anything at all. We hope to be part of an environment that supports that sort of expression without fear of persecution, intimidation and most importantly, annoyance. As always, in our own AIB way we'll continue to strive towards creating that very environment. We encourage any and all conversation on the subject of freedom of expression, for our own silly selves, and for people better, smarter and more courageous than us. . . . Our job is to raid the newspapers, pop culture and life for observations and analogies and it's okay if you think we're juvenile or unfunny. We respect arguments that are critical, and as for the arguments we don't, we respect your right to make them without impediment. This Knockout shouldn't matter. In a secure culture it wouldn't matter.

AIB and the *Kavi Sammelan* tradition

It is true that the format of the AIB show was modelled on the American Roast show. However, a platform where jokes are cracked filled with irony, satire and humour is not uncommon in India or foreign to Indic traditions. At any *Kavi Sammelan* for example, prominent poets used to recite couplets called *shers*, or poems or jokes on life, women, politics, the state of affairs, etc. Occasionally the participants of a *Kavi Sammelan* would address each other and humorously pull each others' legs. Of course, the jokes were made about women and sexuality in a subtle manner, whereas the jokes made in the roast were crass and not subtle. For instance, while in a *Kavi Sammelan*, a person might crack a joke suggesting sexual activity by pointing out that a person's kid resembles his neighbour, the joke in the roast made direct references to sex, for instance, by suggesting that the last good thing a certain named actor was in, was another actress.

But thinking about the idea of 'subtlety' from a philosophical point of view, why would 'obscenity' ride upon lack of subtlety? Whether subtle or not, if the message is the same, and that message is understood (the vulgar form by the masses, the subtle form by the elite), then are they not both equally 'obscene'? It is possible that there is an inegalitarian element hiding in our belief that subtle sexual jokes are acceptable (that is, deemed as non-corrupting) whereas explicit ones are obscene. Are the elite beyond being corrupted by the very same message that corrupts the masses?

Conclusion

It is possible that due to clause (2) of Article 19, the free expression of the organizers of AIB Knockout might not be protected under the Indian Constitution. This is because it may be considered to be against public order, decency or morality and the state has a right to restrict such expression. However, from the vantage point of Mill's *On Liberty*, the case of AIB Knockout clearly represents a liberty which must not be interfered with. Culturally, it represents a transformation of Indian middle-class society through the presentation of private jokes in public spaces. While legal prosecution is underway, social prosecution is significant too. The AIB organizers have said, 'We can live with abuse, hate, anger, fury, rage, ignorance, bigotry and perhaps even bullying. But we don't want anybody to get hurt because of us.' Together with the Desi Voltaire comment, the AIB group represent thoughts in defence of wide freedom of speech. The case of the AIB Knockout is an example of unregulated free speech and the consequences of what may happen as a result of it.

Notes

1 John Locke. (1824). 'A Letter Concerning Toleration.' www.constitution.org/jl/tolerati.htm (accessed 18 October 2017).

2 As per the format of a 'roast' guests are subjected to humorous insults by a panel of comedians and the show host; towards the end they get a chance to take a dig at the members of the panel and the host. In the roast, there was no censorship of content and everyone on stage sportingly put up with being ridiculed and insulted. It was a forum where political incorrectness, etc. could be exhibited while the roast was on.

3 Actors Ranveer Singh, Arjun Kapoor were the guests and director Karan Johar, maker of popular big budget family films and also subject of gossip regarding his homosexual inclinations, was the roast master of the show. Among those who were also eventually dragged into the controversy were actors Deepika Padukone, Sonakshi Sinha, Alia Bhat and Sanjay Kapoor. All India Bakchod. www.facebook.com/IndiaBakchod/posts/859141927463136 (accessed 2 August 2017).

13 Equality and reservation

In order to maintain justice in a pluralistic society, especially one known to be a nation of 'unity in diversity', those who framed the Indian Constitution realized the importance of borrowed but necessary concepts such as justice, liberty and equality to hold the country together. This is validated by the Preamble of India which talks about securing its citizens 'justice in the social, economical and political sphere, liberty of thought, expression, belief, faith and worship and equality of status and of equal opportunity'. From the Indian Constitution, it is Article 14 that is quoted to address questions of discrimination and inequality. It is important to note that in order to have equality in society, the value of equality is read in conjugation with other positive concepts of justice and liberty. The moment anyone seeks equality before law, all three concepts come into play – there is a demand for equality, the demand itself can be made due to liberty of thought and expression and the goal is to acquire justice before the law. In this chapter, we shall discuss the need for equality within India and how the Indian Constitution and the courts protect its citizens or attempt to guarantee equality. Relevant cases concerning discrimination will be discussed in the light of examining answers to primary questions regarding equality, such as 'Why Equality?' and 'Equality of What?' which reflect in some of the verdicts given by the law courts in India.

Equality in philosophical perspective

In his book *Inequality Reexamined*, Amartya Sen ([1992] 2006) presents his reader with two essential and interlinked questions: 'Why Equality?' and 'Equality of What?' (Sen, 2006: 12). His argument is that both these questions are interdependent and the more significant question is 'Equality of What?' (Sen, 2006: 12). In *Inequality Reexamined* as well as *The Idea of Justice* (2010) Sen presents the capability theory, which talks about ideas like equality and justice in terms of freedom to achieve instead of actual achievements. In *Inequality Reexamined*, there is a section called 'Gender and Inequality' where he quotes statistics of how the state of Kerala has a very good quality of life for women despite being one of the poorest states in India in terms of distribution of income. Sen gives an elaborate reason in support of the capability theory:

> The explanation of Kerala's success in the important space of basic capabilities has to be sought in the history of public policy involving education (including female literacy) and health services (including communal medical care) and to some extent, food distribution (including the use of public support of food consumption of the rural as well as the urban population), in contrast with the rest of India. There are also other factors involved, including a more favourable position of women in property rights and in inheritance among a substantive and influential section of Kerala's population, and the greater public activism connected with educational campaigns as well as politics in general. The history of public action in Kerala goes back a long time, with remarkable literacy campaigns in the native states of Travancore and Cochin in the nineteenth century.[1]

Without deviating completely from Sen's approach, we can opt to arrive at a positive conclusion by an alternate route, considering very simple answers to the questions 'Why Equality?' and 'Equality of What?'. The answer to 'Why Equality?' would be 'Clearly, because of rampant inequalities'. As for the question 'Equality of What?', let us consider possible answers. Suppose someone answers, 'Equality of welfare'. In so answering the question what is being suggested is that all persons deserve to be equal in terms of welfare, or the ability and opportunities to satisfy their preferences. However, there are some serious criticisms to this position. What if a person's preferences are harmful, offensive, or sadistic – why should we seek to help satisfy such preferences? Here a case comes to mind, namely *Suchitra Srivastava v. Chandigarh Administration*. The verdict in this case recognized the reproductive rights of a woman who was intellectually challenged, 'mentally retarded'. Such a woman was raped by a staff member in a government-run institute in Chandigarh. The Chandigarh administration sought a petition to terminate the pregnancy. The woman wished to bear the child and appealed to the Supreme Court. This became a case where the legal capacity of a mentally retarded woman was brought into question. It is possible that some can question this verdict for it is possible that the woman, despite her wish, was incapable of taking care of the child. According to that argument, the preference of the woman in this case could be deemed harmful for the welfare of her baby.

Some have argued for equality of resources. Sen would completely disagree and his example of Kerala as being a rich state in terms of quality of life instead of low income per head is meant to oppose this view. Moreover, while the problem of a person's harmful preferences will not be solved from this answer, there are several other criticisms to consider instead. In the conception of equality of resources, people are not responsible for unchosen circumstances, or brute luck. The ideal here is that, for all persons, initial circumstances should be completely equalized, including appropriate compensation for unfortunate brute luck. But from that point on, the persons remain responsible for the consequences that result from their own choices. Here society would have no obligation to then equalize the differences in resources that results from these choices. First, this idea to completely equalize initial circumstances for everyone seems highly improbable if not impossible. Moreover, the implementation of the equality of resources is complicated by several problems inherent in the concept of responsibility. For example, if some of our preferences are genetically determined, would that not put our preferences into the category of brute luck, for which we are not to be held responsible?

Perhaps the solution lies in equalizing the opportunities for welfare. This would mean that each person faces a set of options that is equivalent to every other person in terms of the prospect of satisfaction of their preferences, whatever they may be. Thus, if people are entitled to equal opportunity for welfare, any actual inequalities in welfare would be due to factors within each person's control. This position also faces some objections. For example, a person confined to a wheelchair, and a physically normal person, both equally share the opportunity to climb a flight of stairs. The person in the wheelchair does not have access to that activity. So what good is an opportunity? This problem has led some to reformulate equality of opportunity as 'equal access to advantage'. If one analyzes most of the legal cases in India where the right of equality is cited, when the verdict takes place in favour of respecting Article 14, judges generally tend to consider whether a person who is being subjected to inequality in some form will be able to get equal access to an advantage, be it in the sphere of employment, education, health care or identity. In the next section we will see how the Constitution of India and some Acts combat inequality to uphold the ideals maintained in the nation's Preamble.

Special privileges necessary to ensure equality for all: caste, sex, disabled individuals

Abolition of untouchability and need for reservation

There has been and continues to be rampant discrimination against socially and educationally backward classes, castes, as well as what may be regarded as the weaker sex, be it women, gay, lesbian, bisexuals or transgender individuals. B. R. Ambedkar, deemed chief architect of the Constitution of India, was aware of and rather sensitive to caste and sex discrimination within the country. Special privileges or provisions such as reservations and the abolition of untouchability were included in the Indian Constitution. In India, lower castes and some minority groups were considered Untouchables. They were shunned from various social practices and had no access to any economic benefits. It was therefore a requirement in the Constitution of India to abolish such a practice that reeked of discrimination and inequality.

The metaphysical need for actualization of concepts like equality arises from the fact that due to sheer chance or what may be regarded as morally arbitrary 'brute luck', some people are born rich, some poor, some are associated with high class, some with low class, some are born as male or female and so on. The harm or benefit as a result of such brute luck is not well deserved.

The positive outcome of unequal treatment is referred to as positive discrimination. Different countries have policies favouring positive discrimination, such as affirmative action in the United States of America, positive action in the United Kingdom, employment equity in Canada and reservation in India. Special provisions are made to compensate for the unequal treatment or inequality accorded to some sections of the community, in order to balance the scales of justice. Opportunities for education and employment are given to certain socially and economically deprived groups, castes, races and classes to bring them at par with the general category citizens who do not face such injustice. However, it may be argued by a libertarian that reservation quotas are an unjust way to pursue justice. In fact, in India, reservation was introduced as a temporary solution to kick-start the process of equality for a generation of economically and socially backward classes. However, the system of reserved quotas in education and employment still continues. In time, reverse discrimination was also seen, as members of the general category, who have no reservation quotas for them, felt that they were at a disadvantage for having ancestors who had had the good fortune of not being discriminated against. Despite a debate on whether reservations should be continued for backward classes, India does not seem to be legally ready to challenge reverse discrimination. The Constitution of India also includes exceptions to Article 14 so that discrimination of deprived groups of individuals does not take place.

It is interesting to note that under the Right to Equality section of the Indian Constitution, the term 'equality' is used only twice, at the following places:

Article 14 reads, 'The state shall not deny to any person equality before the law or the equal protection of the law within the territory of India.'

Article 16 reads, 'There shall be equality of opportunity for all citizens in matters relating to employment to any office under the State.'

Do note how Article 14 is framed by the use of negation in the case of being discriminated. The nature of discrimination is not mentioned and can therefore include a variety of factors. It is also noteworthy that Article 16 grants a positive sanction of equality but is restricted to cases of employment to a state-held office. In contrast, within the same sections, the phrase 'Nothing in the article shall prevent' is repeated eight times.

Article 15 mentions how the state is against discrimination. Article 15(2) mentions that:

> No citizen shall, on grounds only of religion, race, caste, sex, place of birth or any of them, be subject to any disability, liability, restriction or conditions with regards to (a) access to shops, public restaurants, hotels and places of public entertainment, or (b) the use of well, tanks, bathing ghats, roads and places of public resort maintained wholly or partly out of State funds or dedicated to the use of the general public.

To an average contemporary urban Indian citizen residing in any metropolitan city, Article 15(a) and Article 15(b) might appear futile. However, it is important to then inform such a citizen that prior to Independence and even to date a number of people of lower castes are subjected to discrimination and are not allowed to use basic public facilities like footpaths, wells or water sources. Despite many positive laws being made in the colonial times, due to the *shastric* nature of Hindu Law, gross discrimination was observed even within the courts when injunctions were issued to disallow a person of an inferior caste from visiting public facilities and some religious temples. The incorporation of these articles also reflects the specific context in which the Constitution of India was so framed. However, today, there is a need to observe equality in many other spheres formally. It is the ambiguous and inclusive nature of the wording of Article 14 that gives space within the legal system to grant equality, which was not conceived of when the Constitution was first framed.

Discrimination of disabled citizens

There is no mention at all of special privileges for the physically handicapped or differently abled individuals within the Constitution of India. However, in some court cases, mention of Article 14 has been made to grant justice to the differently abled or disabled members of society.

What is available for this section of Indian citizens is the Persons with Disabilities (Equal Opportunities, Protection of Rights and Full Participation) Act, 1995. Despite the presence of this act, there was a need for a court-ordered mandate to the Union of India to make sure that there is no discrimination of individuals with hearing impairment and speech challenges in comparison to blind and orthopedically handicapped individuals in terms of transport allowance to be granted to those who were employed with the government. The particular case was called *Deaf Employment Welfare Association v. Union of India*. As per an official memorandum, the argument put forward by the Ministry of Finance was that it was 'not fair and just to equate the disability of deaf and dumb persons with those of blind persons in so far as transport allowance was concerned'.[2]

Despite recommendations from the Ministry of Road Transport and Highways as well as the Ministry of Health and Family Welfare, the allowance was not granted. In 2006 when the Ministry of Finance advised the Ministry of Health and Family Welfare to refer the issue to the 6th Central Pay Commission, double the normal rate of transport allowance was granted to blind or orthopedically handicapped government employees. However the same was not done for those with impaired hearing. In February 2013, the Ministry of Finance was approached again by the Ministry of Social Justice and Empowerment. The Ministry of Health and Family Welfare argues in favour of similar travel allowance for individuals with hearing impairments mentioning that according to the Disability Act 1995, hearing impairment is classified as a disability and travelling risk for hearing impaired employees can be equated to that of any other disability. Moreover they cannot communicate and more time and effort is required for them to reach any destination. And, of course, The Disability Act did not discriminate between persons with different disabilities.

According to the judgement of Justice K.S. Radhakrishnan:

> There cannot be further discrimination between a person with disability of 'blindness' and a person with disability of 'hearing impairment'. Such discrimination has not been envisaged under the Disabilities Act.

It was also found to be in violation of Article 14 of the Constitution of India, which is concerned with the right to equality. It was also mentioned that comparing the suffering of an individual with a hearing impairment with that of an individual with a visual impairment violated Article 21 of the Indian Constitution, which assures protection of life and personal liberty.

Discrimination against third gender

In 'India: Implementing Sex Equality through Law' Martha Nussbaum (2001) makes the critical observation that 'the framers [of the Indian Constitution] understood the goal of equality in terms of an end to systematic hierarchy and discrimination, based on both caste and sex' (Nussbaum, 2001: 39). However, when Martha Nussbaum wrote this article, she thought particularly about gender equality for women and not the third gender. It is only in 2014 that a decision was taken by the Supreme Court of India regarding legal gender recognition of transgender people in *National Legal Services Authority v. Union of India*. The case was that positive development for pre-existing Indian laws had only recognized the genders 'male' and 'female' and there were no provisions for the 'third gender' and this prohibited third gender individuals from claiming legal rights in relation to marriage, inheritance, taxation, adoption and general welfare. The absence of legislation in this case was what discriminated the third gender against recognized binary genders. In the judgement given by Judge K.S. Radhakrishnan, which was endorsed by Judge A.K. Sikri, there was acknowledgement that members of the transgender community, comprising *Hijras*, eunuchs, *Kothis*, *Aravanis* and the like, had been subjected to both prejudices and disadvantages since at least the 18th century. Discrimination faced by this community in different sectors, be it health care, employment or education, led to social exclusion, which violated Article 14. Article 14 is gender neutral, and grants the right to equality to 'any person'. It should be and is, applicable to men, women and the third gender alike, so a transgender group is also entitled to equal protection under the law.

The judgement found that the right to choose gender identity also falls within the scope of Article 21 that grants all citizens the right to life and personal liberty. Moreover Article 15 and Article 16 of the Constitution of India prohibit various types of discrimination, including on the basis of sex. The judgement equated sex with gender and declared that any gender bias or gender-based discrimination is also prohibited. It was declared that it was a fundamental right to not be treated differently just because one does not conform to binary genders. It was also recognized that the transgender community qualifies as socially and educationally backward; hence affirmative action should be taken by the state to rectify the injustice done to this group for centuries. It was also recognized that gender expression and presentation was protected by another fundamental right, the right to freedom of expression, mentioned in Article 19(a) of the Constitution of India. Despite the absence of any statutory guidelines, both the central and state governments must grant legal recognition of gender identity as male, female and the third gender. The Indian government was also directed to address issues pertaining to education, society and health with respect to the third gender.

Conclusion

Equality is an important concept in philosophy and is of incredible importance in the Constitution of India. Special provisions have been made to ensure that certain groups who have faced inequalities in various forms get an equal advantage as others who are not discriminated against. While drafting different acts pertaining to equality, the framers of the Constitution had focused on aspects such as caste-based discrimination or gender inequality, where women were the only victims. In time, a lot of other groups have used Article 14 to fight inequalities like discrimination against the third gender or physically disabled individuals. An analysis of the cases mentioned would show that when one asks the question 'Equality of What?', the answer that Indian courts have most often given is tantamount to the idea that it is 'Equality of opportunities, which is to be read as an equal access to advantage'.

Notes

1 Amartya Sen. (2006). *Inequality Reexamined*, p. 128.
2 Writ Petition Civil Number 107 of 2011.*The Supreme Court of India*, p. 4; http://judis.nic.in/supremecourt/imgs1.aspx?filename=41072 (accessed on October 8, 2015).

14 Queering law[1]

A queer perspective on law seeks to recover lost voices through a re-reading of law and legal history from a queer subaltern viewpoint and to highlight new voices which have emerged in the process of political engagement. This chapter will attempt to track the process of legal change and to systematically develop such a perspective.

The first part of the chapter will focus on the colonial period which seamlessly spills over into the post-Independence era. During this period, there were no vocal and visible queer voices and colonial powers introduced Indian laws which defined queer as 'unnatural'. Key to this period was the introduction of Section 377 of the Indian Penal Code and the Criminal Tribes Act respectively.

The second part focuses on the contemporary era of the queer struggle. By this time, initially isolated queer voices had gathered momentum, after having challenged the socio-political and legal basis of their subordination. This period is marked by rich internal debates on the differences between gender identity and sexual orientation and the understanding of how class, gender and sexuality intersected in the lives of *hijras*, *kothis* and other transgender people. This period also saw inclusiveness of sexuality as the result of recognizing a whole range of identities such as *kothis*, *hijras*, *jogappas*, besides gays and lesbians. This period can roughly be dated from the dismissal of two hitherto unknown policewomen, Leela and Urmila from their jobs in 1987 on the perception of them being lesbian and culminates in the decision of the Delhi High Court in *Naz Foundation v. NCR Delhi and Others* in 2009.

The final part will make an argument regarding possible future directions of the queer struggle in India after the overturning of the *Naz* decision by the Supreme Court.

History of the queer subject of law

The historical existence of queer people is rendered invisible through silence, by a dismissal of the same-sex tradition as completely irrelevant and by a wilful attempt to heterosexualize existing queer traditions. Queer historians such as Ruth Vanita and Saleem Kidwai undertook the task to focus on stories of same-sex love in Indian history against the dominant trend of Indian historiography. In their book *Same-Sex Love in India* (2008) these authors look at mythology, literature and history and question silence and misinformation on the queer aspect of our past. They point to an array of texts in which the closest relationships are between men and men or women and women.

While homosexuality was subject to some strictures in pre-colonial texts such as the *Manusmriti*, it is unclear whether it was homosexuality per se that was sought to be punished or more general sexual transgression or the violation of caste norms. It was only colonial law which introduced clear strictures against homosexuality. This is enforced by laws like the notorious Section 377 of the Indian Penal Code, the Criminal Tribes Act, 1871 and numerous prohibitions under the broad guise of preventing nuisance, obscenity and enforcing public morality, all colonial codifications, which sought to enforce a conservative hetero-normative sexual order.

Section 377 of the IPC

It was through Section 377 that for first time homosexuality was criminalized explicitly as 'unnatural sex', punishable with up to life imprisonment. It was drafted by Lord Macaulay in 1837, but came into force in 1860. Section 377 of the Indian Penal Code, the dreaded source of homophobia throughout the former British Colonies read:

> Section 377: Unnatural offences – Whoever voluntarily has carnal intercourse against the order of nature with any man, woman or animal shall be punished with imprisonment for life, or with imprisonment of either description for a term which may extend to 10 years, and shall be liable to fine.

The core problem with Section 377 has been its blanket inclusion of both coercive and consensual sex within its prohibition. The wording of carnal intercourse remains vague and encompasses all sexual acts which are non-procreative in nature. The wording of the provision itself gives the police a chance to target queer people arbitrarily. Along with creating social stigma, the vague and general nature of Section 377 made the provision akin to a blackmailer's charter. Section 377 also acted as a significant marker of second-class citizenship for queer people both during the colonial period and significant parts of the post-Independence era as the queer voice was entirely absent.

The Criminal Tribes Act, 1871

The Criminal Tribes Act, 1871 which specifically targeted *hijras* remained relatively unnoticed. The Criminal Tribes Act, 1871, is a product of repugnance of the British administration towards certain tribes and communities who were, 'addicted to the systematic commission of non-bailable offences'. These communities and tribes were perceived as being criminals by birth, with criminality being passed on for generations. This idea was based on the notion that 'crime as a profession passed on from one generation of criminal caste to another: like a carpenter would pass on his trade to the next generation, hereditary criminal caste members would pass on this profession to their offspring' (Radhakrishna, 2001: 5).

The link between sexual non-conformity and criminality was made more explicit in the 1897 amendment to the Criminal Tribes Act of 1871, which was subtitled 'An Act for the Registration of Criminal Tribes and Eunuchs'. Under the provisions of this statute, an eunuch was 'deemed to include all members of the male sex who admit themselves, or on medical inspection clearly appear, to be impotent'. The local government was required to register the names and residences of all eunuchs who were 'reasonably suspected of kidnapping or castrating children or of committing offences under Section 377 of the Indian Penal Code'. Any eunuch so registered who appeared

> dressed or ornamented like a woman in a public street . . . or who dances or plays music or takes part in any public exhibition, in a public street . . . [could] be arrested without warrant and punished with imprisonment of up to two years of with a fine or both.

If the eunuch so registered had in his charge a boy under the age of 16 years within his control or residing in his house, he could be punished with imprisonment of up to two years or fine or both. An eunuch was considered incapable of acting as a guardian, making a gift, drawing up a will or adopting a son.

The invidious role played by the Criminal Tribes Act was also recognized by the Naz judgement when the judges noted that, 'While this Act has been repealed, the attachment of criminality to the *hijra* community still continues.'

The contemporary era: creating a queer legal consciousness

Political consciousness of queer people in India emerged forcefully with Section 377 of the Indian Penal Code, 1860, which conceptualized 'queer' as unnatural. Nearly four decades after independence India saw the beginning of an indigenous opposition to an alien law through the emergence of a queer community which was politicized by the sheer injustice of the law. Section 377 brought a range of communities together through a commonality. This commonality was a 'state of injury', and a condition of marginality. The opposition to this state of marginality gave birth to a queer political consciousness forged in the crucible of struggles around the law. This emergence of a queer political consciousness is signposted by activist publications like the *Less than Gay Report* (1991), *Campaign for Lesbian Rights* (CALERI Report) (1997), *Humjinsi* (1999) and the *PUCL-Karnataka* reports on human rights violations against sexuality minorities and the transgender community in 2001 and 2003. These documents which articulated a greater vision for queer rights were both significant milestones for change that created a foundation for demanding rights.

When ABVA (AIDS Bhedbhav Virodhi Andolan) organized the first public protest against Section 377 in 1992, not too many people knew what was being protested. However by 2006, Shefali Vasudev could write in *The Outlook* that Section 377 of the IPC no longer needed a qualifying line. An open letter in 2006 by Vikram Seth and Amartya Sen arguing for decriminalising an expression of romantic love made a turning tide. It built upon over a decade of work by LGBT activists in the form of Fact Finding Reports, activist interventions, conferences and writing in the media on the pernicious effects of the law.

Naz Foundation v. National Capital Territory of Delhi and Others

In 2001 Lawyers Collective HIV/AIDS Unit, on behalf of Naz Foundation filed a constitutional challenge to Section 377 in the Delhi High Court on the grounds of equality, privacy and freedom of expression. This Public Interest Litigation was a unique example of the consultative mode for it kept the community involved and informed about the many decisions to be taken during various stages of the litigation.

The petition soon became more visible in the public eye. The proceedings in the case were widely reported and keenly followed by newspapers. The fact that after seven years of filing, the final arguments actually began in September 2008, made the possibility of change more imminent. The seven years served as an important gestation period garnering more supportive public opinion and seeing the emergence of a more articulate queer political voice. For example, before the arguments began in September 2008, the first Pride marches across the country were still fresh in public memory. The fact that the judgement in 2009 was preceded by a second year of Pride marches, although coincidental, foregrounds the uniqueness of the struggle against Section 377, which was simultaneously a political demand and a legal battle.

The *Naz* judgement came at a fortuitous moment of convergence between legal and political thinking and social attitudes:

- Homosexuality and homosexuals were more visible in 2009 than in 2001. More queer people spanning multiple professions had 'come out' as gay, bisexual, transgender or lesbian. The most fitting illustration of the role that coming out played in changing social attitudes was the fact that in 1986 when the US Supreme Court voted to retain the anti-sodomy law in *Bower's v. Hardwick*, not a single judge knew anyone who was gay or lesbian. However by 2003 in *Lawrence v. Texas*, when the US Supreme Court voted to strike down the anti-sodomy law every judge knew someone who was gay or lesbian. By 2009, due to the nature of media publicity and the interaction with gay and lesbian judges from other jurisdictions it was likely that judges in India as well knew people who were queer.
- The judgement had come at a time when mainstream culture was increasingly being queered. Literature, plays, movies, dance performances and other forms of entertainment increasingly had queer themes and openly queer characters. Mainstream Bollywood cinema is perhaps the best symbol of how queerness has found a representation in mass culture. With the 2008 hit film *Dostana* the word 'gay' began being used in an almost casual everyday sense for the first time. *Dostana* introduced queerness to the Indian public and initiated conversations around sexuality in homes and offices.

- Combined with this change in public culture was a growing sense of entitlement in the queer community. While in 1996 there was a palpable sense of fear, by 2008 the community itself had become more visible and vocal.

The 105-page judgement itself has inaugurated a new discourse on queer people moving away from the terms of 'carnal intercourse' and inhabiting the new language of dignity, privacy, equality and inclusiveness. The judges overturned a 149-year-old discourse which saw homosexuality merely within the frame of unnatural sexual intercourse. The Court held that criminalization of consensual sex between adults in private violates the Constitution's guarantees of dignity, equality and freedom from discrimination based on sexual orientation (Articles 21, 14 and 15). In technical terms, the judges 'read down' or interpreted Section 377 so that it no longer criminalized consensual sex between adults in private.

The judgement was unique in that it drew closely from the experience of the queer community and was able to reflect the lived and existential realities. The judgement quoted instances of violence faced by the queer community. Firmly anchored in the experiences of the queer community, it empathized with its pain through sustained legal reasoning.

The judgement adopts a view of human dignity that privileges the ability to freely make choices about how to live one's life. From this notion of dignity, the court derives a concept of privacy that 'deals with persons and not places'. The right to privacy is not merely the right to do what one wants in 'private spaces', but also a right to make choices about how to live one's own life. Privacy protects personal autonomy, both zonal and decisional. This includes the right to sexual expression, which necessarily entails being able to choose sexual partners without unjustified interference by the state. As the Court eloquently put it, 'The expression of sexuality requires a partner, real or imagined. It is not for the state to choose or to arrange the choice of partner, but for the partners to choose themselves' (para. 47).

The judgement emphatically recognizes that even without actual enforcement, laws like Section 377 stigmatizes an entire section of society and violates their dignity as citizens. By making a specific reference to the colonial-era Criminal Tribes Act, the judgement notes the horrendous instance of the criminalization of sexual minorities. The judges also note how Section 377 has the effect of viewing all gay men as criminals.

In furtherance of the equality argument, the Court finds that 'sexual orientation is a ground analogous to sex and that discrimination on the basis of sexual orientation is not permitted by Art. 15' (para. 104). The justices thus construe the meaning of 'sex' in Article 15 to include not merely biological or physical sex, but also sexual orientation.

The justices note that the Supreme Court has read the right to life in Article 21 of the Constitution to include a right to health. This right to health includes various entitlements, such as an equal opportunity to access a functioning health care system. The Justices concluded that Section 377 infringed on the right to health of LGBT persons because it hampered HIV/AIDS prevention efforts.

The Court held that the public's opinions on morality cannot be used as a justification for limiting LGBT persons' fundamental rights. This 'constitutional morality' that the Court identified was based on the liberal democratic ideals at the core of the Indian Constitution, not on any particular religious or cultural tradition. They derived the concept from Dr Ambedkar, who in the Constituent Assembly noted, 'Constitutional morality is not a natural sentiment. It has to be cultivated. We must realize that our people have yet to learn it. Democracy in India is only a top dressing on an Indian soil which is essentially undemocratic'.[2] The judges conclude that to stigmatize or to criminalize homosexuals only on account of their sexual orientation would be against constitutional morality.

Reinforcing their commitment to constitutional morality, the judges highlighted the role of the judiciary in a constitutional framework as being 'to protect the fundamental rights of those who may dissent or deviate from the majoritarian view'. The judges thereby asserted the responsibility of the judiciary in protecting fundamental rights regardless of the opinion of the legislative majority. Thus the judiciary as an institution has a responsibility in ensuring that 'legislative majorities in tantrum against a minority' did not 'sterilize the grandiloquent mandate' (para. 125).

In conclusion, the Court drew upon the notion of equality which underlay the Indian Constitution and made an organic connection between the intention of the founding fathers and the need to ensure that LGBT persons were not discriminated against in the present day.

By asserting that Sec 377 ran contra to the prohibition against discrimination under Article 15, it opened the door for queer people to claim further constitutional protection. By bringing in a notion of morality which must be 'constitutional' the Court extended its protection to 'unpopular minorities'. By reading Indian society as embodying the very value of inclusiveness the Court tried to set itself up as only elucidating the best values of the Indian tradition. The Court asserted that queer people were indeed a part of the Indian nation and also stated that the judiciary remained an institution committed to the protection of those who might be despised by a majoritarian logic. It initiated a fundamental debate on notions of choice, personal autonomy and our fundamental right to love.

The overturning of Naz: now what?

On 11 December 2013, Justice Singhvi's decision in *Suresh Kumar Koushal v. Naz Foundation* upholding the validity of Section 377, effectively recriminalized the lives of LGBT Indian citizens. This was most eloquently described by Vikram Seth as a 'bad day for law and love'.[3]

The decision in Suresh Kumar Koushal fails the law in three important ways: 1. It ignores the fact that reasoned arguments should guide judicial decisions, 2. it fails to appreciate the philosophy underlying the Indian Constitution and 3. it lacks a sense of constitutional humanism.

When judges pronounce verdicts, they demonstrate the power of reasoned argument. It is this form of deliberative reason which nourishes and sustains the legitimacy of the judiciary. The judges in *Suresh Kumar Koushal* failed in exercising this most fundamental tool of a deliberative democracy, which is public reasoning. On the three key limbs of the case of the respondents the judges choose not to come to a reasoned finding. The key question before the Court was whether Section 377 did violate the right to equality, the right to privacy and dignity as well the right to non-discrimination.

With respect to the right to equality, under Article 14, the courts have laid down two tests. For a law to be valid under Article 14 it can classify between groups or classes, but the classification must be based upon intelligible differentia. The classification must have a reasonable nexus to any objective. In *Koushal* the Supreme Court came to the conclusion that there was a valid classification between 'carnal intercourse in the ordinary course' and 'carnal intercourse against the order of nature'. It is debatable whether this classification lacks any kind of intelligible differentia particularly as the judges say, 'it is difficult to prepare a list of acts which would be covered by the section'. Their failure is astounding. This failure leads to the speculation that the reason the judges did not address the second limb of the test was that then they would be forced to state publicly that their actual reason for upholding law under section 377 was morality. With respect to the question of privacy, the High Court had noted the development of the law on privacy by stating that what was protected under Article

21 was not just the right to privacy as the right to freedom in the zone of your home, but equally the right to make decisions about your intimate life. As such, Section 377 violated both the zone of the home and unconscionably intruded into the realm of decision-making about such intimate questions as who one's partner might be. The Supreme Court did not engage with the debate on privacy initiated by the High Court and came to no finding as to whether the right to privacy (both zonal and decisional) was violated at all.

The reasoning in the *Naz* and *Koushal* judgements – a comparison

As far as the *Naz* Court was concerned, Section 377 by criminalizing an intimate aspect of the human personality, in effect 'denied one the right to full personhood'. This argument of the link between privacy and dignity and how both formed an integral aspect of the right to life under Article 21 formed a key argument of the *Naz* Court. However when it came to the Supreme Court, in spite of voluminous submissions on how Section 377 was an attack on the very selfhood of individuals, the Court did not come to any finding at all.

The answer *Suresh Kumar Koushal* gives to narratives of torture, rape and other violations, all of which demonstrate the impact of Section 377 on the right to life of LGBT persons, is to blandly conclude that 'harassment, blackmail and torture' of LGBT persons is 'neither mandated nor condoned' by Section 377 and the mere fact of misuse is not a 'reflection of the vires of the section'.

Another important innovation of the *Naz* Court was to read sexual orientation as an analogous ground to sex and hence opening out Article 15 to protect possibly every kind of group facing discrimination not currently expressly covered by the Constitution. This was an important jurisprudential innovation and was hailed as perhaps the central and most far reaching ruling of *Naz* and had the potential of being good for all minorities. The *Koushal* Court did not even raise the question of why Article 15 did not apply and concluded that 'High Court was not right in declaring Section 377 IPC ultra vires Articles 14 and 15 of the Constitution'.

As an exercise in reasoning, the *Koushal* judgement failed to demonstrate why it reached the conclusion that Section 377 was constitutionally valid. Perhaps even beyond the questions of equality, privacy and dignity, *Naz* had developed the conceptual notion of constitutional morality. Justice Shah made a point that a notion of public morality cannot be used as a basis for depriving a minority of rights. In other words, if India was a form of democracy based upon majority rule only, then 'any legislative transient majority in tantrums against any minority' could discriminate at will against women, Muslims, Christians and disabled people. The *Naz* court underlined that India was a constitutional democracy rooted in a tradition of inclusiveness which meant that the fundamental rights of all persons of whatever stripe or persuasion were non-negotiable. The *Naz* Court extended this notion of constitutional morality derived from Dr Ambedkar and the notion of inclusiveness as derived from Jawaharlal Nehru to LGBT persons. As such the ruling was based on a profound appreciation of the deepest meaning of the Indian Constitution's commitment to protect the fundamental rights of all persons and groups however 'miniscule' they might be.

The *Koushal* judgement failed to appreciate this understanding of the role of the Constitutional Courts. By arguing that it was duty bound to respect the will of Parliament which represented the 'will of the people' it abdicated the responsibility of the judiciary to protect all minorities from the vicissitudes of majority opinion. Its conclusion that a 'miniscule fraction of the country's population constitute lesbians, gays, bisexuals or transgenders' and hence it was unnecessary to adjudicate the validity of Section 377 did disservice to Indian constitutionalism.

While reason is a key component of the law, emotion is not alien to it. Judicial decisions at their best are not cold and unfeeling, rather they display empathy for human suffering. A court which is moved by human suffering produces judgements like the pavement dwellers judgement (*Olga Tellis*) and bonded labourers judgement (*Bandhua Mukti Morcha*). One can argue that by responding to human suffering, judges embody a form of humanism which should really be at the heart of the judicial function.

This idea of humanism as being central to the very purpose of the Constitution finds a place in Jawaharlal Nehru's famous 'Tryst with Destiny' speech in the Constituent Assembly welcoming India's independence. Nehru said, referring to Gandhi that,

> the ambition of the greatest man of our generation has been to wipe every tear from every eye. That may be beyond us, but as long as there are tears and suffering, so long our work will not be over.
>
> (Moraes, 1959: 2)

Clearly constitutional functionaries like the judges of the Supreme Court are enjoined to keep in mind the idea that they have a high constitutional responsibility to redress the causes of 'tears and suffering'. In *Suresh Kumar Koushal*, the narratives of rape, torture and harassment suffered by LGBT persons did not move the court, nor did narratives of parents of LGBT persons who stated that the law induced a profound sense of fear and was destructive of the ability to enjoy family life peacefully. The judgement embodies a profound failure of Constitutional humanism.

Suresh Kumar Koushal also does disservice to the idea that law and love can meet. The unspoken articulation in *Naz* was of 'the right to love'. Although *Naz* never used this phrase, it did open an imaginative horizon where law could meet love. Till the *Naz* judgement, the question of the lives of LGBT persons was understood in terms of the freedom to perform certain sexual acts in the privacy of bedrooms. *Naz* was instrumental in breaking open the closet doors and strongly asserting that 'the sense of gender and sexual orientation of the person are so embedded in the individual that the individual carries this aspect of his or her identity wherever he or she goes'.

Thus *Naz* developed the right to love as a public right, and succeeded in asserting that questions pertaining to sexual orientation and gender identity were not really about the freedom to perform sexual acts in private, but rather about the identity and personhood which flows from the freedom to form profound intimate attachments with others of one's choice. It is this right to love regardless of the barriers of gender identity and sexual orientation which is deeply imperilled by the judgement in *Suresh Kumar Koushal*. For all those who believe that the right to love should not be constrained by the barriers of caste, religion and sexuality, the decision in the *Suresh Kumar Koushal* case represents a major setback.

The most important conclusion of the Delhi High Court which found no mention in Koushal was the theme of inclusiveness. As the High Court noted,

> If there is one constitutional tenet that can be said to be underlying theme of the Indian Constitution, it is that of 'inclusiveness'. This Court believes that Indian Constitution reflects this value deeply ingrained in Indian society, nurtured over several generations. The inclusiveness that Indian society traditionally displayed, literally in every aspect of life, is manifest in recognising a role in society for everyone. Those perceived by the majority as 'deviants' or 'different' are not on that score excluded or ostracized.

Conclusion

Indian law seems to have traversed from colonial times to the *Naz Foundation*, from persecution for intimacy to making some space for the 'little communities of love'. However, the victory has seen a set-back with the decision in *Suresh Kumar Koushal.*

This reversal is hopefully a temporary one. In support of this hope lies the fact that Naz Foundation has done its job. Indian society has changed dramatically in the time period since *Naz* and it is really very difficult to turn the clock back on seemingly irreversible changes. The fact that LGBT people are now increasingly a part of the mainstream culture signals that this is not an issue which can simply be put back in the closet again.

It was the Delhi High Court judges' fitting conclusion that

> If there is one constitutional tenet that can be said to be underlying theme of the Indian Constitution, it is that of 'inclusiveness'. This Court believes that Indian Constitution reflects this value deeply ingrained in Indian society, nurtured over several generations. The inclusiveness that Indian society traditionally displayed, literally in every aspect of life, is manifest in recognising a role in society for everyone. Those perceived by the majority as 'deviants' or 'different' are not on that score excluded or ostracized.

The theme of 'constitutional morality' has also brought about a paradigm shift in the way LGBT persons may be thought about in relation to the law. The struggle for the rights of LGBT persons is not only about guaranteeing a despised minority its rightful place in the constitutional shade. It has great relevance in the context of the vision of the kind of country we all want to live in and what that vision might mean for the majority.

If India is to be an inclusive democracy in which the rights of all minorities are protected, then the nullification of *Koushal* is a national imperative. Early in 2016, The Supreme Court referred petitions against Section 377 of the Indian Penal Code to a five-judge Constitution Bench for a possible in-depth hearing. As this chapter has shown, there is a great deal hanging in the balance.

Notes

1 The material for this chapter was written by Arvind Narain. The original is considerably longer than what appears here, which has been abridged, edited and slightly reworked by us, with the kind permission of the author.

The original is available on e-PGPathshala | Free PG Courses, http://epgp.inflibnet.ac.in/ and may be found at http://epgp.inflibnet.ac.in/ahl.php?csrno=27 (accessed 01 January 2018).

2 *Naz Foundation v. NCR Delhi.* (2009), p. 277 para. 79.

3 Interview available on ndtv.com dated 12 December 2013 and on https://www.youtube.com/watch?v=nnVG1Mn6dj0 (accessed 1 December 2017).

15 Rape and security

A Buddhist vantage point

Violence against women in the Indian national capital saw a heinous embodiment on December 16, 2012 which has now been referred to as the *Nirbhaya* rape case. In this chapter, we are going to discuss this case with the purpose to understand criminal behaviour against women and the subsequent need for and ways to implement effective risk mitigation. Concepts of Buddhism will help us understand this in a methodical manner.

The four noble truths to understand criminality and risk mitigation technique

In Buddhism, there are four noble truths to self-discovery pertaining to suffering. The path is as follows:

1 There is suffering,
2 There is a cause of suffering,
3 There is cessation of suffering,
4 There is a path that leads to the cessation of suffering.

If we replace *suffering* with *crime* in this statement, one may say:

1 There is crime,
2 There is a cause of crime,
3 There is cessation of crime,
4 There is a path that leads to the cessation of crime.

There is crime – the *Nirbhaya* rape case

While there are a number of cases of violence against women, we are mainly going to discuss one particular case. Consequent to this particular case, a lot of positive changes were brought about by the Indian government and a social movement for change initiated. Some other cases and some statistics will be shared, as relevant.

The *Nirbhaya* rape case refers to a brutal rape which took place on December 16, 2012, in a bus during evening hours, of a young female student accompanied by a male friend. The victim and her male friend entered this bus, which had three more individuals onboard, in order to travel back to their home. The people on the bus had been prowling the city with the intention to find someone to rape. Their *modus operandi* was simple: to rape and then to throw the victim out of the bus. Due to the stigma associated with rape, the assailants thought that the act would probably not get reported. They first thrashed the male friend of the victim. The girl protested. And she was raped. According to one of the accused, had she not resisted so much, the incident would not have been as brutal as it had become. The rape was of an extremely gruesome nature to the effect that the victim's intestines were removed and thrown along with her and her friend's naked bodies after multiple assaults. There were four men accused in this case including a juvenile. The form of rape was therefore gang rape. The vehicle in which the incident took place passed three Police Control Room (PCR) vans of the Delhi Police and the incident went unnoticed till it was reported.

There is a cause of crime

In order to understand why violence against women takes place, it is important to know what are the actual causes of crime. Very often, especially in the context of rape, there is lack of clarity regarding its cause. Quite often, victims of rape are victimized and their features, body language, actions, wardrobe and so on are considered to be causes of them being targets. Before blame can be assigned to anyone for the crime, or the reasons can be revealed about why such crimes take place, it is important to know what does *not* cause crime.

Philosophically, this myth that victims are to be blamed for crimes also points to an informal fallacy of logic, that of false cause. And dress sense is certainly one such false cause. In a 2011 trend analysis study conducted by Garima Goswamy in the capacity of a research analyst for the Risk Monitoring and Advisory Centre of a multinational private risk management company, violent crimes against women of different age groups were analyzed. It was observed that the majority of victims were in the age groups of 18 years and below, and 38 years and above. It is hard to believe that minors and considerably mature women, who made up the majority of victims of sexual crimes, wore provocative clothes and invited trouble.

Playing the devil's advocate, one may argue that considering that 50% of victims of sexual harassment victims belonged to North Eastern States of India, as asserted by a senior police official in a media report published in 2011, the dressing style of such women, as well as their distinctive features might be factors which allowed them to be victimized. It turns out, however, that there is a more causal link to be found, which is shared in common between North Eastern women in Delhi, girls below the age of 18 years, and women more than 38 years – *vulnerability*.

A criminal needs to know that his acts will not be easily detected. This is why he would *choose* a victim who is less likely to inform authorities. Be it an underage child, or a foreigner who has lost her way in Connaught Place, a 5-year-old child brutally raped and strangled by migrant workers or a woman from the North East, targeted by groups of men from the border areas of Gurgaon or Noida. As rape is associated with shame, rapists and many who attempt rape abandon their victims assuming that no complaints will be made against them.

In the case of child abuse there are other complexities. Quite often, children of very young age are not able to realize that they are being violated and are unable to communicate what has happened to them. Mentally challenged persons suffer in the same way. At times, abusers try to instil fear in their victims and threaten them that if they tell their parents or guardian, the abuser will kill the child's parent and/or guardian. Most cases of child abuse are perpetrated by adult family members who terrorize the victim child into staying silent.

In Bangalore, the *modus operandi* of a gang, which was eventually busted, revealed how criminals became confident that their acts would not be detected. They would target North Eastern Indian women to rape. Choosing of victims involved days of surveillance. They would choose women who worked in multinational companies and stayed by themselves in paying guest accommodations. They would rape these women and make videos; to buy their silence they would threaten to post the videos on the internet. They would scare the women by reminding them of the shame they would bring to their families, should the incidents be revealed. In North Eastern India, where the community is close-knit and has a lot of say in family structures, these threats put considerable pressure on the victims.

Women of North East Indian origin who stay in the Indian Capital are also chosen precisely because often they lack the requisite social support in the city. Criminals assume that it will be hard for these women to go to the police with a complaint. Moreover, even if they were to try to make a complaint, language could be a problem for them as many such women cannot speak fluent *Hindi*, the language most understood by law enforcement officers in Delhi. In one such case in 2010, positioning of Police Control Room Vans in the city and the inability of policemen to understand English was criticized by the media once this case was publicized. This is because when an eye witness went to make a complaint following the abduction of a girl, there was delay in the flashing of the message about the incident to the control room primarily due to a language problem.

In most cases of crime, the criminals incapacitate their victims and potential eye witnesses (by beating them up, confiscating wallets and mobile phones) with the effect that they cannot lodge a complaint easily. Rapes are also being carried out in moving vehicles precisely to avoid eye witnesses, so that the crime cannot be detected. Moreover, as in the case of the *Nirbhaya* rape, mobility was a major factor which allowed the criminals not only to lure the victim inside the vehicle but also to escape. Delay is not only physical but also procedural and judicial. Justice delayed is justice denied. And delay in getting justice is often taken advantage of by criminals and potential criminals for conducting their activities. In certain cases, crime then becomes a habit as the criminal uses the loopholes and slowness of the justice system in his or her favour.

As per media statistics, in 2012 there were 705 other cases where no conviction had taken place. Also, between December 16, 2012 and January 2013, only four inquiries were launched when in fact there were as many as 64 rape cases and nearly 500 cases of harassment filed with the Delhi Police. This suggests that despite there being fast track courts, justice in India regarding gender issues still witnesses significant delay.

More significant than delay is deterrence, for by imposing harsher deterrent punishments on convicted criminals, potential criminals are unlikely to commit similar crimes. While in order to combat delay, both police officials and judicial authorities are required to form a good security setup; to ensure effective deterrence the onus of responsibility lies on an effective judicial system.

Besides delay, lack of deterrent punishments for crime against women give the criminals the confidence that even if they were to commit a crime and should their crime be detected and should they be prosecuted, the consequences would not be too severe. Many criticize that what probably led to the severity of the crime in the *Nirbhaya* rape case was the result of a *procrastination of the Indian government* over issues of gender equality and gender violence. This was also evident in a parliamentary session of the *Rajya Sabha* where sufficient time was not being allotted to a member of Parliament to discuss this case, because – to quote the speaker – 'there were other important issues and other ministers of parliaments deserved their turn.'

Very often, crimes of a sexual nature are brushed under the carpet because society does not provide the appropriate response such a crime deserves. The way in which society responds to criminals and crimes has a major impact on the increase or reduction of crime. India's social set up is such that victims of criminality are scrutinized and their behaviour is subject to criticism. So, for instance, rape victims are often blamed – for dressing provocatively, for 'provoking' criminals, for being out of home during 'inappropriate' hours in inappropriate company.

This is perhaps because for years, women who live in a male-dominated society have to make adjustments according to the protocols set by men. Such adjustment often leads women to be invented in the image of how a man views a woman. Very often this leads to lack of acknowledgement of a problem or lack of *response* when crimes against women by men take place, because even women, at times, perceive victims of crime as those who may have provoked the men to victimize them. And eventually it may lead to a worrying proposition that women are to blame for the fate they bring upon themselves, not conforming to social norms or treading with caution. Luckily, this had been a matter of discussion and debate with respect to bringing reforms in perceiving women in India.

In March 2015, a BBC Documentary called *India's Daughter* paved way for a debate whether women are to be blamed for being raped or men are to be blamed for raping them.

In this documentary, a rapist on death row, convicted in the infamous *Nirbhaya* rape case, blamed the victim who was subjected to brutal rape. He blamed her to have been out late at night with a male friend when the accused and his fellow accused were on the prowl, looking for a victim to rape. Moreover, during 2012 protests over the *Nirbhaya* rape case, Abhijit Mukherjee, the son of President Pranab Mukherjee, made sexist comments about women protestors at India Gate. He had called them 'dented and painted' and mentioned these women frequent discotheques suggesting a promiscuous non-Indian behaviour of these protestors. Besides the rapist and the president's son, defence lawyers A. P. Singh and M. L. Sharma were also known to have made tasteless remarks both during trial, in the documentary and after the release of the documentary in India was under discussion.

One comment made was that women are like diamonds and men are like dogs, and diamonds need to be protected or else dogs will devour them. What was implied was that women should not stay out late hours and unaccompanied by family members. Singh made even more radically offensive remarks about women in India who invite trouble by imbibing Western culture and staying out during late hours. He is also known to have gone on record to say that if his daughter ever engaged in shaming the family name by going out with a boy which he equated to having engaged in pre-marital sex, he would shoot her in his farm house in front of all his relatives as an act of justified honour killing. This is an example of how lack of appropriate social response can lead criminals to commit crimes.

To put it simply, why does a criminal commit a crime?

To the criminal mind, it is important that . . .

1 The crime is not detected.
2 If detected, there is delay in arrest or prosecution.
3 The crime should entail minimal loss in the event of a prosecution.
4 Even if prosecuted, there should still be support in society despite the criminal.

These are the most basic tenets of criminal thought as articulated in the philosophy of security. It is the criminal's motivations in each of these, and not the protection of the victim, that the current situation (legal, judicial, police, social) in India caters to. It is no wonder that we are suffering under an epidemic of rape.

There is cessation of crime – risk mitigation

Risk mitigation is an important tool in a world where criminality has been increasing consistently, in particular during the first two decades of the 21st century. Just as the criminals choose their targets to commit a crime, by understanding the cause of crime, the cessation of crime can take place. So, an effective risk mitigation technique would be one which would understand the value of concepts of detection, delay, deterrence and response. Effective implementation after comprehending their importance of this concept results in or is bound to result in stable risk mitigation. Laxity in such implementation may result, as it has before, into increase or continuance of criminality. The role of the government and the judiciary is of paramount importance in effective implementation of control measures.

While the *Nirbhaya* rape case did not lead to cessation of crime, it did pave the path for it. This is perhaps because of the gruesome nature of the crime, the location and the hour and the manner in which the incident took place, or perhaps just because it was the last straw for the civil society to take, the aftermath of this case saw tremendous change in society, which, in turn, resulted in their being constructive steps taken by the administration to attempt at providing better laws for women.

The *Nirbhaya* case led to a nationwide outcry and India saw a mass movement not led by any particular leader as the aftermath of the same. Such form of protest over gender violence was unprecedented. The student population at Jawaharlal Nehru University (JNU) were among few who started the protest. Water cannons, baton charge and tear gas were used at peaceful protestors at India Gate, who kept on coming back to join the protest till a resolution was sought.

Despites loopholes in the administrative systems, some relief was observed with respect to cases of crime against women after the Criminal Law (Amendment) Act 2013 was enacted. For speeding up rape prosecutions, the government's response was formation of six 'fast track' courts.

In a significant 2014 verdict the Supreme Court held that delay in filing FIR is not a basis on which an accused can defeat a complainant's testimony. Social stigma, psychological trauma and delay in medical treatment were recognized as causes for delay in reporting a case of rape. Moreover, considering the social structure of society where often the practice is to discuss the issue within the family prior to filing a report, delays were considered understandable. In the particular case which led to this verdict, a married Indian woman delayed informing her husband that she had been raped by a neighbour in Chandigarh.

Moreover, the Sexual Harassment Act of Women at Workplace (Prevention, Prohibition and Redressal) Act 2013 has set a number of timelines on employers with respect to effective implementation of the salient provisions of this Act. These steps may actually help to avoid delay in cases regarding violence against women and help in effective risk mitigation.

As mentioned before, another significant aftermath of the *Nirbhaya* rape case was the Criminal Law (Amendment) Act 2013. The definition of rape, which previously was restricted to vaginal penetration, was broadened. Another significant change was that lack of physical resistance was made immaterial to the act of rape. This suggests that the victim would not be blamed for not trying to prevent being raped by physically resisting the criminal. Definition of statutory rape was also changed as the age of consent was increased to 18 years. As there were increasing cases of acid attack, sexual harassment, voyeurism, stalking, new offences punishable under the Indian Penal Code were introduced. The law has extended punishment for gang rape to a minimum of 20 years, extendible to life imprisonment. This is really a step in the positive direction because gang rapes are increasing. And the reason why this is probably the case is that previously such strict punishment was not there in the law for gang rapes.

There is a path which leads to cessation of crime

To come back to the controversial documentary *India's Daughter* (banned in India), the views of the defence attorney Singh expressed in it led to a bet between Singh and a radio jockey of radio channel 91.1. While the advocate's claim was that majority of Indians would support his views and if that was not the case, he would not defend the accused in this case. He lost as most viewers did not share his thoughts. However, before he could revert, the Bar Council of India issued show cause notices against both lawyers to have made such offensive remarks in public.

India's Daughter which was centred around these protests in the context of the infamous rape case, was censored in India not only because the case was *sub judice* (it could have interfered with the appeal against capital punishment), but because to interview a rapist was considered reprehensible by many leaders discussing the issue in the *Rajya Sabha*. Akhtar pointed out that this view was expressed openly by many men in gatherings of *Rajya Sabha*.

While better surveillance, policing, adopting safety measures, deploying of CCTV cameras in colonies, institutions, residential complexes, cameras in cars, better administrative and judicial procedures can provide some form of relief, the path which may really pave way to cessation of this particular type of crime against women in the national capital and subsequently in India, is the appropriate response of society towards such crime. As mentioned above, there was and is a dichotomy of social response for rape cases. On one side of the debate are individuals who blame women to objectify themselves and provoke men to rape, on the other side of the debate are individuals who see rape as an act of violence, power and oppression and hold only the criminal responsible.

Awareness about crimes, laws protecting women, helplines, phone applications with GPS trackers, technological surveillance tools and so on may help to prevent crimes. Perhaps such tools will also lead to the reduction of public apathy and to the increase of public disapproval of crime against women.

Conclusion

Buddhist four noble truths can help explain why crimes occur and also help develop a method to curb crime, for what is crime, if not suffering. And nirvana or liberation would be to live in a world free of such crimes. While in practical life, it seems to be a difficult task to achieve in this lifetime, it is not too ambitious an aim considering that it is achievable if the effective risk mitigation steps can be taken by the government and society.

16 The ethics of organ donation

Advances in both medical research and ongoing surgical practices which involve organ transplants are preconditioned upon human subjects giving their body parts for such a cause. The ultimate cause is usually to save a life or to enhance the quality of life of a patient who is in need of a better-functioning organ.

There are several ethical issues involved with respect to organ transplantation and organ donations. The first is the problem of consent. There are two kinds of consent in these procedures – informed consent and presumed consent. The former is when the patient or family members of the patient give consent for removal of organ upon brain death. In the latter case, the consent is 'presumed' in the absence of any objection from the deceased during her or his lifetime or from the deceased's family member. Like many other countries, in India, organ donation from cadavers is legal. A practical problem is that cadaver donations are less in number. So, in cases of kidney transplantation, donations from live donors are encouraged.

The second ethical problem which arises due to the practice of organ transplantation and organ donations in an unregulated fashion is that of exploitation of the poor, or fraudulent practices which were prevalent prior to the ban of sale of organs for money. The racket of transnational organ trafficking in India was met with tremendous public outrage when discovered. Altruism is considered a legitimate standard of organ donation in India and in most parts of the world. In the shortage of supply of organs in comparison to the demand for such organs, the idea of compensated organ donation is visited. The questions this chapter wishes to address are: is it morally feasible to make a case for compensated organ donation in India? Is altruism, as a legitimate reason for acceptable organ donation, a morally viable standard for it?

Ethics of care and justice

In Moral Philosophy, two perspectives are popular, the justice perspective, or what is known as 'ethics of justice'; and, care perspective, or what is commonly described as the 'ethics of care'. The justice perspective is often associated with application of ethics in the legal sphere which emphasizes universality and impartiality. Care ethics lays stress on the fundamental elements of relationships and dependencies.

Care ethics endorses contextualization by 'promoting the well being of care givers and care receivers in a network of social relations' (Seibt et al., 2015: 149). Organ donation presents an interesting case when examined in the light of these two perspectives. This is because in countries like the United States and India, altruism is considered to be a standard to decide whether an organ donation is acceptable or not. For instance, in India the law requires that organ donors must either be related to the recipient (genetically or legally) or else must be willing to sign an affidavit stating 'affection or attachment' as a motive for donating an organ if the donor is not related to the recipient. Should money change hands when non-related parties are involved in organ donation (donor and recipient), the act is punishable under the law, applicable to all impartially. The outcome is thus as per the justice perspective. On the other hand, if altruism is considered the criterion for donation in cases of non-related donors, then the care perspective is at play.

While organ donation and organ transplantation are relatively new concepts, most religions do not seem to have any objection to this practice, since benevolence, compassion, sacrifice and so on are virtues endorsed in many religious texts. One reason why altruism as a motive is not questioned by moralists is because many people endorse what is known as a social conception of morality. According to Paul Bloomfield in his book, *Morality and Self Interest* (2008), this social conception can be opposed to a Socratic conception of morality. The social conception of morality considers concern for others or altruism as a primary moral criterion, while a Socratic conception of morality considers living well or flourishing as a primary moral criterion. Living well might include altruism but it might also exclude it. Proponents of the Socratic conception of morality would probably deem altruism as a legal and moral criterion for organ donation or organ transplantation as open to question. Some scholars, including Sally Satel (2008), for instance, ask the question, What is wrong with compensated organ donation? Does it take away the act of altruism if the organ donor gets something in return in consideration? These are important questions and the need to discuss this becomes very urgent considering that while there is/was a problem of organ trafficking without the consent of the donor, many poor people in India willingly donate/wish to donate an organ for monetary reimbursement. They believe that an organ is like any other property they own which they have a right to sell.

Body/organ – is it a property?

Should a person have the right to sell a human organ, such as a kidney, just as he or she has a right to sell his car? It is with this understanding that many people chose to sell their kidneys for money. There have been several arguments made against the sale of body parts in society (just as with the lease of the body itself in prostitution) as it is said to undermine the dignity and integrity of the body. But what about corpses? Could not a corpse be profitably harvested for saleable organs? Proponents of compensated organ donation will have to consider the further question of whether or not a donor's next of kin has any right or say, then, over the organ to be donated/sold.

If the answer is *no*, that organs are not 'personal property' like cars, and cannot be donated for compensation, neither those of living persons by their own choice, nor those of corpses by next of kin, then it becomes more challenging to defend a case for compensated organ donation. In this case, the only way organ transplantation would be possible is if the *state* has control over deciding who gets to give his or her kidney and the state has indiscriminate control over dead bodies, to use cadavers for organ donation. This is clearly not the case.

As per English Common Law, there are no property rights of a dead body. However, American common law grants quasi property right belonging to the spouse or next of kin to prevent mutilation or damage to a dead body and allows them to possess the same for a proper burial. This was primarily due to the practice of unauthorized mutilation of human cadavers for medical science which was prevalent at the end of the 19th century. It is noteworthy that this is a negative right and no court has granted a positive absolute property right to a dead body. As opposed to this, in a living body, while property rights are not granted, there is what is called 'liberty interest'. This includes the right to use, possess and exclude others from one's body while one is alive. This is evident by there being laws against slavery, presence of false imprisonment penalties, criminal penalties for assault and battery. Right to use one's body can be highlighted by employment contracts. Here the exception is probably made for underage individuals where consent is taken from parents or guardians regarding their medical treatment. However, in a living body, guardians and parents are not allowed by law to misappropriate the body of an individual into prostitution, slavery, etc. As there is no general right to sell the body, some argue that property rights cannot be attributed to a living body. However, this does not take away a property interest of a living body as is evident from the US judgement in *Andrus v. Allard* case which concerned the ban on sale of eagle feathers. The Supreme Court's verdict had implied a right to possess, use and dispose, although the right to sell was not entertained.

In India there is absence of a clear legal rule over whether a dead body is property or not, as is evident in the *Prabhat Balotiya* case – 2009 where the quarrel was between Hindu parents and a Christian wife over who had rights over the body of their convert son/husband. However, precedent might have been set by the *Khushboo* case of 2007 in the context of an accident claim where a vehicle was involved which was transporting a corpse. It was held in *Khushboo* that the body could be defined as goods. There are several cases and laws which protect the dead in India. Definitions of death are found in the Registration of Births and Deaths Act (1969) and the Transplantation of Human Organs Act 1994. Moreover, there are several provisions of Indian Penal Code (IPC) which recognize and/or give due respect to the dead, such as Sections 404, 1860, 499, 503. Moreover, dignity and fair treatment as per Article 21 of the Constitution of India was extended to a dead man's body after his death in *Parmanand Katara v. Union Of India*.

The Transplantation of Human Organs Act 1994 and The Transplantation of Human Organs Rules 1995 are the guiding principles in the Indian Constitution regarding organ transplantation. It is clearly implied that in India, presumed consent is the practice of organ retrieval. While nothing has been specified with regards to whether or not a body or body parts such as organs are considered to be property, it can be read that there is recognition of body and organs as things which can be possessed, and not necessarily with respect to burial procedures. As per the Organs Act, the person lawfully in possession of the body can donate the dead body for organ transplantation unless there is any objection from any near relative of the deceased. Presumed consent would be there with the hospital authorities of an unclaimed dead body after 48 hours. People at a cremation ground have no right to dissect a dead body for organ retrieval.

It is safe to assume then that in India complete negation of right over one's organ might not be entertained. After all, we do get to use our body and we are at liberty to alter it in a variety of ways, cosmetic, dietetic, surgical and so on. What is objectionable generally is intentional harm done to one's body, as is in the case of drug and alcoholism abuse or suicide. There are social provisions to prevent harm to one's body. This suggests that ethically one is not entitled to cause harm to oneself. Removal of an organ or a spare organ may or may not lead to harm, depending upon a number of factors such as health post such an operation of kidney removal. Even though many individuals who volunteer to be donors do not mind suffering the negative repercussions, one of the reasons there is a public outcry is precisely because harming oneself is condemned. In India, it seems that there is nothing to prevent one from assuming the notion that we have property right to one's body and body parts. It is there even in presumed consent, where objections, if any from family members of a deceased, would be entertained.

Charles C. Dunham who supports an incentive system for organ donors believes that legislature should recognize property rights to organs. According to Dunham, the reason why sale of organs is banned in the United States is out of concern of public health and not necessarily because sale of organs as property is condemned.

But if we answer in the affirmative, like Dunham, that individuals have a right over their organs to dispose of them like property at will, then the next question is, is it ethical to put a price tag over one's organ?

Condemnation of for-profit organ donation

Dr H. Barry Jacob, the founder of International Kidney Exchange Limited, had proposed a for-profit plan of organ retrieval by introducing a brokerage system wherein kidneys would be purchased from developed countries to treat patients in the United States. His medical licence was revoked and he was convicted for engaging in such practices. In the National Organ Transplantation Act 1984, Section 301 was introduced which made acquiring, receiving or otherwise transferring any human organ for valuable consideration in use in human transplantation unlawful.

Most countries have imposed a ban on organ trade, for such trade has led to a lot of exploitation. India had become the 'Great Organ Bazaar'. Scandals were uncovered where organs were retrieved from the poor without their knowledge or consent, who were initially tempted with job prospects and sedated before they were operated upon. In other cases, brokers sought for donors and paid them less than what was initially promised. Soon the Indian government drafted a bill which then became the Transplantation of Human Organs Act 1994, earlier mentioned.

The Transplantation of Human Organs Act: criticisms

The main criticism of this Act is its failure to prevent illicit organ trade as organ trade continued way past 1994. There are so many scandals which exemplify that the act has failed to prevent organ trade; for example, the Gurgaon Kidney Scandal of 2008, where it was revealed that more than 600 kidney transplants took place over a decade by fraudulent manner. The Central Bureau of Investigation (CBI) convicted some of the accused but the main accused including Dr Amit Kumar were released due to lack of proper evidence. In 2014, four arrests were made after the death of a person who had willingly flown to Sri Lanka along with agents of 'kidney retrieval' for transplant operation. While in the Gurgaon Scandal the price used to tempt potential donors with job pretext was INR 30,000, in the fraud unveiled in 2014, potential donors were lured by INR 300,000 for organ retrieval. Clearly, the legal ban on kidney donation increased the offering price, even though perhaps only a small percentage or no amount is actually paid in such cases.

In real time, ineffective investigation of unrelated donors facilitates organ trade. As involvement in organ trade is a non-cognizable offence, police officials have to wait for appropriate authorities set up as per the act or an authorized officer appointed by such authority or by an individual who has given prior notice to the requisite authority within a set time frame. In 2015, Justice Ashim Kumar Roy and Justice Ishan Chandra Das of Calcutta High Court directed the state to investigate matters concerning 'kidney rackets'.

As a culture of bribery and corruption prevails in most Indian states, the vetting procedure by appropriate authority is inefficient. Moreover, medical professionals lack investigative skills to be able to access the authenticity of one's 'affection and attachment' towards a recipient. Forged paperwork, perjured affidavit and interviews with false testimonies not only allow brokers to continue the trade but blackmail, if need be, the donors so fooled, for many a time they are unfamiliar with the law prohibiting organ trade. So not only are they not compensated for their services, but they become criminals. In a case which surfaced in the media in 2015, one of the 'accused' donors arrested from R.B. Tagore Hospital wanted to lodge a case of cheating as per Indian Penal Code Section 420. His logic was that he was not paid the amount which was promised by the middlemen and his clients. Probably unaware of the law, the donor felt cheated.

Arguments against and for compensated organ donation

Several arguments are levied against compensated organ donation. Some of these, as pointed out by Sally Satel in *When Altruism Isn't Enough*, put forth as a devil's advocate are as follows:

1 Poor people will be forced to donate organs in order to get incentives.
2 Donors will not give informed consent.
3 Individuals may misrepresent their eligibility to donate.
4 Fewer organs for transplantations would be secured for free.
5 The poor will supply the rich and discrimination will result due to unjust preferences of race, class (caste considerations can be extended in the Indian scenario).
6 Donors will be worse off financially.
7 The quality of medical conditions will be unreliable.
8 A legal organ market shall pave the way for a black market.

However, these criticisms can be argued against if there are further regulations made to prevent such activities from happening should the legislature allow buying and selling of organs. A lot of emphasis given in setting up such a regulatory system to facilitated compensated organ donation is on:

1 Education of potential donors.
2 In-depth assessment of their medical history and psychological assessment.
3 Provision of less invasive procedures.
4 Long-term surgical and medical compensation instead of a one-time cash amount.
5 State incurring expenses including lost wages during recuperation and guarantee of job availability post-surgery.
6 Equal access to health care and setting up of a fair system to match donors and recipients irrespective of consideration of class, race, etc. All potential recipients would be equally favoured.
7 The donor compensation proposal would have no space for a middleman or organ broker. This will prevent fraud and exploitation.

8 The donor compensation proposal would contain provisions for binding legal contracts. This would prevent cheating.

In 'Donor Compensation without Exploitation' James Stacey Taylor and Mary C. Simmerling argue that legalizing a kidney market will not encourage sale in a black market because the only customers of a black market probably could not afford to buy organs there. On the contrary legalizing organ trade might reduce problems related to organ trafficking by providing a buyer with a legal and safer option (Satel, 2008: 50–5).

Although altruistic donations might be less, there is no reason to believe that these will stop completely. A person may be offered incentives to donate; he or she can always refuse any such incentives too.

The degree of exploitation of donors is higher in the case of uncompensated organ donation as per Virginia Postrel, a kidney donor. According to her, 'Expecting people to take risks and give up something valuable without compensation is a far worse form of exploitation than paying them' (Postrel, 2007).

Iranian model

An actual model for compensated organ donation is seen in Iran, the only country where organ trade is legal. This suggests that such a case is possible. Previously the Ministry of Health in Iran funded dialysis patients to receive transplants abroad. This practice soon became very expensive and a long renal waiting list was created. Post-1985, renal transplant facilities were developed in Iran and between 1985 and 1987, 274 renal transplants from live donations were performed. In 1988, when a deceased donor organ transplantation program was a distant reality, a government-funded, regulated, compensated living unrelated donor renal program was established in Iran. As many as 25 transplant teams were set up. By 1999 the transplant waiting list was eliminated. By 2005, 19,609 renal transplants were performed out of which 15,365 were from living unrelated donors and 823 from deceased donors.

Some of the salient features of compensated organ donation in Iran are as follows:

1 All potential donors contact Dialysis and Transplant Patients Association (DATPA) as there are no organ brokers in Iran. Most DATPA members are patients who have End Stage Renal Disease

and receive no incentives for finding or referring a live unrelated donor to a renal transplant team.

2 DATPA members find a living unrelated potential kidney donor for a patient without any related potential kidney donor.
3 Government funds all renal transplantation costs and all transplant teams are affiliated to university hospitals. It also provides immunosuppressive drugs to transplant recipients at subsidized rates.
4 There are no incentive schemes for renal transplant teams.
5 Living unrelated donors receive an award and health insurance from the government of Iran. Many also receive a rewarding gift either from the recipient or from a charitable organization in case of poor recipients. The nature of rewarding gift is pre-decided and arranged by DATPA.
6 Charitable organizations are active in providing financial support to poor patients.
7 Transplant teams scrutinize the program for any possible ethical issues.
8 Foreigners can be operated on in Iran after acquiring proper authorization from the Ministry of Health. However, they are not allowed to either give or take kidneys from Iranian citizens.

The elimination of the waiting list suggests that in Iran equal medical care is offered to poor and rich alike. A study on 1,000 individuals comprising of renal transplant recipients and their living unrelated donors was conducted to determine if there was discrimination with respect to the socio-economic class receiving transplants from paid kidney donations. The findings revealed very insignificant differences suggesting no or rather less exploitation of the poor to serve the rich. This program decreased related living donors, some of whom were forced to give their kidneys due to lack of option or availability of an alternative.

Conclusion

In India, owing to exploitation of poor and cases of fraud and cheating, the government banned sale of organs for commercial gains. However, the act turned out to be ineffective. Instead of banning organ sales, an alternative can be to formulate a regulatory mechanism, perhaps inspired by the Iranian model to facilitate ethical regulated compensated organ donation. But we may still ask, are the ethical issues circumvented by the legal solution? What does the organ trade tell us about the connect or disconnect between law and morality?

17 Indian Supreme Court jurisprudence

Five exemplary cases

This chapter offers a brief overview of five of the most important cases of the Indian Supreme Court. We concentrate especially upon those that continue to have abiding socio-legal relevance, and particularly serve to relate the internal dynamics of Indian Supreme Court jurisprudence to the Philosophy of Law as such. In this sense we are beginning to transition from applying legal philosophy to Indian cases, which was the broad aim of Part III of this book, to applying Indian cases to legal philosophy, an equally important task.

Within the earlier chapters of the book, we have already had occasion to discuss various landmark cases, such as *Naz Foundation v. Government of National Capital Territory of Delhi* (in Chapter 14), *National Legal Services Authority v. Union of India* (Chapter 13), *S. Rangarajanv. P. Jagjivan Ram* (in Chapter 12), among many others. This chapter turns to the following additional cases, which are widely regarded to be of crucial importance:

We begin with *Kesavananda Bharati v. the State of Kerala*, which established the 'basic structure' doctrine. This holds that the essential principles of the Constitution are beyond amendment by Parliament.

Another important case is *Olga Tellis v. Bombay Municipal Corporation*, where the Court ruled that the right to life granted under Article 21 includes the right to livelihood as well.

Next presented is *Indra Sawhney v. The Union of India*, which laid down one of the most basic and central judicial decisions with respect to the constitutionality of reservation.

We then discuss *Mohammed Ahmed Khan v. Shah Bano Begum*, where the Supreme Court ruled, in the absence of a Uniform Civil Code, that Muslim women can file divorce petitions under the Code of Criminal Procedure, 1973, or – as later cases lay down – under the Muslim Women (Protection of Rights on Divorce) Act, 1986.

Finally, we end with *Vishaka v. State of Rajasthan*, where the Court arrogates to itself the duties of legislation and lays down rules to prevent sexual harassment at the workplace.

Each of these cases is very briefly but systematically presented with a fourfold method. We first provide the facts of the case along with its background. Then we lay out the decision of the Court. Next we put the facts of the case and the decision into broader context. And finally we link up the case with wider aspects of the Philosophy of Law, especially in terms of the topics of earlier chapters of the book. Let us begin, then, with *Kesavananda*.

Kesavananda Bharati v. the State of Kerala

Starting with the background of the case, this particular appeal arose following upon land reforms enacted by the Kerala government, whereby restrictions were imposed that adversely effected a religious leader named Kesavananda Bharati. In 1970, as the head of a religious group named 'Edneer Mutt', he challenged the state reforms in court. Bharati filed a petition challenging various constitutional amendments (the 24th, 25th and 29th amendments to the Constitution) that had provided the legal basis for the land reforms that he was opposed to and seeking relief from.

Moving on to the decision, it is somewhat ironic that the Court's verdict yielded no direct relief to the petitioner, while at the same recognizing to a great extent the validity of his claims. This case is not of ultimate historic importance because of the particulars with respect to land reform and its clash with property rights. Rather, it is through this decision that the 'basic structure' doctrine gets propounded. The Court maintained that while Article 368 does grant the Parliament the power to make amendments to the Constitution (including to fundamental rights, such as property rights), this power is not without limitation. Amendments can be made, but the 'basic structure' or the essential nature of the Indian Constitution cannot be altered. What exactly constituted the basic structure of the Constitution was not defined, and numerous judges gave a different set of features. At heart, most of the judges honed in on the Preamble, the fundamental rights and the directive principles of state policy as the trihedron of the basic structure. In a later case (*Indira Nehru Gandhi v. Raj Narain* –1975), free and fair elections and the rule of law were regarded as part of the basic structure of the Constitution, the effect being that the 39th Amendment to the Constitution was invalidated by the Court. Ironically, this desire to preserve the rule of law was instead the catalyst for the declaration of Emergency by Prime Minister Indira Gandhi that year.

To put *Kesavananda* further into context, the case saw assembled a 13-judge bench tasked with deciding whether constitutional amendments brought about by procedurally flawless means (i.e. in line with article 368 of the Constitution) were limited or unlimited, and whether they were subject to judicial review. The result was the articulation of the basic structure. This doctrine operated as a win-win scenario, insofar as the loggerheads that the Parliament and judiciary were locked up in was dissolved by granting both institutions more robust powers within their own spheres. Parliament was fully free to amend, and yet the Court was fully free to review. During the Emergency, the existence of the basic structure doctrine helped to prevent India from transforming into a totalitarian regime, though it was nevertheless only very dimly present during those dark years of Indian democracy, and the Court refused to face off against the executive, standing by as spectator as the government systematically violated the fundamental rights of its citizens. But thankfully *Kesavananda* was there as a precedent, so following the Emergency there was a firm foundation for the rebuilding of the priority of fundamental rights, along with the reputation of the Court.

From the philosophical point of view, this case is one of the richest in the history of Indian jurisprudence. There are countless ways to approach it. From the basic question of legal ontology (what does it mean for something to *be* a law?, as discussed throughout Part I of the book), to the most sophisticated questions of legal reasoning (e.g. we can see this case as a classic example of exploring legal reasoning at the highest tier, as discussed in Chapter 4), an entire course on the Philosophy of Law could be taught just by reading the decision reached in *Kesavananda* – and of course, since the printed judgement amounts to nearly 800 pages, with a historically unprecedented 11 separate opinions expressed by the 13 judges, it would take a full semester just to get through it!

But perhaps one of the most salient aspects of this case is the way it reveals the underlying tension that is always present, and always vague and ambiguous, between law and morality (as we discussed in depth in Chapter 1). At the strictly legal level, the case propagates the doctrine of the basic structure as a way of delineating the judicial and legislative spheres and preventing usurpation of one by the other. But the basic question posed – *Can there be judicial review of constitutional amendments that are procedurally flawless?* – would tend to be answered quite differently by the positivist (who would be more inclined to answer *no*) and the natural law theorist (more inclined to answer *yes*).

Olga Tellis v. Bombay Municipal Corporation

To begin the background to this case, in 1981 the Chief Minister of Maharashtra was cited by newspapers as announcing that pavement dwellers in Mumbai would be forcibly evicted and deported to where they came from or to other places outside Bombay. Evictions and demolitions began to take place in accord with a municipal order issued under the Bombay Municipal Corporation Act. In 1985, journalist Olga Tellis petitioned the Supreme Court on behalf of Bombay slum and pavement dwellers. In the Maharashtra government's counter affidavit, it asserted that no one had been deported and that such a proposal had not in fact been made. Regarding evictions, it argued that no one had the legal right to encroach upon public pavements. It further contended that the refusal to allow the petitioners to use pavements was not unreasonable, unfair or unlawful. By living on the pavement, the slum dwellers were bereft of basic civil amenities.

In the Supreme Court's decision, the Chief Justice famously mentioned that 'human compassion (happiness) must soften the rough edges of justice in all situations.' Although the Court held that the eviction orders were valid, the judges took a humanitarian approach and held that alternative shelters must be provided to slum dwellers who had been evicted. The eviction procedure prescribed by the relevant sections of the Bombay Municipal Corporation Act was not unreasonable, unjust or unfair. The writ was thus disposed of. However, in the process, a somewhat radical idea was introduced and given traction: that is, that the right to *livelihood* was recognized as a fundamental part of the constitutionally guaranteed right to life, established as an organic part of an individual's liberty.

The basic idea that arises from *Olga Tellis* is that the right to life includes the right to livelihood. To place this into the context of rights jurisprudence, we see here a case where the classic idea of fundamental constitutional rights being limited to first generation (that is, civil and political) rights gets overcome with the introduction of second generation rights (e.g. the right to health or social security). Through this judgement, the state is not merely prohibited from infringing in liberties of its citizens, but is positively bound to take certain measures: liberties as negatively conceived transform into positive obligations of the state. The (second generation) right to shelter places a positive duty to be performed by the state. However, subsequent cases (an infamous one being *Almitra Patel v. Union of India* – 2000, as well as the many decisions surrounding the Narmada river dam), have significantly backtracked on this important innovation.

In terms of the philosophical implications, most commentary within the field of jurisprudence has tended to highlight the utilitarian aspect of the decision. As we saw in the quote above, the Chief Justice appealed to the principle of utility in his judgement, 'the greatest happiness to the greatest number'. But within the broader contours of the philosophy of law, we think it would be far richer to explore this case from the vantage point of Chapter 5, the debates within the philosophy of human rights. On the one hand, the chief justice made remarks serving to enlarge the substantive meaning of abstract rights, for example when he wrote that 'no one can live without the means of living'. He thus recognizes here that rights can be seen as meaningless in comparison to the material conditions that govern whether they may ever be realized. This is a profoundly important recognition. But is mere recognition enough? For, on the other hand, as subsequent case law (like the cases mentioned just above) has often shown, it is also possible to witness the firm support of human rights simultaneous with an agenda that in no way helps the plight of the poor. Indeed, as the legal scholar Balakrishnan Rajagopal has argued, the Supreme Court jurisprudence since *Olga Tellis* can be characterized as 'pro human rights but anti poor' (Rajagopal, 2007: 169).

Indra Sawhney v. Union of India

This is one of those cases that is deeply tied into the dynamic politics of the nation. As everyone is well aware, the Indian government has implemented a (evolving) reservation policy related to various dimensions of employment and education. In the 1970s, this required investigation about backward classes in India and recommendations to improve their status. In 1978, Prime Minister Morarji Desai commissioned B.P. Mandal to form a backward classes' commission. By 1980 the report was prepared. A decade later (in 1990), orders to implement numerous aspects of the report was issued by Prime Minister V.P. Singh. This led to widespread civil disturbance throughout India. Prime Minister P.V. Narasimha Rao issued another memorandum related to reservations. Cumulatively, by means of the memorandums and pre-existing legislation, there was now to be 59.5% reservation in central government posts: there was already in effect 22.5% reservation for SC/STs; now was being added 27% for OBCs; and 10% reservation was created for other economically backward sections not included in the Scheduled Caste/Scheduled Tribe/Other Backward Class (SC/ST/OBC) schemes. A Public Interest Litigation (PIL) was filed by Indra Sawhney to challenge the memorandums.

In the decision, the Court observed that the Constitution did not define backward classes but an integral relation between caste, occupation, poverty and social backwardness was observed. The Court held that Article 16(4) (which allows special provisions for backward classes) was not a violation of Article 16(1) (which guaranteed all Indian citizens equal opportunity in matters of public appointment), and that it contemplated social backwardness. It further laid down that reservations were not applicable in promotions (later, Parliament enacted legislation that circumvented this restriction), and generally should not exceed 50%. The Supreme Court struck down the 10% reservation that had been established for other economically backward sections that were not covered in the existing schemes of reservation.

It should be noted that the landmark judgement in this case is a proof of the power of the PIL (refer to the discussion of PIL in Chapter 6). But more pertinent, while upholding the need of a reservation policy for uplifting the backward classes, in this case the Court attempted to balance the threat of reservation policy to result in unjustifiable reverse discrimination. In other words, the case illustrates the basic tension built in to the concept of equality discussed at length in Chapter 13. Reservation is beyond doubt a need in this country in order to permit a substantial population to be in a basic position to experience minimal equality. But the politics of reservation proceeds blind to the ambiguities inbuilt within the concept of equality itself. Philosophers and jurists need to come together to make progress on a viable concept of equality that can serve to diffuse the politics of reservation and contribute to the teleology of reservation: a life of equal dignity for all citizens. This is one urgent challenge facing the Philosophy of Law in India.

Mohammed Ahmed Khan v. Shah Bano Begum

Here is another case, like *Indra Sawhney*, deeply entrenched in the politics both of its day and our own. In this case, it is not the politics of caste, but of community. Shah Bano, former wife of Ahmed Khan, was divorced by triple *talaq*, and evicted from her matrimonial home after over 40 years of marriage. Khan paid her INR 3,000 as *mahr* (marriage gift) in addition to some small amount for an *iddat* (i.e. three-month) period. His counsel argued that as per the Muslim personal law, Khan had paid his dues upon divorce and was not liable to make further payments. However, lower courts sided with Shah Bano holding that a maintenance was legally required as per enactments falling beyond Muslim personal law. Khan appealed to the Supreme Court.

The decision of the Supreme Court was reached in 1985 by a five-judge bench. The Court dismissed Khan's appeal after consulting with Muslim bodies, including the All India Muslim Personal Law Board. The verdict held that divorced Muslim women had the right to alimony or maintenance under Section 125 of the Code of Criminal Procedure (CrPC). In case of conflict with personal law, precedence must be given to the CrPC. Going further, the Court mentioned that it would be unjust if the Quran were to be understood to exclude provisions for economically destitute women who could not remarry. Consequently, the Court extended the duties of an ex-husband beyond the *iddat* period. It also made remarks to the effect that it was high time for a Uniform Civil Code to be introduced in order to rationalize personal law and other domains of law within the constitutional legal system.

The Supreme Court judgement unfolded within a context of communal unrest. The Court's audacity in interpreting the Quran also became a political issue fomenting further unrest. Consequent to this case, the Muslim Women (Protection of Rights on Divorce) Act, 1986 (or, MWA) was passed. Contrary to the title of the Act, the provisions actually undermined the rights of Muslim women rather than protecting them. The MWA gave precedence to Muslim personal law interpreted as disallowing payment of alimony beyond the *iddat* period. Subsequently, however, the Supreme Court creatively reinterpreted the MWA (most notably in the judgement on *Danial Latifi* – 2001) as requiring a fair and reasonable alimony to be paid *within* the *iddat* period.

This case reopened the debate of a uniform civil code, initially begun most saliently by Dr B.R. Ambedkar. One step behind this debate looms the larger question of the relationship between religion as such and law as such. As can be gleaned from Chapter 2, Chapter 7, Chapter 8 and Chapter 9, this is no small or negligible issue. Does the secular law introduced during British rule contain traces of its origins in Christian tradition and long historical relationship to canon law? Does the contemporary secular setup secretly favour elements of the majoritarian Hindu religion? Given that within society today, women cannot yet claim to enjoy equal rights and opportunities with men, is it unfair to women to bind them to a particular religious community rather than allowing them free and total entry into the realm of uniform secular law? The legal challenges posed in *Shah Bano* reduplicate into both numerous political questions (as highlighted in Chapter 9) and deep philosophical questions, all of which must be untangled and addressed within an Indian Philosophy of Law.

Vishaka v. State of Rajasthan

This case arose within a horrific background. Bhanwari Devi was a social activist who worked in the Women's Development Project for the Government of Rajasthan. In 1992, as retaliation for her breech of caste norms and her attempts to introduce social change, she was gang raped by a number of high-caste men, who also unleashed their rage on her husband, Mohan, an eye witness to the rape who was himself brutally beaten. While attempting to report the event and seek justice, Bhanwari Devi faced hostility from policemen, neighbours, medical professionals and judges. In 1995, a court in Jaipur acquitted the accused of charges of rape. They were instead sentenced to six months' imprisonment on minor charges, two of the accused being released against time already served. This case and the hostility of the unjust system that it displayed resulted in national protests. The agitations provoked women's groups and NGOs to file a petition in the Supreme Court of India under the name *Vishaka* asking the Court to give directions regarding sexual harassment of women at the workplace.

The Supreme Court of India acknowledged the violation of fundamental rights of working women otherwise guaranteed by Article 14, 19 and 21 of the Indian Constitution. While Bhanwari Devi's case was acknowledged to be the immediate reason for filing this petition, it was made a matter of separate judgement. In 1997, the Supreme Court laid down the Vishaka Guidelines. These included defining sexual harassment, holding employers responsible to prevent or deter sexual harassment at the workplace by spreading awareness, and implementing a complaint mechanism.

As discussed at length in Chapter 15, social change is required to prevent or curb crime against women. Often it is the victims who are blamed, and thus further victimized. The Bhanwari Devi case is intersectional, as she was attacked both on account of her gender and her caste. Both gender and caste biases were reflected not only by her assailants, but even amongst those who were tasked with the job of defending her and restoring justice. While from the social vantage point, it is welcome that the Court took initiative to legislate the Vishaka Guidelines, but from the jurisprudential perspective, we are led to wonder why Parliament, administration and police have been silent about this need for so long. Can the tail of judge-made law wag the heavy dog of state and nation?

Conclusion

In this chapter we have discussed *Kesavananda* – 1973 as it relates to the theme of Chapter 1 (law and morality), *Olga Tellis* – 1985 as it relates to the theme of Chapter 5 (human rights), *Indra Sawhney* – 1992 as it relates to the topic of Chapter 8 (equality and reservation), *Shah Bano* – 1985 as it relates to the subject of Chapter 9 (Islamic law and politics) and *Vishaka* – 1997 as it relates to Chapter 15 (rape and sexual harassment). Our aim has been threefold.

First, looking at these cases is meant to serve the broader comprehension of the reader, by introducing a broader unity and continuity to the material in this book by linking real cases with philosophical query.

Second, as a worthwhile activity in itself, this chapter has briefly introduced some pivotal cases within the jurisprudence of the Indian Supreme Court. As should be clear by just this cursory glance, several of these cases warrant books individually devoted to them.

Finally, and most importantly, our aim has also been to show how there exist numerous deep sources for philosophical reflection within such case law, as well as how judicial decisions might themselves benefit from the cultivation of a robust Indian Philosophy of Law upon which it could turn for clarification and insight. At present, the Indian Court has nowhere else to turn other than foreign jurisdictions and trans-Atlantic (i.e. North American and European) Philosophy of Law. As we shall take up once again in the Conclusion, the standard model of jurisprudence taught in Indian law schools only exacerbates this problem, serving not to address but instead to perpetuate the shortfall.

Conclusion

Where things stand

The Philosophy of Law, as the reader has by now seen, has posed foundational questions about the law – *What is the law? What is the source of the law? What is the law for? How does law differ from other norms or codes of conduct? What is the difference between law and morality? Who is obligated to follow the law? What is the difference between moral and legal obligation?* and so on and so forth. Thus we have been concerned with the nature of the law, the origins of the law and also the direction in which it is going, the aims or ends which it seeks to realize. But in this book, we have not been exclusively concerned simply with the nature of law, but also with the nature of law in India, the India of today and the India of the future. To put this in another way, we have not simply been engaged with some totally abstract Philosophy of Law as such, but also always with Indian Philosophy of Law too.

In the Introduction, a standard model of the syllabus for jurisprudence classes around India was presented. (Recall that jurisprudence refers to the way the Philosophy of Law is taught in law schools, and a great deal of the material is overlapping, covering the same concepts, arguments, traditions, etc.) Prominent Indian legal theorists (e.g. S.N. Dhyani) as well as judges (e.g. V.R. Krishna Iyer) have argued that jurisprudence as presented in the standard model is saturated with Anglo-American legal theories that were cultivated on foreign soil. These concepts and principles emerged from contexts profoundly dissimilar from the Indian one, but they have been superimposed upon Indian academic treatment of the nature of law in India. For this reason, the approach that we have taken in this book has differed considerably from the standard model.

We have attempted to pay particular attention to the context-sensitive application of the philosophy of law throughout the book, and structured it to ensure that it did not suffer from the same critiques as are levied against the standard model. Thus there were three broad divisions of all the material in the book:

1 Part I, devoted to the Philosophy of Law as it is taught and understood more or less around the world as a consequence of the overwhelming influence of Anglo-American jurisprudence, both in theory and practice. As students have seen, this is a tradition that stretches from John Austin to Joseph Raz.
2 Part II, devoted to the particularities that contextualize the Philosophy of Law in India, which have allowed us to theorize and comprehend the distinctiveness of Indian Philosophy of Law. Such lessons are very rare and usually non-existent within the standard model. This has been one of the most distinctive features of this book on the Philosophy of Law, and we hope the reader has duly focused on these chapters, as we are in urgent need for a new generation of philosophers and jurists to really put their mind and energy towards this domain and labour to flesh it out.
3 Part III, functioning as case studies illustrating the diversity and wide-ranging scope of the Philosophy of Law. These chapters attempted to merge specific thematic/conceptual issues with cases peculiar to India. Of course, both the concepts and the contexts within which we grounded them are relevant both to India and to numerous other jurisdictions across the globe. These case studies were conceived in order to introduce students to contemporary cases, controversies and conundrums.

In summarizing the logic behind the organization of this book, the reader would do well to keep in mind that the future task of cultivating an authentic Philosophy of Law in India lies with them. What this would suggest is, in the first place, that in future work on the Philosophy of Law, the second domain (number 2 above) should eventually substitute and phase out the first domain (number 1 above). Eventually, all the cases in the third domain (number 3 above) could be adequately and fruitfully theorized not on the basis of foreign schools of thought, but within the horizon of our own fully ripened tradition.

Review of the chapters – Part I

Chapters 1 to 5 fell broadly into the first domain above-described, treating of the dominant traditions and discourses of legal theory from primarily, though not exclusively, the Anglo-American world. In this section, we shall review some of the important points from chapters appearing within the first domain.

- In Chapter 1, we learned that legal philosophy is a distinctive field of knowledge at the crossroads between Law and Philosophy. Its main purpose is to explore the nature and function of the Law in its most general sense. This chapter identified the two main traditions that have held the field in contemporary debate, natural law theories and legal positivism. The chapter focused on the main philosophical conundrum of legal philosophy, the distinction between law and morality, and outlined the most important contributions to this debate in historical perspective. We focused on the debate engaged in between H.L.A. Hart and Lon Fuller. As a legal positivist, Hart insisted on the separation of law and morality. However, he developed a much more sophisticated model than Austin's to explain the nature of law. Fuller, however, attempted to show that Hart's position, as indeed the law as such, depends upon at the very least a minimal content of appeal to morality.
- In Chapter 2, the Christian sources of secular law, most saliently, Canon Law, was introduced. Although primarily meant for theological purpose or control of the Church over its jurisdiction, Canon Law is significant in the history of Western legal and political developments, not only in historical perspective, but also, as the great jurist Carl Schmitt had argued, in shaping the legal structure of modern nation states.
- Chapter 3 introduced students to diverse legal theories through the fictitious case of the Speluncean Explorers. What students learned is that different decisions are not just the result of different facts. On the contrary, the same facts can lead to widely different results, all because of the central importance of the underlying philosophies (of law) brought to bear in the process of judicial interpretation.
- Chapter 4 explored the fate of legal reasoning amidst critiques of reason. Legal reasoning turned out to be not only salvageable, but also possibly a source of some comfort for disciplines beyond the law. In the first place, turning away from the substantive inability for us to confidently adjudicate between rival axiomatic sets, an earlier privilege enjoyed by reason that has now been undermined by critiques of reason, through a turn to natural justice, we recuperated at the procedural level what we lost at the substantive level.

- Chapter 5 enumerated the long tradition of critiques of human rights. Contemporary critiques of human rights, like those formulated by Arendt or, later, Agamben, have focused on the paradoxical tension between 'man' and 'citizen' as the bearers of rights. This original tension had the effect that precisely those most in need of protection – the stateless, the refugees, 'man' as such – were denied these rights that apparently apply only to citizens. Postcolonial theory also accused the false universalism of human rights, which is an expression of its Western bias and which obscures the suffering of the non-Western other. Finally, the chapter showed that Žižek and Rancière have also emphasized the tension between the abstract universalism of the *Declaration* and its particular application, but saw in this tension the very source of its political efficiency.

Review of the chapters – Part II

Chapters 6 to 11 fall into the second domain, devoted to the particularities that contextualize the Philosophy of Law in India, which allowed us to theorize and comprehend the distinctiveness of Indian Philosophy of Law. In this section, we shall review some of the important points from the chapters appearing in Part II.

- Chapter 6 addressed the meaning and scope of the term 'Indian' within the title 'Towards an Indian Philosophy of Law'. We looked at the nature and status of the Philosophy of Law in India today (the 21st century). This put the focus on the idea of law in a post-independence context. But as we saw, what law in India is today owes an immeasurable debt to the era of colonization, and above all, British rule. After all, the very idea of law as we presently conceive of it in India is largely a transplant of 17th–20th century British developments. Thus when we consider jurisprudence in India – from Constitutional law and its philosophical interpretations, to criminal law, the law of contracts and so on – we generally envision this wide historical epoch, and within it circulate our attention back and forth from the present 21st century developments back to their 19th- or 18th-century origins, and then again return to the contemporary developments.
- Chapter 7 focused on Hindu Law, from early on as Dharmashastra to Modern Hindu Law. We showed how Hindu Law has its

own history of transformation from what was known as Classical Hindu Law, where its rules were applicable in all civil and criminal matters, to Modern Hindu Law where Hindu Law became narrowed to the sphere of personal law or family law.

- Chapter 8 focused on the persistence of caste within Hindu society and thus its tension with Hindu Law. The significance of Hindu Law in India is important considering that as personal law, it governs matters such as marriage, adoption, succession, divorce and so on. Some aspects of Indian philosophy were misconstrued and led to social discrimination and exclusion. In the British era, the courts did not pass any law discouraging such discrimination in cases which involved religious practices as they had adopted a policy of non-interference relating to matters of religion and caste. However, post-Independence, national leaders took sufficient measures to ensure that the Indian legislature does not recognize negative social discrimination due to caste.
- Chapter 9 focused on the place of Shariat in postcolonial Muslim political discourses, exploring the ways in which the constitutionally granted minority rights are identified as potential sources for articulating political arguments and positions. The chapter raised two conceptual questions: What are the forms in which Shariat is represented as a political issue? And, How do these varied political forms draw legal-constitutional legitimacy?
- Chapter 10 was devoted to M.K. Gandhi. It discussed and analyzed Gandhi's engagement with law over the course of his life. The law undoubtedly played a major role in Gandhi's life and arguably his training as a lawyer contributed to his larger persona as the father of the nation.
- Chapter 11 turned to another giant of Indian history, B.R. Ambedkar. The question the chapter explored was whether there was something which could be called an Ambedkarite vision of the law, which was not limited to the epithet of being 'the father of the Constitution'. Three points were taken up: that the idea of law in Dr Ambedkar's corpus extends beyond state law; that the key Ambedkarite conceptualization of law is as a counter majoritarian force to be mobilized on the side of the Dalits against 'the law of Hindu society'; and, legal concepts Dr Ambedkar espoused such as constitutional morality have been re-discovered as tools to combat new forms of oppression as the history of the nation unfolds.

Review of the chapters – Part III

Chapters 12 to 17 fall into the third domain, treating of legal concepts and thematic studies that functioned as case studies illustrating the diversity and wide-ranging scope of the Philosophy of Law. Again, we shall present key ideas that represent the thrust of the chapters.

- In Chapter 12, we discussed the important concept of free speech in terms of philosophy, law, and used the case of the AIB Knockout. Due to clause (2) of Article 19, the organizers of AIB Knockout might not be protected under the Indian Constitution. However, from the point of view of Mill's *On Liberty*, the case of AIB Knockout represents a liberty which must not be interfered with. More practically, it also represents a transformation of Indian society through the presentation of private jokes in public spaces. AIB Knockout is an example of unregulated free speech and the consequences of what may happen as a result of it.
- In Chapter 13 we saw that equality is an important concept in philosophy and is of incredible importance in the Constitution of India. Special provisions have been made to ensure that certain groups who have faced inequalities in various forms get equal advantage as others who are not discriminated against. While drafting different acts pertaining to equality, the framers of the Constitution had focused on aspects such as caste-based discrimination or gender inequality. In time, a lot of other entities have used Article 14 to fight inequalities, like discrimination against the third gender or physically disabled individuals. An analysis of the cases mentioned would show that when one asks the question 'Equality of What?', the answer to it by Indian courts has been, 'Equality of opportunities as an equal access to advantage'.
- Chapter 14 introduced Queer Legal Theory. A queer perspective on law can inform about political engagement, the process of legal change and also give a way to read its legal history. It calls to recover lost voices through a re-reading of law from a 'queer subaltern viewpoint' and highlights new voices which have emerged in the process of political engagement. This chapter uniquely attempted to systematically develop a queer perspective on law.
- Chapter 15 addressed the Buddhist four noble truths in order to help explain why crimes occur and also help develop a method to curb crime, for what is crime, if not suffering? And nirvana

or liberation would be to live in a world free of such crimes. While in practical life, it seems to be a difficult task to achieve in this lifetime, it is not too ambitious an aim considering that it is achievable if the effective risk mitigation steps can be taken by the government and society.

- Chapter 16 on the ethics of organ donation reflected on this issue in the wake of exploitation of the poor and cases of fraud and cheating. The government has banned sale of organs for commercial gain. However, the act turned out to be ineffective. Instead of banning organ sales, an alternative could be to formulate a regulatory mechanism, perhaps inspired by the Iranian model to facilitate ethical, regulated, compensated organ donation.
- The final chapter turned to some of the most important cases decided by the Indian Supreme Court, especially those that have had lasting importance for reflection within the Philosophy of Law. We discussed *Kesavananda* – 1973 as it relates to the theme of Chapter 1 (law and morality), *Olga Tellis* – 1985 as it relates to the theme of Chapter 5 (human rights), *Indra Sawhney* – 1992 as it relates to the topic of Chapter 8 (equality and reservation), *Shah Bano*–1985 as it relates to the subject of Chapter 9 (Islamic law), and *Vishaka* – 1997 as it relates to Chapter 15 (sexual harassment).

Conclusion

Students of Contemporary Indian Political Philosophy are likely to be familiar with the most recent orientation of that discipline. That is, a collective attitude that Indian political thought should articulate its concerns through native, vernacular or indigenous ('experience-near') conceptions, and begin the process of sloughing off the conceptual apparatus hitherto worked with, which has too often ensured that Indian political philosophy was realized as a derivative discourse incapable of addressing the realities of the ground situation as they seemed to present themselves. The most recent thinking in the Philosophy of Law matches this very same concern.

Indian legal theorists have argued that Indian jurisprudence is saturated with Anglo-American legal theories that were cultivated on foreign soil. Not only has India seen legal transplantation, but also the transplantation of legal theories and the overall philosophy of law. But it has not at all been established that this transplantation of concepts from alien contexts bears relevance to the Indian ground situation, to

Indian conditions, legal, political, social, cultural or whether they possess any real validity in India at all.

The same forces behind the development of Indigenous Indian Social and Political Philosophy have been serving as sources of momentum and inspiration for scholars of Indian Philosophy of Law, who have been trying, against the odds, to inaugurate and cultivate a new tradition of Indian legal theory in recent years. They believe that the teaching of jurisprudence in India within law schools does not meet any of the basic tests of need or utility, as these ideas are of no use, or of ground realities, as these ideas are oblivious to the actual Indian situation. According to them, the philosophy of law tradition from John Austin to H.L.A. Hart to Joseph Raz needs to be toppled. Indian Philosophy of Law, rather, should look to reflect the real ideas and best practices of the Indian people. Indian jurisprudence should be Indian in origin, in content, in application – it should be *sui generis* and not merely borrowed or derivative. Further, they recognize that in India, the law has been mostly imposed from above. And certainly within the last several hundred years, it has had no roots in the authentic Indian soil, with a foreign vocabulary totally distanced from the common people. Both the actual legal system as well as the theoretical reflection related to it have lacked the imprimatur of India's cultural, climatic or geographical conditions.

But just as in the search for an authentic, indigenous political philosophy, how we identify the authenticity and indigeneity of Indian Philosophy of Law is open to contestation and dispute. For, indigenous could be equated to ancient, which was a common way of conceiving it for many swarajists, like Gandhi or Swami Vivekananda. This has been a central position in Indian political philosophy. However, within the Philosophy of Law, although there has been a temptation to link indigenous and authentic with ancient (at times, even simply Hindu), for the most part, jurists and legal theorists recognize the fundamental modernity of our primary legal (and political) institutions, and opt rather for a hybrid approach, which fuses some of the values and traditions of the ancient view, with the profoundly egalitarian, pluralist and progressive elements enshrined in the Indian Constitution.

But the question, *What is authentic or indigenous Indian Philosophy of Law?*, is a challenging one, and the temptation of leaping back to a presumed glorious age, that 'wonder that was India', remains strong in current theoretical discourse.

What this book has tried to achieve instead is to conceive of the task of authenticity within the Philosophy of Law in India as a project to continue to broaden the sweep of humane and egalitarian legal thought and practice that has been consistently developing in Indian jurisprudence, while at the same time reforming and rewriting our laws in a manner that reflects the best practices of our own traditions, both customary and written. We must balance our ancient law and values with our modern sentiments and institutions. At the same time, the indigenous legal system and thought must continue to evolve and adapt to newly emerging shared values and new needs, based on the experience of our own people, but even including those developed in other progressive countries or jurisdictions, if they have inherent worth.

In conclusion, one of the foremost elements of India's newly emerging indigenous Philosophy of Law is that it must be consistent with our plural society – with the common, shared fate of our diverse internal cultures and traditions. The essence of Indian unity and the best part of our heritage has been a continuous evolution and acceptance of diverse religious beliefs, linguistic habits, regional variation and so on, harmonizing all this within the mosaic of an Indian nation. When legal philosophy seeks authenticity, it does so with diversity and not exclusion in mind.

Bibliography

Agamben, Giorgio. *Homo Sacer. Sovereign Power and Bear Life*. Stanford, CA: Stanford University Press (1998).

Agnes, Flavia. *Women and Law in India*. Delhi: Oxford University Press (first published in 1992 (2004).

Agrawal, C. M. *Golu Devata, the God of Justice of Kumaun Himalayas*. Almora: Shree Almora Book Depot (1992).

All India Bakchod. www.facebook.com/IndiaBakchod/posts/859141927463136 (accessed on 2 August 2017).

———. Archdiocese of Bombay's Post (February 9, 2015). https://www.facebook.com/IndiaBakchod/posts/861394710571191 (accessed on 1 December 2017).

Ambedkar, B. R. 'The Annihilation of Caste' in Vasant Moon (ed.), *Babasaheb Ambedkar: Writings and Speeches*. Vol. 1. Mumbai: Government of Maharashtra (1979), 23–96.

———. Constitutional Assembly Debates: Official Reports Vol.VII: November 4, 1948.

———. 'India and the Prerequisites of Communism' in Vasant Moon (ed.), *Dr. Babasaheb Ambedkar: Writing and Speeches*. Vol. 3. Bombay: Government of Maharashtra (1987), 99–111.

———. 'Their Wishes and Laws Unto Us' in Vasant Moon (ed.), *Babasaheb Ambedkar: Writings and Speeches*. Vol. 5. Mumbai: Government of Maharashtra (2014) (first Published in 1989), 272–86.

———. 'What Congress and Gandhi Have Done to the Untouchables' in Narendra Jadhav (ed.), *Ambedkar Writes Vol I*. New Delhi: Konark Publishers (2014).

———. 'What Path to Salvation?' in Narendra Jadhav (ed.). *Ambedkar Speaks*. Vol. 1. New Delhi: Konark Publishers (2013).

———. *Words of Freedom: Ideas of a Nation*. New Delhi: Penguin Books. (2010).

———. in Vasant Moon (ed.), *Babasaheb Ambedkar: Writings and Speeches*. "Chapter 23: Their wishes are laws Unto us" in Vasant Moon (ed.) Babasaheb Ambedkar: Writing and Speeches. Vol 5. Mumbai: Government of Maharashtra (1989). Reprinted January 2014.

———. in Vasant Moon (ed.), *Babasaheb Ambedkar: Writings and Speeches*. Vol. 15. Mumbai: Government of Maharashtra (1997). Reprinted January (2014).

Aquinas, Thomas. *The 'Summa Theologica' of St. Thomas Aquinas*. Part I QQI-XXVI.Vol 1(1256). http://oll.libertyfund.org/titles/1979 (accessed on 2 August 2017).

Arendt, Hannah. 'The Decline of the Nation-State and the End of the Rights of Man' in *The Origin of Totalitarianism*. New York: Harcourt, Brace & Co. (1973).

Augustine, Charles. *A Commentary on the Code of the Canon Law*. London (1918), https://archive.org/details/1917CodeOfCanonLawCommentary (accessed on 28 November 2017).

Austin, J. *The Province of Jurisprudence Determined*. W. Rumble (ed.), Cambridge: Cambridge University Press (1995) (first published in 1832).

Baruch, Yehuda and Stuart Jenkins. 'Swearing at Work and Permissive Leadership Culture: When Anti-Social Becomes Social and Incivility Is Acceptable.' *Leadership & Organization Development Journal* 28, no. 6 (2007): 492–507.

Bavinck, Maarten *et al.* 'From Indifference to Mutual Support – A Comparative Analysis of Legal Pluralism in the Governing of South Asian Fisheries.' *European Journal of Development Research* 25, no. 4 (2013): 621–40.

Baxi, Upendra. 'Critiquing Rights: Politics of Identity and Difference.' *The Future of Human Rights*. Oxford University Press (2002).

———. 'People's Law, Development and Justice' *Verfassung und Recht in Übersee / Law and Politics in Africa, Asia and Latin America* 12, no. 2 (1979): 97–114.

Benda-Beckmann, Franz von. 'Who's Afraid of Legal Pluralism?' *Legal Pluralism & Unofficial Law* 37 (2002): 37–82.

Bentham, Jeremy. 'Anarchical Fallacies: Being an Examination of the Declaration of Rights Issued during the French Revolution' (1791); republished in J. Bowring (ed.), *The Works of Jeremy Bentham, Vol II*. Edinburgh: William Tait (1843).

Bix, B. 'Legal Positivism' in Martin P. Golding and William A. Edmundson (eds.), *The Blackwell Guide to the Philosophy of Law and Legal Theory*. Oxford: Blackwell Publishing Ltd. (2005).

Bloch, Marc. *Feudal Society* (two vols.). London: Routledge (1965).

Bloomfield, Paul. *Morality and Self Interest*. New York: Oxford University Press (2008).

Bradon, Hammer. 'Smooth Sailing: Why the Indian Film Industry Remains Extremely Successful in the Face of Massive Piracy.' *Journal of Sports and Entertainment Law* 5, no. 1 (Winter 2014): 147–87.

Brown, Wendy. 'The Most We Can Hope For.' *South Atlantic Quarterly* (Spring/Summer 2004): 451–63.

Burke, Edmund. *Reflections on the Revolution in France*. Oxford: Oxford University Press (2009) (first published in 1790).

———. *Select Works*. E. J. Payne (ed.). New Jersey: The Lawbook Exchange (2005).

———. *The Works of the Right Honourable Edmund Burke*. Vol. XV. London: C & J. Rivington (1827).

Cahn, Naomi *et al*. 'The Case of the Speluncean Explorers: Contemporary Proceedings.' *George Washington Law Review* 61 (1993): 1754–811.

Carrin, Marine and Harald Tambs-Lyche. '"You Don't Joke with These Fellows." Power and Ritual in South Canara, India.' *Social Anthropology* 11(2003): 23–42.

Chiba, Masaji. (ed.). *Asian Indigenous Law in Interaction With Received Law*. London and New York: KPI (1986).

Cistelecan, Alexandru. 'Which Critique of Human rights?' in Alexandru Cistelecan and Aakash Singh Rathore (eds.), *Wronging Rights? Philosophical Challenges for Human Rights*. New Delhi and London: Routledge (2010), 3–22.

Claus, Peter J. 'The Siri Myth and Ritual: A Mass Possession Cult of South India.' *Ethnology* 14 (1975): 47–58.

Cohn, Bernard S. 'Anthropological Notes on Disputes and Law in India.' *American Anthropologist* (Special Number: *Ethnography of Law*) 67, no. 2 (1965): 82–122.

Coleman, Jules. 'Negative and Positive Positivism.' *Journal of Legal Studies* 11(1982): 139–64.

Constituent Assembly Debates, December 1, 1948 Part 1; https://indiankanoon.org/docfragment/1107530/?big=0&formInput=sedition. dated 18 December 2017

The Constitution and Constituent Assembly (Some selected speeches), India: Lok Sabha Secretariat Publications (1990).

Coughlin, John J. 'Canon Law.' *Notre Dame Legal Studies Paper No. 07–27* (April 23, 2007). Available at SSRN: http://ssrn.com/abstract=982132 or http://dx.doi.org/10.2139/ssrn.982132 (accessed on 11 August 2017).

———. 'Canon Law and the Human Person' Scholarly Works. Paper 726. http://scholarship.law.nd.edu/law_faculty_scholarship/726 (accessed on 28 November 2017) (2003): 1–58.

The Criminal Law (Amendment) Act, 2013. Ministry of Law and Justice. Government of India. Delhi: Controller of Publications. http://indiacode.nic.in/acts-in-pdf/132013.pdf (accessed on 11 August 2017).

D'Amato, Anthony. 'The Speluncean Explorers – Further Proceedings.' *Stanford Law Review* 32 (1980): 467–485, DOI: 10.2307/1228393, Stable URL: www.jstor.org/stable/1228393, (accessed on 11 August 2017).

Daniel, Charles E. 'Review of Strauss (1986).' *The Sixteenth Century Journal* 18, no. 3 (1987): 429–30.

Davies, Brian. *The Thought of Thomas Aquinas*. New York: Oxford University Press (1993).

Davis, Jr. Donald R. 'Law and "Law Books" in the Hindu Tradition.' *Social Science Research Network*. (September 2005). Available at SSRN: http://ssrn.com/abstract=924581 or http://dx.doi.org/10.2139/ssrn.924581 (accessed on 31 January 2015).

———. *The Spirit of Hindu Law*. Cambridge: Cambridge University Press (2010).

Declaration of the Rights of Man (1789), http://avalon.law.yale.edu/18th_century/rightsof.asp, (accessed on 28 November 2017).

Derrett, J. and Duncan M. 'The Administration of Hindu Law by the British.' *Comparative Studies in Society and History* 4, no. 1 (November 1961): 10–52.

De Roover, J., Sarah Claerhout and S.N. Balagangadhara. 'Liberal Political Theory and the Cultural Migration of Ideas: The Case of Secularism in India.' *Political Theory* 39 (2011): 571–99.

de Silva, William Robert. 'Cult of Bhuta' in *From Rta to Dharma. The Symbolic and Diabolic of the Systems of Production and Representation in Kinship and Tributary Societies. Transition as Structural Transformation*. Mangalore: Pragati Prakasan (1985), 121–190.

Deutsch, Kenneth and Joseph Fornieri. *An Invitation to Political Thought*. New Jersey: Princeton. (2008).

Dhyani, S.N. *Jurisprudence and Indian Legal Theory*. 4th ed. Allahabad: Central Law Agency (2002).

Dimock, Susan, 'The Natural Law Theory of St. Aquinas' in Joel Feinberg (ed.), *Philosophy of Law*. CA: Wadsworth (2000).

Dunham IV, Charles C. 'Body Property: Challenging the Ethical Barriers in Organ Transplantation to Protect Individual Autonomy.' *Annals of Health Law* 17, no.1 (2008): 39–65.

Dwivedi, O.P. and V. G. Julie Rajan (eds.). *Human Rights in Post Colonial India*. New York: Routledge. (2016).

Dworkin, R. *A Matter of Principle*. Cambridge, MA and London: Harvard University Press (1985).

Ehrlich, Eugen. *Fundamental Principles of the Sociology of Law*. Cambridge, MA: Harvard University Press (1936) (first published 1912 Grundlegung der Soziologie des Recht).

Engineer, Asghar Ali. *The Shah Bano Controversy*. Hyderabad: Orient Longman (1987).

Feinberg, Joel. *Philosophy of Law*. Wadsworth (2000).

Finnis, J. *Natural Law and Natural Rights*. Oxford: Clarendon Press (2011) (first published in 1980).

———. 'Natural Law: The Classical Tradition' in Jules Coleman and Stuart Shapiro (eds.), *The Oxford Handbook of Jurisprudence and Philosophy of Law*. Oxford: Oxford University Press (2004), 1–60.

——— *Philosophy of Law: Collected Essays, Vol. IV*. New York: Oxford University Press. (2011).

Fuller, Lon L. 'The Case of the Speluncean Explorers.' *Harvard Law Review* 62, no. 4 (1949): 616–45. http://w.astro.berkeley.edu/~kalas/ethics/documents/introduction/fuller49.pdf (accessed on 13 January 2015).

———. *The Morality of Law*. Revised Edition. New Haven: Yale University Press (1969) (first published in 1964).

———. 'Positivism and Fidelity to Law – A Reply to Professor Hart.' *Harvard Law Review* 71, no. 4 (1985): 630–72.

Gajendragadkar, P. B. *Law, Liberty and Social Justice*. New York: Asia Publishing House (1965).

Galanter, Marc. 'Hinduism, Secularism, and the Indian Judiciary' in Rajeev Bhargava (ed.), *Secularism and Its Critics*. Delhi: Oxford University Press (1998): 268–96.

———. 'Law and Caste in Modern India.' *Asian Survey* 3, no. 11 (1963): 544–59.

———. 'Personal Law Systems and Religious Conflict: A Comparison of India and Israel' in Gerald James Larson (ed.), *Religion and Personal Law in Secular India: A Call to Judgment*. Bloomington and Indianapolis, IN: Indiana University Press (2001).

Gandhi, M.K. *An Autobiography: The Story of My Experiments with Truth*. Mahadev Desai (trans.). London: Penguin Books (1987).

———. *Freedom's Battle: Being a comprehensive collection of writings and speeches on the present situation*. India: Floating Press (2013) (first published in 1922).

———. *Hind Swaraj*. Suresh Sharma and Tridip Suhrud (eds.), Orient Black-Swan (2010).

———. *Hind Swaraj and Other Writings*. In Anthony Parel (ed.). UK: Cambridge University Press. (1997) (first published in 1909).

———. *The Law and Lawyers*. S. B. Kher (ed.), Ahmedabad: Navjivan Publishing House (2001) (first published October 1962).

'Gangrape Case: Jaya Bachchan threatens to protest in Rajya Sabha.'www.youtube.com/watch?v=_fLoph-ALEo (accessed on 13 April 2015).

Geary, Patrick J. *The Myth of Nations. The Medieval Origins of Europe*. Princeton: Princeton University Press (2002).

Geras, Norman. 'The Controversy About Marx and Justice.' *New Left Review* I, no. 150 (March–April 1985): 47–85.

Gharpure, J.R. *Hindu Law*. 4th ed. Bombay: Office of the Collection of Hindu Law Texts (1931).

Ghods, A. J., and S. Savaj. 'Iranian Model of Paid and Regulated Living-Unrelated Kidney Donation.' *Clinical Journal of the American Society of Nephrology* 1, no. 6 (2006): 1136–45.

Ghosh, Dwaipayan. 'Calcutta HC concerned over kidney rackets.' *Times of India*, May 15, 2015. http://timesofindia.indiatimes.com/city/kolkata/Calcutta-HC-concerned-over-kidney-rackets/articleshow/46570140.cms (accessed on 15 June 2015).

Goebel, Julius. 'King's Law and Local Custom in Seventeenth Century New England.' *Columbia Law Review* 3, no. 3 (1931): 416–48.

Gray, Phillip W. 'Political Theology and the Theology of Politics: Carl Schmitt and Medieval Christian Political Thought.' *Humanitas* XX, no. 1 and 2 (2007): 175–200.

Griffiths, Anne. 'Pursuing Legal Pluralism: The Powers of Paradigms in a Global World.' *Legal Pluralism & Unofficial Law* 43, no. 64 (January 2011): 173–202.

Griffiths, John. 'What Is Legal Pluralism?' *Journal of Legal Pluralism* 24 (1986): 1–55.

Gruber, Robert. 'Perimeter Security: Deter, Detect, Delay, Deny.' *Master Halco Security Solutions Group*. www.plantservices.com/assets/wp_downloads/pdf/master_halco_deter_detect_delay_deny_wp.pdf (accessed on 15 January 2015).

Guha, Ramachandra. *Gandhi Before India*. India: Penguin Publications (2013).

Hart, H.L.A. *The Concept of Law*. Oxford: Oxford University Press (1994) (first published in 1961).

———. 'Positivism and the Separation of Law and Morality.' *Harvard Law Review* 71, no. 4 (1958): 593–629.

Helmholz, Richard H. 'The Legal Framework of the Church of England: A Critical Study in a Comparative Context' *Texas Law Review* 75, 1455 (1997). http://chicagounbound.uchicago.edu/cgi/viewcontent.cgi?article=6165&context=journal_articles (accessed on 28 November 2017).

The Hindu Marriage Act 1955. http://bokakhat.gov.in/pdf/The_hindu_marriage_act.pdf (accessed on 11 August 2016).

Hoebel, E. A. *The Law of Primitive Man*. Cambridge: Harvard University Press (1954).

Ignatieff, Michael. *Human Rights as Politics and Idolatry*. Princeton University Press (2003).

Jain, M.P. and S.N. Jain. *Principles of Administrative Law*. New-Delhi: Lexis-Nexis, Butterworths Wadhwa Nagpur (2010).

Kapur, Ratna. 'Human Rights in the 21st Century.' *Sidney Law Review* 28, no. 4 (2006): 665–87.

Kaserman, L. David. 'Should We Sell Human Organs – Correction of a Faulty Analysis.' *International Journal of Social Economics* 32, no. 10 (2015): 893–98.

Kaviraj, Sudipta. 'Gandhi's Trial and India's Colonial State' in Lloyd Rudolph and John Kurt Jacobsen (eds.), *Experiencing the State 308*. New Delhi: Oxford University Press (2006), 293–308.

———. *Imaginary Institution of India: Politics and Ideas*. New York, NY: Columbia University Press (2010).

Kelsen, H. *Pure Theory of Law*. Max Knight (trans.). Berkeley, CA: University of California Press (1967).

Kozinski et al., 'The Case of the Speluncean Explorers: Revisited.' *Harvard Law Review* 112, no. 8 (June 1999): 1876–923.

Larcom, Shaun. 'Problematic Legal Pluralism: Causes and Some Potential "cures".' *The Journal of Legal Pluralism and Unofficial Law* 46, no. 2 (May 2014): 193–217.

Lelyveld, Joseph. *Great Soul*. New York, NY: Vintage (2011).

Lenin, V.I. *State and Revolution*. www.marxists.org/archive/lenin/works/1917/staterev/ (accessed on 15 March 2015).

Locke, John. 'A Letter Concerning Toleration' in William Popple (trans.), *The Works of John Locke in Nine Volumes*. London: Rivington (1824).

Lok Sabha Debates, Secretariat, 1985.

Mahmood. 'Muslim India.' *Islamic and Comparative Law Quarterly* 5, no. 1 (March 1985).

———. *Muslim Personal Law: Role of the State in Subcontinent*. Delhi: Vikas (1977).

Mahmood, Tahir. *Islamic Law in the Indian Courts Since Independence: Fifty Years of Judicial Interpretation*. Delhi: Qazi Publishers and Distributers, IOS Series, Readings in Islamic Law (1997).

Malik, Aditya. 'Petitioning the God of Justice. Modernity, Democracy, and the *Darbar* of Goludev' in Helene Basu and William Sax (eds.), *Law of Possession. Ritual, Healing, and the Secular State*. Oxford: Oxford University Press (2015).

Maneka Gandhi v. Union of India 1978 AIR 597.

Marx, Karl. 'Conversion of Surplus-Value into Capital' in Ben Fowkes (trans.), *Capital*. Vol. 1. England: Penguin Classics (1990) (first published by Pelican Books in 1976), 410–33.

———. *Critique of Hegel's Philosophy of Right*. Annette Jolin and Joseph O'Malley (trans.). New York, NY: Cambridge University Press (1843) (first published 1970, reissued in digitally printed version 2009). www.marxists.org/archive/marx/works/1843/critique-hpr/ (accessed on 13 March 2015).

———. *Critique of the Gotha Programme, Marx/Engels Selected Works Volume 3*. Moscow: Progress Publishers (1999) (First published in 1970). www.marxists.org/archive/marx/works/1875/gotha/ (accessed on 14 March 2015).

———. 'Debates on Law on Thefts of Wood' in Clements Dutt (trans.), *Rjeinische Zeitung* Nos. 298, 300, 303, 305 and 307 (first published in 1842, transcribed for the internet 1996).

———. *Grundrisse*. London: Penguin Books in association with New Left Review (1993) (first published in 1973), 83–8.

———. *On the Jewish Question*. Paris: Deutsch-Französische Jahrbücher (1844). www.marxists.org/archive/marx/works/1844/jewish-question/ (accessed on 16 June 2015).

———. 'Preface' to *A Contribution to the Critique of Political Economy*. S. W. Ryazanskaya (trans.). Moscow: Progress Publishers, (1859). www.marxists.org/archive/marx/works/1859/critique-pol-economy/index.htm (accessed on 15 June 2015).

Marx, Karl and Friedrich Engels. *Manifesto of the Communist Party*. www.marxists.org/archive/marx/works/1848/communist-manifesto/ (initial publication *Marx/Engels Selected Works, Volume 1*. Moscow: Progress Publishers [1969] [first published in February 1848], 98–137) (accessed on 15 June 2015).

Massey, I.P. *Administrative Law*. Lucknow: Eastern Book Company (2001).

Mayne, John Dawson. *A Treatise on Hindu Law and Usage.* Madras: Higginbotham, Stevens and Hynes, Harvard Law Library Series (1906), 191.

Media Correspondent. 'Hyderabad: Kidney Selling Racket Busted Three Arrested.' *NDTV*, April 23, 2014. www.ndtv.com/south/hyderabad-kidney-selling-racket-busted-three-arrested-558436 (accessed on 12 June 2015).

Menski, Werner F. *Comparative Law in a Global Context: The Legal Systems of Asia and Africa.* 2nd ed. Cambridge: Cambridge University Press (2006).

———. *Hindu Law: Beyond Tradition and Modernity.* Delhi: Oxford University Press (2003).

———. 'Postmodern Hindu Law.' *SOAS Law Department Occasional Papers* (2001): 1–42.

———. 'The Role of Custom in Hindu Law.' *Recueils de la Société Jean Bodin pour l'Histoire Comparative des Institutions, Vol. LIII: Costum, Part 3: Eastern Europe, Asia and Islam.* Bruxelles: De Boeck Université (1992), 311–417.

———. 'Sudra Sannyasis: A Piece of Realism in Hindu Law.' *Madras Law Journal* (1981): 25–26. www.wernermenski.co.uk/images/publications/2a%20piece%20of%20realism%20in%20hindu%20law.pdf (accessed on 16 July 2015).

———. 'On Vyavahara.' *Indologica Taurinensia* 33 (2007): 124–47.

Merry, Sally Engle. 'Law and Colonialism.' *Law & Society Review* 25, no. 4 (1991): 889–922.

Mill, John Stuart. *On Liberty.* London: Longman, Roberts & Green (1869).

Milton, John. *Areopagitica. The Harvard Classics.* Vol. III, Part 3. New York: P.F. Collier & Son (1643), 1909–14.

Moraes, Frank. Jawaharlal Nehru: A biography. Mumbai: JAICO Publishing House. (2007) (First published in 1959).

Morgan, Thomas Jefferson. *Patriotic Citizenship.* New York: American Book Company (1895).

Murphy Coleen. 'Lon Fuller and the Moral Value of the Rule of Law.' *Law and Philosophy* 24 (2005): 239–62.

'Muslim India.' *All India Muslim Personal Law Board* (1985–86). http://aimplboard.in/index.php?language=english (accessed on 7 May 2015).

Nadar, Nupur. 'Law and Medicine: An Analysis of the Organ Transplantation Law in India.' (2008). www.legalserviceindia.com/article/l224-Organ-Transplantation-Law-In-India.html (accessed on 12 March 2015).

Narrain, Arvind. *Queer: Despised Sexuality Law and Social Change.* Bangalore: Books for Change. 2005.

National Legal Services Authority v. Union of India and Others (Writ Petition No. 400 of 2012 with Writ Petition No. 604 of 2013). http://judis.nic.in/supremecourt/imgs1.aspx?filename=41411 (accessed on 13 August 2017).

Naz Foundationv. NCR Delhi (*Government of National Capital Territory of Delhi and Others*). *Delhi Law Times* 160 (2009). http://indiankanoon.org/doc/100472805/ (accessed on 13 August 2017).

News Bureau. 'How Potholes Saved Delhi Teen from Kidnapping.' *NDTV*. New Delhi: Midday, July 25, 2011. www.ndtv.com/delhi-news/how-potholes-saved-delhi-teen-from-kidnapping-462717 (accessed on 11 July 2015).

Nussbaum, Martha C. 'India: Implementing Sex Equality through Law.' *Chicago Journal of International Law* 2, no. 1 (2001): Article 4. 35–58.

Paone, Tommaso. 'A Critical Adjudication of the Fuller Hart Debate' https://scholar.princeton.edu/sites/default/files/tpavone/files/hart-dworkin_debate_critical_review.pdf (accessed on 28 November 2017).

Pappe, H.O. 'On the Validity of Judicial Decisions in the Nazi Era.' *The Modern Law Review* 23, no. 3 (1960): 260–74.

Parel, Anthony J. *Gandhi's Philosophy and the Quest for Harmony*. UK: Cambridge University Press (2006).

Pashukanis, Evgeny. 'General Theory of Law and Marxism' in P. Beirne and R. Sharlet (eds.), *Selected Writings on Marxism and Law*. London and New York: Evgeny Pashukanis (1980). www.marxists.org/archive/pashukanis/1924/law/ (accessed on 14 June 2015).

Paulson, Stanley L. 'Lon L. Fuller, Gustav Radbruch and the "Positivist" Theses.' *Law and Philosophy* 13, no. 2, Special Issue in Lon Fuller, (August 1994): 313–59 (accessed on 11 March 2015).

Perry, Clifton. 'Human Organs and the Open Market.' *Ethics* 91, no.1, October (1980): 63 71.

The Persons with Disabilities (Equal Opportunities, Protection of Rights and Full Participation) Act, 1995, *Section 33*. https://indiankanoon.org/doc/1950606/ (accessed on 11 August 2017).

Ponty, Maurice Merleau. *Humanism and Terror*. Boston: Beacon Press (1990).

Pospisil, Leopold J. *Anthropology of Law: A Comparative Theory*. New York: Harper Row (1971).

Postrel, Virgina. 'Organ Donation Incentives.' Dynamist.com, http://www.dynamist.com/weblog/archives/002168.html (accessed on November 5, 2007).

Radhakrishna, Meena. *Dishonoured by History: Criminal Tribes and British Colonial Policy*. New Delhi: Orient Longman (2001).

Rajagopal, Balakrishnan. 'Pro-Human Rights but Anti-poor? A Critical Evaluation of the Indian Supreme Court from a Social Movement Perspective.' *Human Rights Review* 18, no. 3 (2007): 157–87.

Rakesh, Vanya. 'Cloud Computing in India: The Current Legal Regime and the Main Issues and Challenges.' *India Law Journal* 7, no. 1, Article 3 (2015). www.indialawjournal.com/volume7/issue-1/article3.html (accessed on 11 January 2015).

Rancière, Jacques. 'Who is the Subject of the Rights of Man?' *South Atlantic Quarterly* (Spring/Summer 2004): 297–310.

Rao, K.L. Seshagiri. 'Practitioners of Hindu Law: Ancient and Modern.' *Fordham Law Review* 66, no. 4 (1998): 1185–93.

Ranciere, Jacques. *On the Shores of Politics*. London: Verso. (1995).

Rathore, Aakash Singh and Alex Cistelecan (eds.), Wronging Rights. Philosophical Challenges for Human Rights. New Delhi: Routledge (2011).

Rawls, John. *A Theory of Justice*. Revised Edition. Cambridge, MA: Harvard University Press (1999).

Raz, J. *The Authority of Law*. Oxford: Oxford University Press (1979).

Rehmani, Maulana Syed Shah Minnatul. *Qanoon-e-Shariat ke masder aur naye masael ka hal*. AIMPLB, Delhi (1999): 7–12, translated from the Urdu.

Rocher, Ludo. 'Hindu Conceptions of Law.' *Hastings Law Journal* 29 (1978): 1283–97.

Rorty, Richard. 'Human Rights, Rationality, and Sentimentality' in *Truth and Progress: Philosophical Papers*. UK: Cambridge University Press (1998).

Russell, Bertrand. *History of Western Philosophy*. New York: Simon and Schuster (2009).

Salvo, Charles Di. *Man before the Mahatma*. India: Random House (2012).

Samuels, R., Stich, S. and Faucher, L. 'Reason and Rationality' in I. Niiniluoto *et al.* (eds.), *Handbook of Epistemology*. Amsterdam: Kluwer Academic Publishing (2004), 131–79.

Sarkar, Subhradipta. 'Right to Free Speech in a Censored Democracy.' *University of Denver Sports and Entertainment Law Journal* 7 (2009): 62–89.

Satel, Sally. *When Altruism Isn't Enough – The Case for Compensating Kidney Donors*. Washington DC: The AEI Press (2008).

Savarkar, Vinayak Damodar. *Essentials of Hindutva*. Create Space Independent Publishing Platform (2016).

Sax, William. 'God of Justice' in *God of Justice: Ritual Healing and Social Justice in the Central Himalayas*. Oxford: Oxford University Press (2009): 25–50.

Schiff Berman, Paul. *Introduction to Global Legal Pluralism: A Jurisprudence of Law Beyond Border*. Cambridge: Cambridge University Press (2012), 3–22.

Schmitt, Carl. *Political Theology: Four Chapters on the Concept of Sovereignty*. George D. Schwab (trans.). Cambridge: MIT Press (1985).

———. *Roman Catholicism and Political Form*. G.L. Ulmen (trans.). Westport, CT and London: Greenwood Press (1996).

Searle, J. *Rationality in Action*. Cambridge, MA: MIT Press (2001).

Seibt, Johanna, Raul Hakli and Marco Norskov (eds.). *Sociable Robots and the Future of Social Relations*. Amsterdam: IOS Press (2014).

Sen, Amartya. *The Idea of Justice*. London: Penguin Books (2010).

———. *Inequality Reexamined*. New York: Oxford University Press (2006) (first published in 1992).

The Sexual Harassment of Women at Workplace (Prevention, Prohibition and Redressal) Act 2013, Ministry of Law and Justice. Government of India. Delhi: Controller of Publications: Delhi. www.iitbbs.ac.in/notice/sexual-harrassment-of-women-act-and-rules-2013.pdf (accessed on 11 August 2017).

Shank., J.B. 'Voltaire.' *Stanford Encyclopaedia of Philosophy*. August 31, 2009. http://plato.stanford.edu/entries/voltaire/ (accessed on 13 August 2017).

Shapiro, David L. and Lon L. Fuller. 'The Case of the Speluncean Explorers: A Fiftieth Anniversary Symposium.' *Harvard Law Review* 112, No. 1913 (June 1999): 1834–917.

Singh, Smriti. 'Ghastly Rapes Delhi's Undoing for Long.' TNN, December 18, 2012. http://timesofindia.indiatimes.com/city/delhi/Ghastly-rapes-Delhis-undoing-for-long/articleshow/17657414.cms (accessed on 13 August 2017).

Sinha, Manoj Kumar. 'Hinduism and International Humanitarian Law.' *International Review of the Red Cross* 87, no. 858 (June 2005): 285–94.

'Software Patent and Copyright Laws in India.' *123HelpMe.com*. 29 March 2015. www.123HelpMe.com/view.asp?id=36962 (accessed on 12 October 2015).

Spivak, Gayatri. "Righting Wrongs" in Gayatri Spivak (ed.), *Other Asias*. Blackwell (2008),14–57.

Stein, Edward. *Without Good Reason: The Rationality Debate in Philosophy and Cognitive Science*. Oxford: Clarendon Press (1996).

Stein, Peter. *European Thought in Roman History*. Cambridge, UK: Cambridge University Press (2004).

———. *Roman Law in European History*. Cambridge, UK: Cambridge University Press (1999).

Strauss, Gerald. *Law, Resistance and the State. The Opposition to Roman Law in Reformation Germany*. Princeton, NJ: Princeton University Press (1986).

Suber, Peter. *The Case of the Speluncean Explorers: Nine New Opinions*. London: Routledge (1998).

———. 'Legal Reasoning after Post-Modern Critiques of Reason.' *Legal Writing* 3 (1997): 21–50.

Summary of Judgments on Disability Rights. https://cis-india.org/accessibility/blog/summary-of-judgments-on-disability-rights (accessed on 13 August 2017).

Tamanaha, Brian Z. 'A Non-Essentialist Version of Legal Pluralism.' *Journal of Law and Society* 27, no. 2 (June 2000). Available at SSRN: http://ssrn.com/abstract=234793 (accessed on 13 August 2017).

Taneja, An. and Vivek. 'Jinnealogy. Everyday Life and Islamic Theology in Post-Partition Delhi.' *Journal of Ethnographic Theory* 3, no. 3 (2013): 139–65.

———. *Nature, History, and the Sacred in the Medieval Ruins of Delhi*. New York, NY: Columbia University Press (2013).

Tercapanchanana, Jagannatha. *A Digest of Hindu Law on Contracts and Successions. Volume 1*. H. T. Colebrooke (trans.) Madras: J. Higginbotham (1864).

Teubner, Gunther. 'The Two Faces of Janus: Rethinking Legal Pluralism.' *Cardozo Law Review* 13, (1992): 1443–62.

Thapar, Romila. 'Imagined Religious Communities? – Ancient History and the Modern Search for a Hindu Identity.' *Modern Asian Studies* 23, no. 2 (1998): 209–23.

Thomas, Abraham. 'Delay in Lodging FIR Natural in Rape Cases: SC' October 2, 2014; www.dailypioneer.com/nation/delay-in-lodging-fir-natural-in-rape-cases-sc.html (accessed on 4 October 2015).

The Transplantation of Human Organs Act 1994 No. 42 of 1994. Ministry of Law, Justice and Company Affairs, Government of India. http://notto.nic.in/WriteReadData/Portal/images/THOA-ACT-1994.pdf, (accessed on 11 August 2017).

Vanderlinder, Jacques. 'Return to Legal Pluralism: Twenty Years Later.' *The Journal of Legal Pluralism and Unofficial Law* 21, no. 28 (1989): 149–57.

Vanita, Ruth and Saleem Kidwai. *Love's Rite: Same-Sex Marriage in India and the West*. India: Penguin (2005).

———. *Same Sex Love in India: Readings from Literature and History*. New Delhi: Penguin Books India (2008).

Varier, Kartik and Ankita Susan Mathew. 'Looking Beyond Hart vs Fuller – Law and Morality in Contemporary Indian Society' (October 26, 2010). Available at SSRN: http://ssrn.com/abstract=1917342 or http://dx.doi.org/10.2139/ssrn.1917342, 1–12 (accessed on 11 August 2017).

Vivekanand, Paper on Hinduism. (1893). http://www.ramakrishnavivekananda.info/vivekananda/volume_1/addresses_at_the_parliament/v1_c1paper_on_hinduism.htm (accessed on 28 November 2017).

Wade, H.W.R and C.F. Forsyth. *Administrative Law*. Oxford: Oxford University Press (2004).

Waldron, Jeremy. 'Positivism and Legality: Hart's Equivocal Response to Fuller.' *NYU Law Review* 83, no. 4 (October 2008): 1135–69.

Walshe, Maurice (trans.), *The Long Discourse of the Buddha: A Translation of the Digha Nikaya*. Sri Lanka: Buddhist Publication Society (1996).

Weber, Max. *Economy and Society. An Outline of Interpretive Sociology*. Berkeley, CA: University of California Press (1968).

———. *Max Weber on Law and Society*. Cambridge: Harvard University Press (1954), 224–31.

Woolf, Harry and Jowell Jeffery et al. *De Smith's Judicial Review*. London: Sweet and Maxwell (2007).

Žižek, Slavoj. 'Against Human Rights.' *New Left Review* (July-August 2005), 115–31.

Index

For Product Safety Concerns and Information please contact our EU representative GPSR@taylorandfrancis.com Taylor & Francis Verlag GmbH, Kaufingerstraße 24, 80331 München, Germany

Batch number: 10725981

Printed by Printforce, the Netherlands